Praise for *The Trigg*

"A provocative, sometimes maddening, occasion: lives of six ordinary Americans who share the experience of having - one. . . The roughly 43 victims of gun violence every day [in the United States] were killed by the kind of people profiled by Patinkin. . . . Each story is self-contained but also illuminates the broader issues surrounding gun violence."

—*Washington Post*

"Patinkin writes about these lives with bracing empathy, and he clearly engaged the trust of his subjects, whose perspective on their crimes is filled with horror and regret. . . [He] has told us six stories that no one else would. He acknowledges that he is in no way trying to overlook the central tragedy of the victims and their families, but he tries his best to force readers to realize that these shootings aren't just random events, but a result of real troubles within the shooters and the society that produces, and generally ignores, them."

—*Chicago Tribune*

"A moving exploration of gun violence . . . With a distressing and challenging set of narratives, Patinkin gives a rare account of the perpetrator's perspective."
—*oxygen.com*, "5 True-Crime Books We Can't Wait to Read This Spring"

"We need stronger conversations around gun violence, and *The Trigger* is an interesting place to start."
—*giggles.com* and *att.net*, "11 True Crime Books That'll Give You Goosebumps and Keep You Up All Night"

"An extraordinary read from first page to last, *The Trigger: Narratives of the American Shooter* will prove to be a welcome, thoughtful and thought-provoking contribution to the present national dialogue over the role of guns in our contemporary American society. . . . Very highly recommended for both community and academic library Contemporary Social Issues collections, and deserving of as wide a readership as possible."

—*Midwest Book Review*

"Timely . . . His narratives, each complex in its own thorny way, humanize shooters for those who, like Patinkin before he embarked on this project, have had no previous exposure to them as people."

—*Publishers Weekly*

"This is a great look at guns, the people that have had to shoot someone, and how it has affected their lives. This is a wonderful book . . . and one that I recommend everyone to read."

—jbronderbookreviews

"Patinkin illuminates hard truths about American society that are not evident in commonly cited statistics or partisan talking points. The narratives challenge the reader to critically examine his or her own beliefs, and to either reaffirm them or abandon them. This is a powerful and unique contribution to the dialogue about gun violence in the United States."

—Andrew Yang, author of *The War on Normal People* and 2020 US presidential candidate

"Patinkin dives behind the headlines to reveal the fine details of the lives of his subjects. He humanizes them through his meticulous investigative process and offers a compelling and gripping work that explores gut-wrenching social issues. Anyone seeking to understand gun violence in America needs to read this intense, intimate book."

—Tony D'Souza, author of *Mule*

"*The Trigger* is a raw and unflinching look at America's gun violence epidemic. Patinkin weaves us through the complicated and emotional backstories that propel people into shootings. This is a sobering and important book."

—Jooyoung Lee, gun violence expert and author of *Blowin' Up*

THE
TRIGGER
NARRATIVES
OF THE
AMERICAN
SHOOTER

DANIEL J. PATINKIN
WITH A NEW FOREWORD BY WILLIAM H. REID, MD, MPH

Arcade Publishing • New York

In memory of Brandon Clancy

First Paperback Edition 2019

For the purposes of privacy and discretion, various names and details pertaining to individuals or events discussed in this book have been modified.

Arcade Publishing books may be purchased in bulk at special discounts for sales promotion, corporate gifts, fund-raising, or educational purposes. Special editions can also be created to specifications. For details, contact the Special Sales Department, Arcade Publishing, 307 West 36th Street, 11th Floor, New York, NY 10018 or arcade@skyhorsepublishing.com.

Arcade Publishing® is a registered trademark of Skyhorse Publishing, Inc.®, a Delaware corporation.

Visit our website at www.arcadepub.com.
Visit the author's sites at www.danielpatinkin.com and www.thetriggerbook.com.

10 9 8 7 6 5 4 3 2 1

Library of Congress Cataloging-in-Publication Data

Names: Patinkin, Daniel J., author.
Title: Narratives of the American shooter / Daniel J. Patinkin.
Description: First Edition. | New York : Arcade Publishing, [2018] | Includes
   bibliographical references.
Identifiers: LCCN 2018000621 (print) | LCCN 2018014775 (ebook) | ISBN
   9781628729207 (ebook) | ISBN 9781628729191 (hardcover : alk. paper) | ISBN
   978-1-948924-55-9 (paperback) : alk. paper
Subjects: LCSH: Murderers--United States--Biography. | Homicide--United
   States--Biography. | Firearms and crime--United States. | Firearms--United
   States.
Classification: LCC HV6785 (ebook) | LCC HV6785 .P38 2018 (print) | DDC
   364.152/3092273--dc23
LC record available at https://lccn.loc.gov/2018000621

Cover design by Brian Peterson
Cover photograph: iStockphoto

Printed in the United States of America

CONTENTS

Foreword by *William H. Reid, MD, MPH*   *vi*

Introduction   1

Chapter 1   In the Spanish Wells: Lester Young Jr.   13

Chapter 2   The Drifter: John Frizzle   71

Chapter 3   The Devil's Bargain: Marvin Gomez   125

Chapter 4   A Man for Others: Alphonsus O'Connor   163

Chapter 5   In Isolation: Brittany Aden   203

Chapter 6   An All-American Boy: Brandon Clancy   239

Epilogue   *291*

Acknowledgments   *301*

Notes   *303*

FOREWORD

I'm asked regularly about our "epidemic" of shootings, particularly mass killings. What makes the perpetrators pull the trigger? How can we stop them?

Those questions miss the point. Mass killings are not the most important topic facing law enforcement, mental health professionals, our culture, or our social structure. Daniel Patinkin "gets it."

That mass shooters and serial killers are the biggest problems in law enforcement is a myth. Nothing could be further from the truth. Many people also believe that those who use firearms to commit mayhem can be pigeonholed into a few neat categories that lend themselves to social understanding and to common-sense prevention. Nope and nope.

Very few shootings, in the United States or abroad, are anything like the sensational events that grab national headlines—their rarity is a big part of the reason mass shootings grab headlines. Far more people are killed in the kinds of shootings described in *The Trigger* than in cinemas, malls, houses of worship, or schools. National crime statistics (and any law enforcement officer or prosecutor) will tell you the same thing, which Facebook, Twitter, Instagram, and the news media won't: Stories of mass shootings are sensational because they're *not* common among shootings overall. People who shoot other people don't fit into a few neat categories—criminals, terrorists, crazies—recognizable and explainable and ready to be filed away in our minds so that we can get back to whatever we were doing before we turned on the news.

There are some similarities, of course, among those who pull the trigger in the kind of shootings that happen most frequently. There are certain situations in which shootings are more likely than others. Some incidents are associated with environment (bars, prisons, severe family strife, drug deals, gang subculture, and the like). Others are loosely correlated with personal characteristics (people with no conscience, drug or alcohol abusers, those with strong persecutory thoughts or jealous delusions, those who are—realistically or not—dreadfully *afraid* of something).

But each person who pulls a trigger against another has a unique story. When you know the person, when you watch the events closely, when you see what came before—sometimes years before—shootings become *individual,* not simply defined by bromides like "drug deal gone bad," "jealous lover," or "senseless gang violence." These stories rarely get told beyond an incomplete, usually inaccurate mention on the evening news or—worse—in social media. That's what makes this book important.

The shooter's *humanity* is another bone of contention in our world of snap judgments and bumper-sticker explanations. Each shooter is a person, often abhorrent for his or her acts but usually not inherently evil. As Dr. Georg Stürup, the late Danish psychiatrist and head of Herstedvester, one of the world's premier institutions for the criminally insane, told me decades ago in his Aarhus home, "Never forget that they are *people.*" Without forgiving the atrocity of their acts or forgetting the tragedy of their victims, Patinkin shows how we must try to understand the people who hurt us or our neighbors, our fellow citizens, and he does it masterfully. Sometimes the *person* shouldn't be defined by one act, no matter how unthinkable that act is.

Daniel J. Patinkin knows these things. His narrative of the six shootings recounted here is compelling and, ironically, entertaining in the way good writing is entertaining, to keep us interested and moving through stories of lives marked by tragedy. Read his book and feel. Read it and weep. Read it and learn.

William H. Reid, MD, MPH
Author of *A Dark Night in Aurora:*
Inside James Holmes and the Colorado Mass Shootings

INTRODUCTION

It occurs to me that I am America.
I am talking to myself again.

—Allen Ginsberg

This book presents the life stories of six individuals who have shot someone in the United States. The narratives recounted to me and relayed here are harrowing and stark—at times disturbing, at times profound. The revelations contained within them, I hope, will have a lasting impact not only on how you, the reader, perceive the issue of gun violence in this country, but also on how you perceive the American experience in a broader sense. The process of researching and composing this book, indeed, rattled and realigned my own world view. This introduction will address the genesis of this book and the somewhat unusual process that brought it to fruition, along with some reflections on how my personal history and point of view may have impacted the project.

But first, a brief narrative of my own.

I returned to Chicago, my hometown, for the Fourth of July weekend in 2016. On that Friday night, my old friends Malachy, Molly, and Steve joined me for a stand-up comedy show at Zanies in Old Town. One of the comedians who performed told a memorable joke about a public service announcement that he heard on the radio. In the announcement, a famous local rapper pleaded with Chicagoans to stop shooting each other, to "put the guns down." The comedian, who was from somewhere else in the United States—somewhere safer—was appalled that the city of Chicago had resorted to begging to resolve its ever-worsening gun violence problem.

After the show, we rendezvoused with another close friend, Al O'Connor (a police officer whose story happens to be featured in this book). Al, Steve, Malachy, and I attended high school together on Chicago's Near West Side, at a Catholic school named St. Ignatius College Prep, before scattering to various Midwestern universities. I was the only one who had later moved away from the city, to Los Angeles. After a few rounds of drinks, Molly called it a night and we—the four guys—decided to continue our revelry at a late-night bar named The Continental, which is on the border of the East Garfield Park and Humboldt Park neighborhoods. During the ride over, our conversation returned to the topic of rampant gun violence in Chicago. I had begun working on this book just a few months prior, and so was curious about how my friends were coping with the widely publicized phenomenon. On this weekend, we were at the halfway point of a year that would see a total of 762 homicides (a 57 percent increase versus 2015) and 4,331 shootings victims (a 46 percent increase) in the city—the worst tally of gun violence in twenty years. My friends were discouraged and aggravated by the carnage and the omnipresent threat, as well as by the extensive and bleak media coverage the issue was getting. Although the situation had been bad in the city since at least the 1960s, the overwhelming, collective sense of despair among Chicagoans in 2016 seems to have reached new heights.

Around two in the morning my group arrived at The Continental, a bar which, despite certain charms, might reasonably be described as a dive. It is patronized in large part by twenty- and thirty-something urban hipsters, many of whom may be hoping for one final chance to get lucky before the sun comes up. We ordered rounds of cheap beer and spent an hour or so reminiscing about our adventures in different parts of the world, including Al's somewhat recent bachelor party in the Dominican Republic.

At about 3:30 a.m., there was a sudden commotion. People began rushing in through the front door and elbowing for space. The four of us noticed, but were so absorbed in conversation that we did not address the development until the crowding became oppressive. Squeezed into a spot next to me was a young woman with a disconcerted look on her face.

"What the hell is going on?" I asked her.

"Someone just got shot out front," she responded, panicked and rather pale.

I giggled and gave her a strange look, partly because, in my condition, I was having a hard time processing what she meant, and partly because it sounded like a joke. Hipsters aren't exactly known for their gunplay.

"What do you mean, 'Someone just got shot'?" I asked.

Now I was irritating her. "Exactly what I just said! Someone just got shot in front of the bar."

The woman sighed and turned away from me. The gravity of the situation sobered me up. I relayed the information to my friends, who, like me, reacted with some alarm. We decided to stay put and see what developed. A few minutes later, the lights came on. A towering bouncer near the front door announced, "The bar is now closed. We need everyone to leave. Please pay your tabs and make your way to the door." My friends and I downed our beers and headed outside.

We emerged onto a crime scene. There were at least a half-dozen police vehicles, along with two ambulances in front of the bar. Down the sidewalk, to the side of The Continental, an area was cordoned off with police tape. A gaggle of bar patrons lingered nearby, waiting for rides and quietly appraising the situation.

"Al, you're a cop. You should find out what is going on," I suggested as we made our way down the street.

"Nah, man. They seem to have the situation under control," he replied.

We hopped into a Lyft and headed home.

The next morning, I found an article about the incident in the online *Chicago Tribune*.[1] A thirty-one-year-old man named Hector Badillo Jr. had been shot in the neck. He was standing outside of his father's automotive shop, next to The Continental, when an unknown assailant emerged from the alley and began firing. Bystanders attempted to treat Badillo, but he was pronounced dead by responding paramedics. One of the stray bullets hit an unaffiliated man in the leg while he sat in a nearby SUV. The motive of the shooter was undetermined.

Hector was one of four men who were shot to death over the course of that weekend in Chicago. Another sixty-two people were wounded. It was a grievous, horrifying tally. However, the body count paled in comparison to the same weekend a year later, when fifteen were killed and eighty-seven wounded throughout the city.

That incident represents my only direct, personal experience with gun violence. In fact, in my life, I have had very few encounters with guns under any circumstances. I have never owned one. I have never gone hunting. Aside from a skeet shooting course that I took in college, guns were never within the purview of my interests or culture.

The home where I was raised, and where my parents still reside, is in Riverside, Illinois. It is an upper-middle-class, western suburb, populated in large part by family-oriented professionals who commute to Chicago for work. A few of my friends had BB guns, and I am sure that plenty of the adults in town possessed real firearms, but I never saw one growing up. Although the political makeup of Riverside is mixed, it, like many of Chicago's suburbs, is rather racially homogeneous. To be precise, 82.1 percent of the 8,859 residents are white, like me. 14.2 percent are Hispanic. Only 115 of the residents, 1.3 percent, are black.[2] I attended grade school and middle school in Riverside before enrolling at St. Ignatius.

High school was a tremendously mind-opening and empowering experience for me. In the previous fourteen years of my life, I had had few interactions with people of a different race, a different socio-economic status, or, in general, a different culture. However, school in the city, with classmates from all walks of life, changed all of that. In particular, the experience exposed me to some of the harsher realities of life outside the suburbs. Every day, I carpooled with friends via Ogden Avenue (part of the original Route 66), which passed through some rough Westside neighborhoods, including Lawndale, Little Village, and Douglas Park. Much of the real estate in those parts was either dilapidated or abandoned. Drug use was rampant, crime rates high. The most prominent visual advertisements were for Old English and St. Ides malt liquor. On a few occasions, we drove past crime scenes in which police officers were processing a dead body on the sidewalk.

The St. Ignatius campus itself was not positioned in the safest of neighborhoods. A section of the notoriously crime-ridden ABLA Homes public housing project was just steps away from the school. We students were advised not to venture south of Roosevelt Road after dark. Yet, despite this environment, urban blight and its related ills were little more than an arms-length curiosity for me and the majority of my classmates. Occasionally we forayed into rougher parts of the city for a party or some other extracurricular activity, but we generally operated within a safety bubble. As long as we stayed on school grounds, on the right side of the street, in our cars, on a well-lit path, we did not have to concern ourselves with the lurking dangers. I look back on this time in my life, proud that I immersed myself in such a diverse culture and geography, but also somewhat ashamed that I did not fully grasp the plight of the communities that surrounded me, that I did not fully empathize with the disadvantaged people who existed thereabouts.

Yet, since those high school days, I have been fascinated by complex social and cultural issues, especially those that are at the root of the major challenges we face as a nation. In recent years, I have begun to incorporate these interests into my work. My first book, *The Crippler: Cage Fighting and My Life on the Edge*, represents one such effort. It is the autobiography (as told to me) of cage-fighting legend Chris Leben. Chris was raised in poverty in Oregon, was illiterate until after high school, went AWOL from the army, suffered from alcoholism, opioid addiction, and mental illness, and made about a dozen trips to jail and prison. Almost every story that he told me dropped my jaw. It was as if he incurred more drama and intrigue in a typical week than I had in my whole life. Consequently, during the year and a half that we collaborated on the book, I developed new, fuller viewpoints on the human experience. My deep dive into Chris's life story—a story that is so vastly different from my own—had a profound moral and emotional impact on me.

Shortly after publishing *The Crippler*, I realized that I had to do it again: I felt compelled to write another book that would investigate unfamiliar life stories and thereby illuminate complicated social and cultural dynamics. Gun violence, perhaps the most fiercely debated and closely scrutinized of American phenomena, I realized, would provide an ideal framework for this endeavor. For me, despite my lack of personal experience with its occurrence or consequences, gun violence is both profanely fascinating and ultra-relevant to an understanding of the contemporary American tapestry. Millions of living Americans have been shot or have a loved one who was shot. In 2016 alone there were 15,083 gun deaths in this country (not including over 20,000 suicides) and 30,616 gun injuries. That amounts to forty-one non-suicide gun deaths and eighty-four gun injuries per day.[3] By comparison, in Japan there were just six—yes, six—gun deaths *in the whole of 2014*. More Americans have been killed by gunshots in the last fifty years (approximately 1.5 million) than have been killed in all wars combined since the Revolutionary War began in 1775.[4] (I could go on listing additional grim statistics.) Many consider the carnage to be an abominable stain on our nation's history and heritage. Many others consider it the price of freedom. In sum, although I am gratified by the process of storytelling, regardless of the broader societal impact of my writing, I am driven by a desire to compel my reader to wrestle with provocative ideas and controversial perspectives. This sort of engagement, I believe, causes a person to grow, to evolve, to become a more understanding and empathetic member of the human race. If I can have that sort of impact on my readers (and on myself), I am fulfilled.

This book—even though it tells the stories of other individuals—is surely, and significantly, a reflection of my personal history. This acknowledgment may sound somewhat paradoxical, even imprudent. I had and have concerns about embedding too much of my own footprint on this book. Therefore, I decided during the planning stages to keep my perspectives, political or otherwise, at arm's length—to conduct my research and interviews dispassionately and, subsequently, to convey what I learned as objectively as possible. Only, I quickly encountered an obstacle to this goal: my decisions about what questions to ask, what events and facts to research, what anecdotes and realizations to convey in the book are inextricably linked to my identity. The subject of gun violence, in particular, is so emotionally charged, so slathered with partisan notions and preconceptions, that an unadulterated appraisal of related incidents is especially hard to come by. Had this book been written by a detective from Philadelphia, or a rancher from Colorado, or an ex-con from Birmingham, the content and tone most assuredly would have been skewed in a different direction.

The six portraits presented here are of people with whom I have relatively little in common. They include a former crack dealer from South Carolina, a navy veteran from Michigan, a troubled young woman from rural Tennessee, a former high school football star from the Pacific Northwest, a working-class Hispanic man from New Mexico. Even Al O'Connor and I, despite our shared history and friendship, have walked very different paths. Under ideal circumstances, these unique individuals would have simply told me their stories from start to finish—unprodded, undirected—unspooling cohesive and thoughtful narratives, relating them to relevant current events and discourse. I, then, could have been a thoroughly impartial conduit of information. However, the interview processes were not quite so streamlined. To varying degrees, I had to coax the information from the subjects and go to lengths to piece together the narratives. I had to dig into their personal histories, drag out memories that had been long buried, and compel them to fill in the gaps and clarify ambiguities. In doing so, I could not help but be guided by the battery of prejudices and under-standings, ignorance and awareness that are the accumulation of my life. After all, curiosity is the byproduct of these things, is it not? This observation may not come as a surprise to my reader, and, I guess, it did not exactly catch me off guard either. However, what I did not anticipate was how *pervasively* my personal experience would mold this project. I hope it was for the better.

Considering the statistics—the great abundance of shooters in America—one might expect that I had an easy time finding candi-dates for inclusion in this book. The process, however, was somewhat arduous. Prior to this project, I knew only two people in the whole world who had ever shot someone: the aforementioned Al O'Connor, and my cousin's husband, who works for the Knoxville, Tennessee police department. I chose not to include the latter. This left me with five more subjects to find. However, there is no centralized resource where an author can readily connect with people who have had the grim experience of shooting another person. There is no smartphone app that offers a browsable database of such individuals. Thus, I had to employ a hodgepodge of recruitment techniques.

Some of my methods bore little or no fruit. I called prisons and sent letters to particular inmates at various institutions. None of the individuals I approached agreed to participate. I inquired with various nonprofit organizations, and criminal attorneys, and bail bondsmen to no avail. I researched specific types of incidents and then attempted to track down candidates via directories and social networking sites. Aside from Lester Young Jr. (featured herein), there were no takers. I found him after Googling the phrase "murderer turned motivational speaker." My search returned an article from a South Carolina news publication. I then used Facebook to connect with him.

To recruit additional candidates, I logged on to online discussion forums, such as Reddit, and posted queries. There were a few marginally helpful replies, but most respondents offered nothing more than a disturbing degree of vitriol. Although I did not plan to advance an overall political position in this book, and although I made that point clear in my online postings, abuse was heaped generously in my direction. Some were incensed that I appeared to be offering a platform to individuals who had committed violent acts. Others were appalled that I had not chosen to focus on the stories of the victims. One angrily demanded that I draw attention, instead, to "how many people are killed as a consequence of gun control." A few others were quite offended by my use of the words "gun violence" in describing the project, the phrase purportedly connoting an unwarranted political bias. I thought, in earnest, about whether I should modify my vocabulary or somehow appease these concerns. In the end, I decided that this sort of accommodation would be cumbersome and unproductive.

Continuing my search, I sent out email blasts, badgering my family, friends, and associates in the hopes that someone had a first- or second-degree connection to a relevant individual. Ultimately, only one of my contacts, out of the scores that I approached, offered a lead. A friend introduced me to his friend, who introduced me to a casual acquaintance: Brandon Clancy. By the way, Brandon Clancy is not a real name. Of the six shooters portrayed in this book, he is the only one who requested that I obscure his true identity—a request that I understand and respect. The rest of the subjects' names are true to life, but there are numerous instances in which I modified other names or details out of a concern for the privacy and welfare of certain individuals.

I found the final three subjects—Brittany Aden, John Frizzle, and Marvin Gomez—believe it or not, via Craigslist. Over the course of a year, I posted classified advertisements in dozens of municipalities throughout the country, from El Paso to St. Louis, from Boise to New York City. The headlines read, "Have you shot someone? Subjects needed for book about shootings." John's ex-wife came across one of the ads and referred me to John. Brittany discovered the ad of her own accord and emailed me.

Marvin also connected with me via Craigslist, although his case was slightly different. I had spent a long time pursuing subjects in the American Southwest, resulting in only a dozen or so inappropriate or uninteresting replies. So, in the summer of 2017, I decided to change the category of the ad. All of my postings, to that point, had been in the "general community" section. And although these, over time, generated upward of one hundred leads, the responses were intermittent at best. In fact, I received zero responses in the majority of the municipalities that I targeted. Also, most of the inquiries that I received were dead ends. As a last-ditch effort, I placed a handful of ads in the "labor gigs" category in cities such as Las Vegas, Tucson, Reno, and Albuquerque. My reasoning was that many candidates for this book were felons who would have a hard time finding steady, traditional employment and, therefore, might monitor Craigslist for temporary work. The strategy (although an apparent violation of Craigslist categorization policy) paid off. In about one week I received at least two dozen responses from individuals. I selected Marvin from that group.

How did I decide which subjects to investigate and which to pass on? I employed four guiding principles. First, I wanted to present geographically distinct stories. As much as this book is about individual life experiences, it is also a guided tour of a diverse America. Second, I wanted the narratives of the subjects to be as dissimilar as possible. Third, I wanted the circumstances of the shootings to have minimal overlap. And fourth, perhaps most importantly, I wanted the stories to be as compelling, as eye-opening, and as robust as possible. Although there are some demographics that I would have liked to incorporate into this book—senior citizens, wealthy individuals, mass shooters—I find the cross section of American society presented here to be wholly intriguing.

Many legitimate candidates, I should point out, did not make the cut: a repo man from Arizona, a prostitute from West Virginia, a former gang member from Alaska, a security guard from Colorado, to name a very few. In most cases, these individuals had stories that did not reconcile with my guiding principles. Sometimes, the individual initiated contact and then reconsidered or disappeared. However, there were at least a few cases that I ruled out because I felt that the individual might reveal things that could put one or the both of us in legal jeopardy or physical danger.

I also want to address potential concerns about the victims who are discussed in this book, and about my attitude toward them. First and foremost, I have great sympathy for the victims and for the friends and families who have suffered so greatly as a consequence of the incidents recounted here. I am horrified by gun violence and the great toll it has taken—physically, spiritually, and otherwise—on my country. I want there to be fewer victims—*many* fewer victims. To that end, I am contributing a portion of the proceeds from this book to nonprofit organizations that seek to reduce gun violence and assist the victims.

Further, I do not celebrate, or approve of, or, in any way, condone the unjustified acts of gun violence that appear in some of the chapters that follow. From certain perspectives, some of the incidents in this book may have been warranted. But, insofar as the shooting was malicious or negligent or immoral, I utterly condemn it. That said, there is clear value in exploring the stories of the shooters. For, overshadowed by the grief, horror, and politicization of every one of these tragedies, there is a sentient, emotional human being who, by choice or of compulsion, pulled the trigger. We must endeavor to understand his or her actions and motivations if we are to improve the situation in America.

I hope that, in laying bare many of the factors that underlie incidents of gun violence in this country, this book will serve as a catalyst for positive change.

I will conclude with a few words about what this book *is*, as well as what this book *is not*. It *is* a collection of biographical portraits of individuals who have shot someone in America. It attempts to provide revealing, in-depth context to a series of tragedies that otherwise might be buried under an avalanche of dehumanizing statistics. This book *is not* a political tome, or a sociological analysis, or an academic text, or a policy recommendation. Many controversial issues and debates arise in the course of telling these stories, and, in some cases, the position of the individual subject is expressed. However, I tried hard not to advance my own biased or partisan agenda, a challenge considering how ubiquitous and inflammatory the issue of gun violence is in America. Nonetheless, I suspect that some readers will infer a certain degree of partiality on my part, and perhaps be agitated or angered by that perception. Indeed, in this country, it seems that the act of openly addressing the issue of gun violence, regardless of one's position or message, is now a political act. If I have provoked an intellectual, emotional, or spiritual engagement with the ideas and perspectives described herein, then so be it.

CHAPTER 1

IN THE
SPANISH WELLS

Lester Young Jr.

On the day after Christmas of 1991, Lester Young Jr. knelt in the grass next to his mother's gravestone. His throat felt as dry as the desiccated, brown leaves that carpeted the Spanish Wells Cemetery. And, although it was not an especially cold afternoon—the climate here was generally subtropical—he shivered as he ran his hand along the flat, granite marker that capped his mother's eternal resting place.

IN LOVING MEMORY
MARY S. YOUNG
JAN. 7, 1952
MAR. 2, 1988

There was also a rectangular slab of loose stone that leaned against the grave marker. Lester was not certain who had placed it there, but he suspected that it must have been his father's doing. It bore a more lyrical message:

A heart of gold
Stopped beating,
Two shining eyes at rest,
God broke our hearts to prove
He only takes the best

Lester thought back on the final days of his mother's life, and hot tears filled his eyes.

In late February of 1988, Mary Young came down with a cough. It was nothing out of the ordinary for that time of year, and, at first, it hardly impeded her ability to carry out her daily obligations. Aside from sixteen-year-old Lester, there were three daughters to care for: Tracy, Suzette, and Evelina, aged fifteen, thirteen, and eleven. An ever-present homemaker, Mary made sure that all four of the children made it to school every day, with lunch in tow or money for a sandwich. She did the cooking and the cleaning for the family and kept their cozy, but nicely appointed, trailer home on Muddy Creek Road in respectable condition. Recently, Mary had increased her workload by taking on a part-time job as the cook at a local diner.

Mary bore the brunt of the domestic responsibilities and chores while her husband, Lester Sr., held down a demanding job as the superintendent of Port Royal Golf & Racquet Club in the northeast corner of Hilton Head Island. He typically worked a good deal more than forty hours per week and, even on his off days, had to respond to urgent situations as they arose. But Mary did not resent Lester Sr. for that. They loved each other, still, after all these years, and the frequent smiles and laughter that they shared revealed how truly they enjoyed each other's company. They were a hardworking, middle-class couple who did everything they could to provide a stable household for their children. They were in this thing together.

Hilton Head Island, where the Young family resided, is located on the Atlantic Seaboard near the very southern tip of the state of South Carolina, approximately twenty miles up the coast from Savannah, Georgia. It is shaped almost exactly like a running shoe, with its toe pointed toward the southwest. Lester Sr.'s Port Royal Club, with its three pristine, eighteen-hole golf courses, lush, sprawling grounds, and upscale clubhouse and facilities, is situated quite squarely in the heel.

The town of Hilton Head, developed in the 1950s on the grounds of a patchwork of former slave plantations, is largely centered around the activities and interests of moneyed residents, vacation homeowners, and upscale tourists who are drawn to the island by its renowned luxury resort culture. Private, gated communities cover 70 percent of the island. A web of twenty-four championship golf courses sprawls across most of its sixty-nine-square-mile area. Hundreds of tennis courts, scores of award-winning restaurants, beautiful beaches, verdant nature reserves, and abundant cultural attractions draw roughly 2.5 million annual visitors to the island. Multi-million-dollar mansions line both the bay and the oceanfront. Hilton Head, then, is a playground for well-to-do people, the vast majority of whom are white.

But a small section of the island, the northwest part, near where the shoelaces of the sneaker would tie into a bow, is occupied primarily by less affluent black people. Spanish Wells, where the Young family lived and where Mary Young is buried, is one of the core neighbor-hoods in this area of Hilton Head. It is characterized by trailer homes and modest frame houses tucked among dense vegetation. Narrow, residential side streets branch off the main thoroughfares and vanish into the trees and shrubbery. Muddy Creek Road runs through the heart of the neighborhood, extending southward from its origin at Spanish Wells Road.

As February of 1988 came to a close, Mary Young's cough grew worse. On the first day of March, she was compelled to miss work and remain in bed. That evening, she asked Lester Jr. to wash the dishes. However, he had plans with his pals down the street and so he protested vehe-mently. They argued about it for a good while. Mary, exhausted by her illness, strained as she confronted her son.

The following morning, Lester Sr. decided he would take his wife to the hospital for some medication. It did not appear to be an urgent situation; Mary was sick, for sure, but lucid and talking and sitting up in bed. Lester Sr. had to take care of some things at the golf club that morning, but planned to return before noon to tend to Mary. He instructed Lester Jr. to stay home and look after her in the meantime. However, the boy was still sore with his mother over their dispute of the previous night. He refused to stay. Tracy, instead, agreed to look after Mary, while the rest of the children went off to school.

Early that afternoon, at Hilton Head Island High School, slender and stern Principal Grant appeared in the doorway of Lester's history classroom, interrupting the teacher, Ms. Wilson. They spoke in hushed tones for a moment before Ms. Wilson said, "Lester, collect your things. You need to go with Mr. Grant now."

As Lester exited the class and followed the gray-haired administrator down the hallway, he was nervous. This was certainly not his first run-in with Principal Grant. Lester initially became a troublemaker in grade school. Then, in middle school, he and his friends began drinking and smoking weed. They became increasingly unruly in the classroom. Lately, it was rare that a week would pass without Lester Sr. receiving a phone call from the school. The boy was frequently disrupting class, incessantly breaking rules, constantly causing problems. His father, a tough man and a disciplinarian, responded as harshly as he could. He grounded his son time and time again, spanked him and smacked him, and did everything he could to scare the boy into getting in line. But it was fruitless. There seemed to be no taming Lester Young Jr.

As the boy trudged down the hallway, he racked his brain to try to remember what he had done of late that would merit top-level intervention. Only a serious issue would prompt a visit from the principal to a classroom. When they arrived at Mr. Grant's office, Lester's older cousin Bernie was there waiting for them. Hands folded and head hung low, he presented a grim countenance. Lester's gut churned. No family member, aside from his father, had ever shown up to the school. Something was wrong.

"Your cousin has some tragic news for you, I'm afraid," Principal Grant said before stepping out to allow them to speak in private.

"What up, Bernie?" Lester asked. He truly had no clue as to what the message from his cousin would reveal. "What's going on here?"

Bernie looked like he had seen a ghost. He hesitated before stammering, "Your mom . . . she passed away. She died, man."

Lester Jr. went numb.

Lester Sr. had not returned from work soon enough. That morning, as Mary lay in bed, she stopped breathing. Tracy walked into the bedroom to discover that her mother had unexpectedly passed. The girl called the ambulance, but beloved Mary could not be resuscitated. The cough, it turned out, had been an acute case of pneumonia.

Lester Jr. was blindsided. The last communication he had had with his mother was an argument over dirty dishes. He'd had no idea that her life was at risk. He'd figured that she would simply go to the doctor, pick up the right pills, and recover in a few days. Now his caretaker, his supporter, his guardian was gone, and he did not know how to carry on. As his sisters sobbed, and as his devastated father spent the next few days making arrangements and notifying family members, Lester Jr. felt completely empty. It was as if all of the life-blood had been drained from his cold body, leaving behind a black, barren void. At the funeral service, he did not cry. As they lowered her wooden casket into the earth, he did not collapse with grief. Lester was lost at sea.

As the days and months passed, different emotions about the tragedy began to affect Lester. He and his little sisters needed a mother. They still had years of childhood left, but no one to tend to them as Mary had throughout their lives. She had been a constant, uplifting spirit within the household, a tireless provider. Lester reminisced about all the times that his mother would make ice pops on hot summer days and pass them out to the neighborhood kids; about the times the whole family would head down to the beach to catch crabs for a special meal; about the way she cackled brightly when Lester Sr. teased her at the dinner table. They had been a happy, tight-knit family. Mary Young was the glue that held them so closely together.

Young Lester grew angry—angry at himself for not recognizing that his mother's life was in danger, and for allowing his final exchange with his mother to be an expression of animosity, and for not being the good, righteous boy that she had always urged him to be. But, to a greater degree, Lester was angry at God for His senseless cruelty. What was the purpose of praying to Him every weekend at church, if He would reward the effort with the untimely death of a saintly woman?

Sometime after the funeral, and after his mother's sisters, who had stayed a while to care for the children, had departed and returned to Boston, Lester finally came to understand the significance of his loss. One night, after brushing his teeth and washing his face and readying himself for bed, he walked into the living room to kiss his sweet mother goodnight. But, this time, the soft armchair, which she had occupied night after night for as long as Lester could remember, was vacant. In that moment, he began to sense that his life would never be the same. He cried himself to sleep. In the days that followed, the grief and the pain and, most of all, the searing guilt washed over young Lester. There were moments when it nearly consumed him, when he felt like he would crumple under the oppressive weight of it all. But, in the end, he found a way to internalize his devastation, pushing the emotions deep down into the recesses of his soul, where he hoped they would stay hidden forever.

For nearly four years after Mary Young's passing, Lester did not return to the cemetery plot where his mother had been lain to rest. But on this day, the day after Christmas 1991, he had nowhere to turn, no one he could confide in. He decided that, before it was too late, he would visit his mother.

Kneeling at the grave site, clutching his hands together in prayer, Lester spoke to her.

"Mom, I never told you how much you meant to me. I never got the chance before you died. I was too selfish, and too caught up in my own thing. You were the best mother I could have had. And I was a horrible son."

As painful as this moment was, Lester knew that if he did not release what was bottled up inside he would not be able to face the challenges the coming days were sure to present. After what had transpired in the last twenty-four hours, his only hope was in the salvation of his mother's mercy.

"And now I have let you down again. I have disgraced your memory by what I have done. You did your best to raise me right, to turn me into a decent man. But, in the end, when you left this world, all of that was lost. I'm too far gone, now, momma. And today I have to leave Spanish Wells. I don't know if I'll ever be able to come back."

Lester looked over his shoulder toward the gravel road that ran through the cemetery, toward the burgundy sedan in which his sister Tracy waited nervously but patiently while her brother paid his respects. Then he bent over and placed his forehead against the cold, hard gravestone.

"I took a man's life, momma," Lester whispered. "I shot a man to death, and they're going to get me for it."

After Mary Young died, Lester's penchant for misbehaving evolved into a criminal tendency. He ran with a crew of guys from the neighborhood who held the old-school, original gangsters of Spanish Wells—the "O-Heads"—in high regard. In that underprivileged pocket of the island, where much of Hilton Head's African American minority resided, in the shadow of the opulent, five-star resorts, there was a bustling black market for narcotics. The O-Heads were the hustlers who emerged in the seventies and early eighties as powerful figures in control of the illicit drug trafficking of the area. Lester and his friends knew these older guys well. Many of them were relatives. The boys grew up watching the dudes do their thing—sling drugs, wield guns, step to anyone who got out of line or stood in their way—and their admiration for this hardcore style soon became a targeted aspiration. Lester and his homeboys agreed that they would become the next generation of O-Heads.

Mid-1988 was near the height of the great American crack epidemic, which had been broadly publicized in the media and by lawmakers and law enforcers throughout the country. The socioeconomic scourge began with a somewhat simple technological development in narcotics. From its emergence as a recreational drug in the

1970s until the mid-1980s, cocaine was consumed almost entirely in its high-priced, powdered form. A single gram of the powerful stimulant cost over one hundred dollars on the street, and so the users tended to be affluent and mostly white. However, faced with a glut of product from South America and plummeting prices, American drug dealers concocted a new, less expensive derivative that would allow them to tap into poorer and much more populous demographics. They mixed cocaine with baking soda and water and heated the concoction. When the mixture dried, it hardened and broke apart into small rocks. Smoking one of these rocks, which typically contained only about one-tenth of a gram of cocaine, would deliver an immediate and intense fifteen-minute high.

During the crack epidemic, a single crack rock traded for less than ten dollars on the street, a price point that appealed to a whole new population of customers. And, because of the highly addictive nature of crack smoking, these customers returned for more with great frequency. From 1985 to 1989 the demand for crack spiked, and new dope markets spread like wildfire across the United States. Researchers who have studied the phenomenon over the past quarter-century have discovered statistically significant correlations between the prevalence of crack abuse and homicide rates, fetal death rates, weapons arrests, and the proportion of American children relegated to foster care.[5] These adverse shocks were of much greater measure and impact in poor black communities than in other demographics. Whites, in particular, experienced only incremental changes in the same statistics.

Most crack trafficking occurred on street corners in urban centers. Large-scale use was first observed in Los Angeles, and soon spread to cities as disparate as San Antonio, Cleveland, Newark, and Dallas. By 1987, the drug was available in all but a handful of states in the union. The epidemic expanded to smaller American communities, as dealers simply had to drive to a nearby metropolitan area to acquire stock. The South Atlantic states, including South Carolina, were not spared from the plague. At the time of Mary Young's passing, crack cocaine had infiltrated Hilton Head, taking root in Spanish Wells, where the O-Heads presided over its marketing and distribution.

Though Lester had no interest in consuming crack himself, he was seduced by the lifestyle that it afforded the local dealers. In the late eighties, O-Heads who were working the corners near the Young house were bringing in five or ten thousand dollars per week. They drove fancy cars and always had the sexiest women tagging along. Most importantly, they had power. The O-Heads were dangerous, influential men, feared and respected by both their rivals and the community at large. When an O-Head rolled down the street in a shiny Cadillac, people paid attention.

Lester, at this time—and really for his entire youth—was extremely limited in his world view. He rarely traveled outside of the Hilton Head and Savannah areas, and he did not care much for his education. School was not so much a place of learning and enlightenment as it was a venue where he and his homeboys could meet up and conspire, chase girls, and get into some shit. Lester never read, never did his homework, never wondered about what life was really like for white people in south Hilton Head, or for the Latinos who worked in the resort kitchens, or for cowboys in Oklahoma, or for the folks who lived in faraway places like Germany and the Philippines. All that Lester knew about, or cared to know about, was the way of the gangster and how it all went down on the street corners of Spanish Wells.

So the choice to become a drug dealer was not much of a choice for Lester Young Jr. He could follow the footsteps of his father, who worked his fingers to the bone just to eke out a living, and who had just lowered his young wife into the dirt because he barely had the time or money to get her the necessary medical care. Or, Lester could become a powerful, rich, revered badass.

Lester did recognize that choosing the latter path could certainly have long-term ramifications. It was illegal, and he was reminded of that every time his father begged him to stay off the streets and to focus on a more legitimate way of life. However, Lester had no moral hesitation or ethical qualms about becoming a drug dealer. Abusers and addicts were going to get their fix one way or another. Whether or not Lester worked the corner would have almost zero impact on that reality. Also, just because it was illegal did not make it wrong. Lester evolved to have a strong distrust for the American legal system. The older guys often talked about how the cards were stacked against the black man. Black folk were much more likely to get busted by the cops than white people were, even when they committed the exact same crimes. Moreover, the punishments seemed to be overwhelmingly discriminatory. The Anti-Drug Abuse Act of 1986 mandated a minimum sentence of five years for anyone caught in possession of just five grams of crack. One would have to be holding five hundred grams of cocaine to receive the same mandatory sentence. Why? In Lester's opinion, the majority of the legal system in the United States was set up to hold the black man down, to create obstacles to his success, and to keep money flowing into the hands of the police departments, the judges, the prosecutors, and the for-profit incarceration complex that emerged during the so-called "War on Drugs." The more black men in jail, the more money contractors made from the outsourcing of prison services including medical treatment, food preparation, and inmate transportation. Private prison operators now had an incentive to stuff full their penitentiaries and to promote long sentences, along with a disincentive to create conditions that would reduce criminal recidivism. If, as it seemed, the purpose of the law was to make the fat cats fatter, then there was no reason for Lester or his homeboys to respect it.

Lester knew a guy from the neighborhood that could help him get started. He was an older dude with an afro that everyone called Big Homie, and he traded out of a run-down shack just down Muddy Creek Road from the Young household. In the fall of 1988, less than a year after his mother's passing, Lester approached the man with fifty dollars cash.

"I need a dealer pack, Big Homie," Lester announced, puffing up his chest to mask his nervousness.

"So you want to get into the game, huh?" Big Homie asked, eyeing Lester appraisingly.

"Yeah, man. You know I hustle."

"Why don't you hustle for me, then? It's easier than going out on your own."

But Lester was never the kind of guy who would want a boss, much less make a good employee. He knew that he had what it took to run his own show.

"Naw, dude," said Lester. "I'm gonna do me."

A "drug dealer pack" was a small amount of crack rocks, about ten in total, separated into plastic baggies, that larger dealers would sell at a discount to rookie distributors. Lester hurried off with the goods and started working his contacts: guys who were crack junkies, other guys who knew guys who were crack junkies. The rocks went like hotcakes. Within an hour or two Lester reappeared in front of Big Homie. This time he walked off with a double pack. It went just as fast.

By the end of his first day of business, Lester had depleted all of Big Homie's supply, and had turned his measly fifty bucks into a whopping one thousand dollars. He walked home and quietly counted his bills, laying them out neatly on his bed. *Damn*, Lester thought. *It's just too easy. This is what I was meant to do!* He fell asleep imagining the stacks of cash he would bring in and the women who would come knocking. He pictured himself in a year or so—a kingpin in the neighborhood, the main man who would set the bar for everybody else.

Several other dealers immediately took notice of Lester's hustle. A few approached him and offered to take him under wing and back his operation. But Lester was already full of confidence. He gave each of them the same reply he gave Big Homie, adding, "I'm not going to risk getting locked up to make somebody else rich."

Lester's solo operation took off. The demand was all but unlimited. In no time, he outgrew what Big Homie could offer. He had to cut out the middleman and find a larger supplier. There was no one in Spanish Wells or even Hilton Head who could meet his needs, so Lester would have to source drugs outside of the safety and familiarity of his home turf. Nearby Savannah was the logical option. However, a few of the older guys, who had been hustling for a while before Lester got into the game, warned him about the dangers of supply runs into the city. Georgia cats were territorial. They were wary of outsiders coming into their neighborhoods and stealing their business. They kept an eye out for South Carolina license plates. O-Heads who showed up on a corner in Savannah looking to re-up faced a very high risk of getting robbed, beat up, or worse.

Lester realized that he would need protection. The good thing was that acquiring a firearm would present no challenge whatsoever. In the Spanish Wells drug game, guns were everywhere. All of the dealers were packing, and a fair number of customers offered to trade their pieces for a few crack rocks. Within a week of his first sale, Lester had both a .357 Magnum and a .45 Colt pistol. He could have built up a much larger arsenal by then, but didn't see the need.

However, a gun by itself wouldn't be enough. If he wanted any assurance of security on a run to Savannah, Lester would need backup. Fortunately, several of the dudes he grew up with were already slinging dope or were ready to start. A few of these guys, in fact, were related to Lester. There was his cousin Damon, who split his time between Hilton Head and Fort Lauderdale, Florida. He was big into nice cars and bling, and wore so many gold chains that his friends referred to him as "Mr. T." As a plus, Damon had learned how to work the street from various run-ins with dealers in Fort Lauderdale. He had a degree of savvy that Lester had yet to develop. Also, there was cousin Sammy, Lester's closest buddy. The two had grown up together and had spent many a night as children sleeping over in each other's beds. Sammy was obsessive about hip-hop fashion, always sported the newest shoes and hats, and always showed up on the block in a color-coordinated outfit.

Sammy had been there when Lester bought his first dealer pack, but was rather hesitant about selling dope himself. His family were shrimpers and worked a few fishing boats. Not long after Lester began slinging, Sammy went away for a week of shrimping. When he returned, he showed Lester the two hundred dollars that his work had earned him. Lester pulled six grand out of his pocket and quipped, "That's nice. I made this while you were gone." Not long afterward, Sammy took a place next to Lester on Muddy Creek Road.

Both Sammy and Damon accompanied Lester on his first run into Savannah. The three were understandably nervous during the drive down. They rehearsed their escape plan in the event that they got jumped during the deal. And, upon arriving at their destination—39th Street and Waters Avenue—they drove a few laps around the block to assess the situation. It was a lower-class, urban neighborhood, more densely populated but not wholly different from Spanish Wells. There was a food mart on that corner, and an old mechanic's shop down the block. The Hitch Village Projects, where most of the city's crack activity was headquartered, were a half-mile away, near the Savannah River.

The boys spotted two brothers in dark hoodies loitering on Waters Avenue. The men watched suspiciously as Damon piloted the car up to them. When Lester rolled down his window, the taller one called out.

"What you want, Carolina boy?"

Lester cradled his .45 in his lap. He assessed the dealers carefully. Both of them had their hands in their jean pockets. It was a certainty that each man was packing heat.

"I need a G," Lester replied, meaning he had a thousand dollars to trade.

The two men looked at each other and giggled.

"You think we're holding a G right here, son?" the taller man replied with a mocking smile.

"Maybe not," said Lester. "But I know you got it somewhere."

The men whispered to each other and then turned serious. The shorter man approached the car slowly.

"Show me what you got," he instructed Lester.

Lester was growing increasingly unsettled. He gripped his gun with his left hand. The short drug dealer came to a halt and waited. The taller man stood back and kept an eye out on the neighborhood, occasionally glancing over at Sammy, Damon, and Lester.

Lester opened the glove compartment and pulled out a rolled wad of twenties. He held it up for the dealers to appraise. For a long moment the short man just stared at Lester. He seemed to be calculating. *Is he thinking about capping the three of us and grabbing the cash?* Lester wondered. He got ready to draw his pistol if the dude made a move.

Finally, the short man turned back and nodded to his taller partner. The tall man then walked over to a nearby garbage can, tilted it back, and retrieved a plastic bag full of crack. He counted out a thousand dollars' worth of small baggies, replaced the larger bag in its hiding spot, and then jogged up to his partner. The short man took the goods, and the tall man returned to his position on the sidewalk.

"You know, Carolina boys have a short lifespan in these parts," the short man said evenly, holding his empty hand out for the cash.

Lester did not reply. He placed the wad of money in the dealer's hand and grabbed the baggies. The dealer removed the rubber band from the cash and began to count it.

"Let's go," Lester said to Damon.

Damon hit the gas and the boys sped off down the street.

Lester, Damon, Sammy, and a few of the other guys from the neighborhood formed a local crew, a kind of informal street gang. They ran territory on Muddy Creek Road, just off of Spanish Wells Road, and pooled their resources to keep a constant supply of crack flowing their way. The boys hung out together, worked the street together, and watched each other's backs. Most importantly, they collaborated to build a hardcore reputation within the community and beyond. This meant confronting rival crews who encroached on the local market or who, for some reason or another, disrespected one of the Spanish Wells Boys, as they came to be known.

In particular, the Spanish Wells Boys had an ongoing beef with crews from Bluffton, a Lowcountry town located just four miles west of Hilton Head via I-278. The rivalry, actually, originated prior to the emergence of Lester and his crew onto the scene. The O-Heads had had some notorious run-ins with the Bluffton hustlers over the years. Lester and his homeboys were more than happy to honor the territorial tradition.

Many of the encounters with rival crews occurred at a joint called Terry's on the west end of Spanish Wells Road. It was a boxing club that turned into an under-21 nightclub on the weekends. It became the preferred venue for settling scores. Booze and guns weren't allowed on the premises, but the Spanish Wells Boys found ways around that. Fistfights and brawls were common on Friday and Saturday nights at the club. Terry, the avuncular proprietor, armed with nothing more than a baseball bat, would do his best to break up the fracas or convince the aggrieved parties to don boxing gloves and settle their differences in the ring. However, as time went on, and as the beef between Spanish Wells and Bluffton heated up, fisticuffs evolved into gunplay. Any little provocation had the potential to turn into a deadly situation. Perhaps a Bluffton guy would flip dope to an off-limits customer, or would hit on the wrong girl, or would hurl an insult across the room. For a time, there were shootouts in Terry's parking lot nearly every other weekend. Lester and his boys would hide pistols in the bushes before entering the club. Then, late at night, around closing time, they would head back out to the parking lot and collect their weapons. If a Bluffton dude showed his face, the Spanish Wells Boys would open fire. Other times, the Bluffton guys would return the favor with an ambush of their own. Miraculously, for a while, no one in Lester's crew took a bullet.

By the time summer of 1989 rolled around, there was no doubt that the Spanish Wells Boys were straight-up gangsters, as feared and respected as any O-Head crew had ever been. The crack trade continued to boom, and the cash poured in hand over fist. Though a fair portion of the business came from local boys who scraped together the occasional twenty-dollar bill on payday, many of the customers were well-off white guys from the south end of Hilton Head. They'd roll over to Muddy Creek Road once or twice a week in their Mercedes and Lexus coupes with five hundred dollars in hand. Every once in a while, a white woman from one of the gated communities would come looking for a score. Some of these ladies had rich husbands who would leave town on business for a week at a time. They'd pass the time by laying by the pool, drinking martinis and smoking rocks. However, their husbands usually only left them with a limited cash allowance. When that ran out, a few of these women would look to trade something else for dope. Some of them turned tricks to get high. They'd pull up and offer to suck a dick or ride one of the boys for a hundred dollars in crack. Young, virile, and perpetually horny, the Spanish Wells crew typically had no objection to that kind of arrangement.

And so, Lester and his crew drank top-shelf booze and smoked primo weed. They bought slick rides and diamond jewelry and heaps of expensive clothing, hats, and sneakers. And the local ladies took notice. It seemed like every girl that Lester met at the club was looking to link up with a bad boy. Many of them, to Lester's surprise, were respectable. But, as advertised, the dysfunctional gangster life was an aphrodisiac. Money, power, respect, pussy—all that Lester had dreamed of when he first dipped his toes in the drug game was coming true.

At the same time, Lester was compelled to do his best to hide his lifestyle from his family. Lester Sr. and the Young girls had their suspicions, and from time to time confronted Lester Jr. about it directly. But the boy always denied the accusations vehemently. Once, however, his youngest sister Evelina walked in on him cutting up some rocks in his bedroom. Luckily, she never outed her brother to their father. Aside from that, somehow, Lester was able to keep the drugs, and the cash, and the guns, and the swag out of sight.

Only seventeen years old, a sophomore in high school, Lester had made a name for himself. The students at Hilton Head Island High

School were well aware of his reputation. Some were his customers. Most knew to simply stay out of his business. Lester continued to cause problems for his teachers, and, as his confidence grew, he became even harder to control.

In September of 1989 Lester was suspended from school for the umpteenth time. This, however, did not sit well with him. There was very little money to be made on the streets during school hours. Moreover, the occasional transactions that he was able to carry out on the premises of the high school provided a nice amount of cash flow. Lester ignored the suspension and returned to school. He went about his business as usual. He attended class and the teachers were none the wiser. They couldn't be expected to keep track of every punishment the administration doled out. A few times during the day, Lester snuck into the bathroom and sold some rocks to his regulars.

However, there happened to be a custodian who was aware that Lester was suspended and temporarily prohibited from entering school property. The man spied Lester in the locker room and notified Principal Grant, who then showed up at one of Lester's afternoon classes. He instructed Lester to leave the class and follow him to the front office.

Lester was not sure what the outcome was going to be. He had never heard of someone violating a suspension order. There was a chance that the school security or even the cops would get involved—a problem, since Lester had three hundred dollars of crack in his pocket. So, as he followed Principal Grant down the hallway, he surreptitiously ditched his stash in a garbage can. Unfortunately, the move wasn't as sly as Lester had hoped it would be. Principal Grant witnessed it, retrieved the bag of crack from the garbage can, and promptly called the police. Fifteen minutes later, Lester was led out of the school in handcuffs.

Lester spent two or three days in the Beaufort County Detention Center before his father showed up to bail him out. Needless to say, the conversation on their drive back to Hilton Head was not the most comfortable. Lester Sr. spent the entire time shouting, near tears, and pleading with his son.

"What do I have to do to save you from this path, boy?" he asked. "How do I save my only son from the disaster that awaits him?"

It was painful to witness his father in such a desperate state, but Lester Jr. relentlessly denied the charges. *The crack wasn't his,* he claimed. *The principal was out to get him. It wasn't his fault.* And so on.

Lester was charged with possession of a controlled substance with the intent to distribute. Because the infraction occurred on school property, the felony charge was a serious one. He faced twenty-five years in state prison. His father asked around for a legal referral, ultimately settling on an influential local attorney named Charles Vance. Mr. Vance was a former state congressional representative who headed a firm based in nearby Beaufort. He was well connected, very familiar with state drug dealing statutes, and had represented numerous clients who had faced similar charges.

Mr. Vance worked his magic for Lester, negotiating greatly reduced charges. Lester pled guilty and was sentenced to only ninety days in Wateree River Correctional Institution, plus five years of probation.

At Wateree, Lester participated in a Shock incarceration program—in other words, a prison boot camp. He and his fellow inmates—mostly young, first-time offenders—were subject to rigorous military drilling. They were roused at the crack of dawn and forced through physical challenges throughout each day. The drill sergeants, who ran the program, were absolutely unforgiving. The inmates were not allowed to speak to each other for the duration of their stay. Rule breakers were dealt with swiftly and severely. For ninety days, Lester did sit-ups and push-ups, went for long runs around the facility, and shined his boots—and that's about it.

Although the program was monotonous and arduous, things could have been much worse. Lester actually enjoyed the physical activity for the most part, and felt good about filling out his normally gangly physique for once. He often received letters from his homeboys, which provided a nice distraction. Sammy once even tried to send Lester some weed. However, the contraband was discovered in the mail room, and Lester was summarily punished.

Also, Lester's cousin Jamal was detained at Wateree when Lester arrived. Jamal was a few years older. He, too, was a dealer, and had an even higher rank on the streets than Lester. Most people were shocked to discover that the two were related because, whereas Lester had a deep mahogany complexion, Jamal looked like a white boy. The product of a Puerto Rican mother and a mixed-race father, he was light-skinned with curly blond hair and blue eyes. Lester often saw Jamal at Terry's club and was impressed by the fact that the older boy never drank or smoked weed. He was remarkably low-key despite his gangster reputation.

Jamal put in a good word for Lester with the correctional officers. And, although the two could not hang out or interact while remanded to the facility, they quietly acknowledged each other whenever possible. This laid the groundwork for a closer relationship, which would develop when Lester and Jamal were both back on the outside.

In the end, the boot camp did little to change Lester's worldview or to deter him from his gangster aspirations. Although the program instilled a new sense of discipline, it offered no counseling or mentoring that would have persuaded Lester to redirect his energies to more legitimate pursuits—quite the opposite, actually. Upon learning that Lester was a dealer, one of the correctional officers made an unexpected proposal. He suggested that, after finishing the stint, Lester set up shop in Sumter County. "I'll call you after you get out and we'll do some business," the correctional officer told Lester. Sure enough, that phone call came a few weeks after Lester's release.

Upon release, Lester was more eager than ever before to rejoin the Spanish Wells Boys and play the dope game with renewed intensity. Lester Sr., however, had other plans. He pulled some strings to secure a low-paying job for his son in the maintenance department at the Port

Royal Club. Also, he imposed a curfew so that, when the boy was not working, he would be confined to the safety of the Young homestead.

"I'm sticking my neck out to help you, son," Lester Sr. told Lester Jr. when they returned home on the day of the boy's release. "If something like this happens again, I will not get your back."

"I understand, Dad," Lester Jr. replied. "It won't happen again."

Rightfully, Lester Sr. seemed to have little faith in his son's affirmations. "I'm begging you, boy," he urged, grabbing Lester Jr. by the shoulders and looking directly and firmly into his son's eyes. "I'm begging you to stay off the streets. I've lost your mother. I cannot lose any of my children."

Moving forward, Lester Jr. went to great lengths to make it appear that he was staying out of trouble, but, in reality, he took every opportunity to run with his crew and remain relevant within the Spanish Wells gangster scene. He would sneak out of the house whenever his father was away. He'd smoke weed and go cruising in his burgundy Monte Carlo, which he secretly kept parked at a friend's house. And, when his father's watchful eye deterred him from hustling on the streets, Lester would have one of his homeboys sell drugs on his behalf.

Later that year, Lester Sr. remarried. As the wound of their mother's passing was still fresh in their hearts, eighteen-year-old Lester and his younger sisters openly protested the union. Their dissatisfaction drove a wedge between them and their new stepmother, Marie. Lester Jr. felt betrayed by his father, and even less inclined to abide by the man's dictates. Soon thereafter, in the hopes of ameliorating the situation, Lester Sr. purchased the house next door and moved into it with his bride. The Young siblings remained in the original home.

Lester eventually enjoyed greater leeway to run with his crew. Soon enough, things were how they were in the early days, before the arrest at school. The boys worked the corners, partied hard, and faced off with their Bluffton rivals. They were emboldened further when Jamal began running with their crew on a regular basis, augmenting the group's street cred. Gun fights continued to occur with regularity, and the Spanish Wells Boys grew increasingly brash. Sammy was expelled and arrested for carrying a .22 pistol on school property. Damon got clipped for shooting up a rival's school bus. Mr. Vance had his work cut out for him.

Lester's crew were heavily influenced by movies and music that glorified the cutthroat gangster way of life. They emulated the bravado of Tony Montana, the fictional, ruthless drug lord portrayed by Al Pacino in the film *Scarface*. They learned about drive-by shootings from the movie *Boyz n the Hood*, and subsequently employed the tactic against one of their local enemies. They reveled in the antiestablishment messages of hardcore rappers such as N.W.A., whose song "Fuck Tha Police" became a gangster anthem in the summer of 1988. They aspired to embody a glamorized vision of the urban American outlaw.

The police presence in Spanish Wells, despite the drug trade and the violence, was not overwhelming in those days. When something went down at Terry's, a few units would appear on the scene. Patrolmen would occasionally cruise through the neighborhood to remind the players that they could not operate with impunity. The Spanish Wells Boys knew to ditch their product as soon as they saw a police vehicle turn up Muddy Creek Road, making it all but impossible for the cops to lock them up on possession or distribution.

"Get the fuck outta here," Lester would snort at any cop who dared ask him what he was doing. "You know you ain't got shit on us, pig."

The patrolmen would cuss and make empty threats in return, before ultimately driving off.

Sometimes the cops would arrest a big user and turn him into an informant. Once or twice, a local dealer got busted this way. A regular customer would show up and make a sizable purchase, all the while hiding the fact that he was wired up and working with the authorities. But, in general, the cops did not interfere in the community too often, and they did not pose an ever-present obstacle to the dope market. When Lester traveled to the nice parts of Hilton Head, where he made regular drop-offs to a few big-spending white customers, the police were far more abundant and visible. That's where the money was, after all. It was essential to the lucrative tourism economy of the island that visitors and residents felt completely secure. It seemed to Lester that the police were content so long as the gunplay and crack peddling remained confined to the black neighborhoods. And he was fine with that.

However, there was one time, in particular, that the police made a notable show of force in Spanish Wells. The boys were hanging out on a Friday night, doing their usual thing. The plan was to head to the Hilton Head Island High School football game later that evening and then hit up a club in nearby Ridgeland afterward. Suddenly, several squad cars appeared at the corner of Spanish Wells and Muddy Creek, their roof lights spinning. Lester and his homeboys scattered as the cars rolled into the neighborhood. Officers jumped out and detained anyone who had been too stupid or unaware to abscond in time. Lester scampered up into a pine tree, where he hid his drugs and watched the events unfold. The police shut down the entire drug market from Spanish Wells Road all the way down to where Muddy Creek Road dead-ended near the Cross Island Parkway.

When the coast was clear, Lester climbed down and ran over to an empty lot on Eugene Drive. Sammy, Damon, and Jamal were hiding in the shrubbery, peeking between the leaves to assess the situation.

"What the fuck is going on here?" Damon wondered.

"It's a raid or some shit," replied Sammy. "This is out of control."

"Way out of line," Lester agreed.

Jamal was equally incensed. "Someone must have fucked up big time. I ain't never seen something like this in all my days in Spanish Wells."

"This ain't right," Lester noted. "Are we going to let these mother-fuckers do this?"

"What are we supposed to do?" Sammy asked.

Lester had an idea. He crouched and snuck over to his Monte Carlo, and popped the trunk quietly. He then reached inside and retrieved a .22-caliber semiautomatic rifle. One of his regulars had exchanged it for forty dollars of crack rocks just a few days prior. Lester returned to where his crew was positioned.

"Watch this," he whispered.

Lester stood up, shouted "Say hello to my little friend!" and began firing into the sky above the distant squad cars. The policemen dove for cover behind their vehicles as staccato blasts echoed throughout the neighborhood. When his clip was empty, Lester and his crew ran over to Jamal's house and hid in the living room with all of the lights off.

They listened as the police shouted to each other and barked into their radios. Ten minutes later, the sound of multiple approaching police sirens began to fill the air.

"Here come the cavalry," Jamal whispered.

That was an understatement. The entire Beaufort County Sheriff's Department—dozens of police cruisers and scores of uniformed men—swarmed the scene, their shotguns and pistols drawn and ready. For the rest of the night, angry packs of policemen were patrolling up and down Muddy Creek Road, banging on doors, and interrogating anyone who had the courage to emerge from his home. The Spanish Wells Boys remained in hiding until everything quieted, then slipped out of the neighborhood.

For the most part, in those days, Lester and his homeboys did not worry about the consequences of their actions. Sure, they wanted to avoid prison. But there were plenty of O-Heads who had done time and had returned to the game stronger than ever. To some degree, a stint in the big house was a rite of passage. The boys didn't worry about killing one of their Bluffton rivals; hell, that was the point of all the gunfights that they got into. Sometimes innocent bystanders got in the way and took a bullet for being in the wrong place at the wrong time. But that was their own fault. If you were worried about that kind of hazard, you shouldn't hang out where trouble brews in the first place.

By mid-1990, however, the chickens started coming home to roost. After another late night of partying at Terry's, the Spanish Wells Boys emerged into the parking lot and were ambushed by the Bluffton crew.

Shots rang out, and people began running every which way. Lester and the guys had long ago learned that the safest way to evade bullets was to crouch real low and scamper to safety. It reduced the surface area of your body, decreasing the likelihood that you'd take a hit. But not all of Terry's customers were quite so battle-tested. A kid from Muddy Creek named Mike heard the gunshots and ran upright, as fast as he could, away from the front door of the club. A bullet hit him right in the chest, piercing his heart and killing him almost instantly.

Mike was the younger brother of a guy named Francis, who was a friend to the Spanish Wells Boys. Young Mike was not a hustler; he was a sweet kid who generally stayed away from the dope game and who most certainly didn't deserve the fate that he received. Francis was inconsolable for a very long time, and his grief was contagious. The Spanish Wells Boys were outraged. Their anguish rapidly turned into anger and a lust for revenge.

For the police and the Hilton Head community, enough was enough. In response to the death, the town shut down Terry's club for good. As a result, the war between the rival crews decentralized and began to spread out across the local region. The Spanish Wells Boys went on a rampage. Over the next couple of months, they made several incursions into Bluffton territory, executing drive-by shootings against any of their foes who were unlucky enough to be hanging out on a corner or a front porch at the wrong time. Shootouts took place wherever the opportunity presented itself. If you spotted an enemy in the convenience store, you'd whip out your piece on the spot and start banging. If you came upon a rival at a late-night diner, you'd shoot the place up. There was one time when the guys took some girls to a local hotel for the evening. In the middle of the night, an extended volley of gunshots rang out. They emerged the next morning to find their Cadillac riddled with bullet holes. From then on, they made sure to park at least a block away from wherever they were planning to hang.

Lester was so accustomed to gunplay that he stopped taking shelter when shots were fired. He would just pull out his pistol and, marching boldly toward his enemies, blast away like a man possessed. It was insane behavior, but his street cred shot through the roof.

Once, Jamal cautioned Lester about being so reckless.

"You gotta think, dawg. You ain't much of a gangster once you're six feet under."

"I'm going to die sooner or later," Lester replied. "Might as well go out in a blaze of glory."

And that was the truth of it. Lester did not expect to see his own twenty-first birthday. Early on he had accepted that the way of the street hustler had a heavy price tag. Rather than live in fear of a violent downfall, he chose to embrace his fate.

The Spanish Wells Boys continued to dance on the edge of a cliff until, finally, it began to give way. One day, in the fall of 1990, Damon ambled up to the corner in an unusual mood. He was brooding and distracted. When Lester inquired, Damon revealed that he had stiffed a big Georgia-based supplier named T-Bone. But, according to some of the O-Heads, this was the wrong devil to dance with. The man had direct connections with the Columbian cartel and zero tolerance for fools who tried to play him. Moreover, T-Bone employed an enforcer, a hit man named Wade. Lester and the guys had heard scary stories about this dude. If a hit was ordered, not only would Wade show up and put a cap in your skull, he'd go after your crew and shoot up your mother's house to boot.

Lester and the guys urged Damon to pay off T-Bone and resolve the issue. But the price tag was too high. Damon owed twenty-five large at this point and barely had a G in cash under his mattress—not a good situation. For the next several days, the Spanish Wells Boys were extremely paranoid. They stayed off the street as much as they could and kept their eyes peeled for unfamiliar visitors. But nothing went down, and, after a while, the specter of impending death began to fade.

Not long thereafter, Lester had a drug deal planned that was to take place at the McDonald's in south Hilton Head. His car was having problems, so he borrowed Damon's Cadillac. Sammy accompanied him. During the drive, Lester noticed a beat-up, red Buick Regal in the rearview mirror. There was a large man with dreadlocks driving. Whenever Lester turned a corner, the Buick followed. Whenever he changed lanes, the Buick did the same.

"Dude," he said to Sammy, "don't look back, but I think this Buick is tailing me."

"Why would someone be following you right now?"

"I don't know, man, but he's been back there since we left the Wells."

Lester and Sammy parked at the McDonald's and pulled out their pistols. The Buick, however, did not follow them into the parking lot.

"I guess he wasn't doin' anything after all, dawg," Sammy said.

"I don't know. Something doesn't feel right about it."

When they finished their business, Sammy and Lester returned to Muddy Creek Road. They parked the car at Damon's house and walked over to their usual spot. It was a chilly evening, so Jamal and Damon had lit a fire of cardboard and wood inside a metal trash barrel. The four boys stood around, keeping warm and shooting the shit until a cloak of darkness descended over the neighborhood.

Soon a pair of headlights appeared at the north end of Muddy Creek Road.

"We got a customer," said Sammy.

The car rolled very slowly toward the boys, eventually coming to a halt a few feet away. It was the red Buick Regal.

"Oh, shit," Lester gasped.

The driver opened his door and emerged with a pistol in one hand and a sawed-off shotgun in the other. He was a heavily muscled man with murder in his eyes, and he loomed over the orange crackling fire like a demon from the depths of hell.

"Where is Damon?" he bellowed. "Tell me now! Where is that motherfucker?!"

There was no doubt that this was none other than Wade. The boys did not respond to his inquiry, and instead took off running for their lives. They darted through some thick foliage and sprinted into the woods, finally huddling in a shadowy spot among some dense bushes, a quarter-mile back from the street. They laid in the dirt, their pistols in hand, and squinted toward the barrel fire, where Wade still stood.

"This is fucked up," Lester whispered.

"We gotta do something about this," Jamal replied. "He's gonna shoot up the neighborhood if he can't find us."

"I know he is. We're gonna have to kill him or he's gonna kill us."

"Then that's what it's gonna have to be."

However, their fears did not manifest. The boys stayed in hiding for an hour until Wade gave up his search, returned to the Buick, and rolled quietly away.

The crew abandoned the street for a full week while they investigated ways in which they could bring the crisis to an end. They looked into borrowing money to pay off T-Bone in full. They considered driving into Georgia and assassinating Wade. They even contemplated skipping town for a few months. But, just a week or so after Wade's appearance, relief came unexpectedly. One of the O-Heads reported that T-Bone and Wade had been apprehended by the FBI on federal trafficking charges. The reason that Wade had come calling in the first place was that T-Bone had been tipped off that there was a sting in progress. They needed to collect as much money as they could to set up a getaway before the feds closed in. But the pinch came quickly, and T-Bone and Wade were thrown into a federal slammer.

The Spanish Wells Boys had again escaped doom by the hair on their chins. However, the episode hammered a deep chink into Lester's armor. Here he was, two years into hustling, and, in terms of wealth or security, he hardly had anything to show for it. A madman had come to the neighborhood to kill all of them, and maybe even their families, and Lester was ultimately, despite his hardcore reputation, helpless. It seemed that, in the end, he was simply spinning his wheels only to sink even deeper in the mud and the shit.

Jamal sensed that Lester was in a spiritual rut, and insisted that his younger cousin join him on a night out to a place called Jack's Club in Jasper County.

"You just need to get this out of your system," Jamal suggested. "You gotta hit the reset button. Let's call up some ladies and forget about everything for a night."

That sounded like the right prescription to Lester. There was one girl in particular, named Tanya, who Lester was excited about. She was classier and more reserved than most of the women he ran with, and very intelligent. She was already working toward a nursing degree. And, on top of it all, she was breathtakingly beautiful. Lester had first encountered Tanya at a party shortly before the Wade incident. They spent the entire night talking and flirting. At the end of the night she kissed Lester and looked into his eyes.

"I want to make something very clear to you, Lester," she said. "I have no interest in associating myself with a street hustler. I've got a lot of things going on, and I don't need any drama like that getting in the way. So, if you're a player or something like that, please tell me now."

Lester knew, of course, that if he revealed even half of the truth, she'd be gone like the wind.

"Naw, girl," he replied. "It's not like that at all. I work in construction. That's how I make my money."

"Really?" she asked skeptically. "You're not playing me, are you?"

"No. No playing. I'm your man." Lester grinned.

When Jamal and Lester arrived at Jasper's that Friday night, Tanya and her friend Lisa were there already. Tanya was a sight for sore eyes. She wore a floral dress, and an updo that revealed her beautiful, slender neck. Lester hugged her deeply, inhaling her sweet perfume.

The group had a few drinks and made their way to the dance floor. The groove was perfect. Jamal was hitting it off with Lisa, twirling her occasionally and holding her close when he could. Tanya shook her body rhythmically and smiled brightly at Lester, who was in a better mood than he had been for weeks.

For once, the boys had completely let down their guard. And, while this allowed them to fully immerse themselves in the joy of the experience, it was a cardinal sin for gangsters—a rookie mistake. *Always watch your back* was lesson one, according to the O-Heads. Lester and Jamal were completely oblivious to the man who was watching them from a shadowy corner of the nightclub. The man was significantly overweight and notably sported a black patch across his right eye. From time to time he leaned over to one of his companions and whispered something, all the while keeping his gaze trained on the boys from Spanish Wells.

As it so happened, Jamal was the reason that this dude, named Ray, had to strap that unfortunate accessory across his face. About a year earlier, the two had a violent run-in at different club. It was over a rather insignificant slight. But the dustup culminated in Jamal stabbing the fat man in the eye. Now half-blind and bent on vengeance, Ray was more than eager for the chance to return the favor.

Tanya's friend Lisa, it turned out, was Ray's cousin. When he saw her cozying up to Jamal he pulled her aside and explained the situation. She agreed to lure Jamal out of the club so that Ray and his boys could jump him. And so, late in the evening, when Lester and Jamal had polished off almost a full bottle of Hennessy, Lisa whispered that she wanted to go somewhere private. Jamal stood up and winked at Lester. Then the sexy girl led him by the hand to the back door of the club.

As soon as Jamal emerged into the cool night air, Ray smashed him over the head with a baseball bat. Jamal, badly staggered and dazed, scampered back inside the club before the big man and his boys could inflict more damage. Blood pouring down his face and neck, he wobbled over to where Lester and Tanya were sitting.

"Dawg!" he shouted to Lester. "They messed me up! They're after me, dawg!"

"What the fuck?!" Lester grabbed his woozy cousin and, with Tanya following, ran out the front door.

Lester helped Jamal into the back seat of their car and gave him a towel to press against the deep gash on the crown of his head.

"Who did this to you?!" Lester demanded.

"It's some big dude named Ray, man. We had beef a year ago. He's in the back of the club."

Lester ran around to the passenger seat, whipped open the door, and dug through the glove compartment for his .357. Half a dozen baggies of crack spilled out of the car onto the ground. Jamal continued to moan in pain and drip crimson onto the cream-colored leather of the rear seats. Lester handed him a vial of cocaine.

"Take a few bumps of this, man," Lester urged. "It'll help with the pain."

Jamal shuddered and snorted the powder. Lester clicked open the cylinder of his revolver and spun it to make sure it was fully loaded. Satisfied, he snapped it shut. His heart was thumping heavily in his chest. Some heavy shit was about to go down. Lester steeled himself, turned around to head for the back of the club, and found himself face-to-face with Tanya.

"You're a thug, Lester!" she cried, shoving him hard against the Monte Carlo. "You're a liar!"

Lester was seething, covered in blood, standing amid a pile of dope bags, clutching a primed silver pistol in his hand. Normally, he would have pushed his way past the girl and taken care of business. But something about the way in which Tanya stared at Lester gave him pause. For a moment, as Lester looked into Tanya's devastated eyes, it seemed to be his very mother staring back at him. Tears welled up and poured over her sweet, brown face. And, when the delicate girl opened her mouth to speak, it was his mother's regal voice that echoed across the dark parking lot.

"What kind of man are you? You're not a man . . . you're . . . you're a monster."

Lester was rendered speechless by the tortured look on Tanya's face. Her shiny, wet cheeks had become mirrors that reflected a shameful reality and foretold an ugly inevitability. Lester had hoped to win her heart with his sophistication and charm. He had even imagined developing an enduring, loving relationship with her, akin to the bond that his father and mother had always enjoyed. Instead, he now offered Tanya an unfiltered glimpse at what he truly was—a reckless, unhinged, murderous gangster. The curtain had been pulled back. Lester was exposed. In the still, midnight air, he heard his mother sigh mournfully.

Tanya then turned and walked away. And, as Lester watched her climb into her car and drive away, something deep inside of him cracked and came loose. It rumbled in his belly, bubbled up through his chest, and stuck painfully in his throat. He tucked the gun away and hung his head. Then he got into the car and drove Jamal to the hospital.

For the first time since he began slinging dope, Lester's confidence faltered. All the balling, and the running around with his homeboys, and all of the cash—those things made the risk more than palatable for a time. But now an acute sense of instability began to plague Lester. The Tanya catastrophe was a wound that would not heal. It stabbed at his heart endlessly, as if someone had crammed a shard of glass deep between his ribs. And the spoils of dope dealing, he now worried, might never repair the damage. The hustler life might not be enough.

As the holiday season of 1990 approached, Lester made preparations to leave Hilton Head. Jamal had decided to relocate to Virginia and was encouraging Lester to join him there and build a whole new operation. But Lester knew that if he didn't get away from the street game soon, he'd end up in a pine box. Disillusioned, he questioned his willingness to pay the ultimate price after all. Lester continued to think about his mother a lot in this time of uncertainty, about the lessons she had tried to teach him and the integrity she had prayed to instill within him. Lord knows what she would be thinking if she were to look down from heaven and bear witness to such depravity.

The shame gurgled in Lester's throat like a vile backwash. He began to toy with the idea that his life should have a renewed purpose—that somehow, someway, he needed to honor his sweet mother's legacy. He began to think that he should start a family and build something positive and lasting. Lester didn't want the only mark he left on the world to be a dirty, bloody, crack-speckled stain on a forgotten street corner.

An older neighbor advised Lester to look into Job Corps, which was a free GED education and job training program administered by the US Department of Labor. He thought about enrolling in Boston, where he had a lot of family, or maybe even trekking to the West Coast where he could start over completely. Perhaps he'd train to become a carpenter, find a decent wife, invest some money in a starter home, and raise a few children. The thought of such a mild, civilian existence slightly depressed Lester, but the fear of a worthless existence had now emerged as a greater motivator.

On a chilly, drizzly day in December, as the four Spanish Wells Boys huddled in Lester's car and waited for customers to roll up to the corner, he decided to let the truth be known.

"I'm tired of this shit," Lester lamented. "I can't do it for one more minute. I'm getting out. For real." And, with that, he opened the car door and headed for home.

On Christmas Eve, Lester, Sammy, and Damon decided it was time to party.

"This may be our last chance to let loose together," Sammy suggested.

"The Spanish Wells Boys gotta send you off right," Damon echoed.

If Lester figured out the whole Job Corps thing, it was possible that he would leave town even before the new year. Time was running out. So he retrieved a few bottles of Cristal champagne from his special stash, along with a bag of the kindest weed that he could find. Some of the other local homeboys joined the party, and they all got busy getting wrecked, right there on their favorite corner on Muddy Creek Road.

At some point in the afternoon, a local dude named Ernie appeared and began barking in Lester's face about some trivial infraction. Ernie was the kind of guy who always had a gripe. This time, though, Lester was in no mood for it. He responded by cracking Ernie in the face with a right hook, sending the whiny crank to the ground. Lester jumped on top, pummeling Ernie furiously.

When he had had enough, Ernie cried out, "All right, dawg! You got me! All right!"

Lester dusted himself off and snapped, "Get the fuck outta here, son," before kicking Ernie in the ribs for good measure. Ernie climbed to his feet with a groan and limped away down the street.

The boys had no sooner resumed their festivities when Ernie, bruised and blood-stained, sauntered up once more. There was a crazed look in his eyes.

"What the fuck you want?" Lester asked, irritated that this chump kept interrupting his last hurrah.

Without a word, Ernie produced a tire iron from behind his back and cracked Lester over the head, hard. Lester dropped to the dirt, clutching his skull, blood gushing between his fingers. Ernie hightailed it out of there.

Sammy took off his T-shirt and pressed it against Lester's head. Blood soon soaked through the cloth. They all piled into Sammy's car and drove to Hilton Head Regional Hospital. Lester guzzled champagne during the ride to numb the throbbing pain.

Two hours later, the boys returned to Muddy Creek Road. Lester was sporting a half-dozen staples in his scalp and had a gauze wrap wound around his cranium like a turban. He ran inside his house to clean up and grab a change of clothes. He also picked up his .22 pistol and shoved it in his pocket. If Ernie showed his face one more time, Lester would put a cap in it.

The boys refused to let the violent episode put a damper on their party. They clinked bottles, lit new spliffs, and redoubled their efforts. By eight o'clock they were flat-out wasted. Lester himself had polished off at least three more bottles of bubbly, and had smoked about as much weed as he had ever smoked in one sitting. The sting from the gash in his head had abated, and the boys were having a good old time. It was turning out to be one hell of a send-off.

Around eleven a white Chevrolet Malibu rolled up Muddy Creek Road and creaked to a stop, not far from where the crew was loitering. There was a white guy behind the wheel. He rolled down his window and signaled that he was looking to buy. He looked to be about thirty years old and had sandy hair that hung over his ears. A black woman of about the same age slouched in the passenger seat. Though none of the boys had sold to this particular customer, Lester was pretty sure that he knew who it was.

The man's name was Darryl, and he was allegedly a "jackboy" from Bluffton. Word on the street was that he had recently pulled a snatch-and-grab of fifty dollars of crack. When the dealer reached into the car to hand off the dope and take the cash, Darryl grabbed his wrist and hit the gas pedal. Darryl dragged the dealer down the street, forcing him to let go of both the money and the product.

"Yo, man. I need some rocks," Darryl shouted from his car. His slurred speech indicated that this wouldn't be the first score he had made today.

Lester eyed the white boy suspiciously. One of the homeboys—a guy named Lee that Lester had palled around with since middle school—began to walk toward the Chevy. Lester grabbed him by the arm.

"Hold up, man," Lester warned. He pulled Lee, Damon, and Sammy aside and began to whisper to them. "I think I heard about this dude. He might be a jackboy."

"I ain't never heard of him," Sammy said. "Are you sure?"

"Someone told me to watch out for a white Malibu. This is the first one I've seen."

Lee looked toward the car and then back to Lester. "Who knows, dude. Lemme see what the white boy wants. Maybe he's holding some real cash."

Lester took a swig from a champagne bottle and leered at the Chevy. "All right. But I'm watching your back."

Lester tucked his .22 into his back pocket, and he and Lee strolled up to the Chevy. Darryl smiled. He seemed a bit loopy, and his eyes were glassy. He had probably smoked a few rocks already that day. The woman in the passenger seat was in similar shape.

Lee approached the window. "How much you want?" he asked.

"Gimme two hundred, man."

Lee looked back to Lester. That was a decent buy. Lester nodded for him to go ahead. Lee pulled five small baggies out of his pocket. But, as soon as he produced them, Darryl grabbed Lee and threw the car into drive. Lester reacted immediately. He pulled his piece out and fired into the car. Darryl let go and the Chevy peeled out down the street. After watching the car disappear around the corner, Sammy, Lester, and Damon packed up their stuff and ran into Damon's house.

The boys spent an hour or two finishing off their last bottle and getting dressed and ready to go clubbing. They talked about crazy Darryl and how Lester's gunshot must have scared the shit out of that cracker. It definitely was a weird situation. They figured that he wouldn't be showing up to the neighborhood anytime soon, much less trying to pull that snatch-and-grab shit again.

They hopped into Damon's Cadillac and headed to a club called Bird's. However, on the way out of the neighborhood, the boys spotted the girl from Darryl's car. She was wobbling down the street by herself, a strange sight. The boys pulled over.

"Where's the dude you were with?" Lester asked.

"Oh! It's you guys!" In her hazy state, it took the woman a moment to recognize that she was speaking with the same men who Darryl had encountered earlier that day. "I left him at the school."

"What do you mean you left him at the school?"

"I mean, I left him in the school parking lot. He's in the car and he's dead."

"What's this crazy bitch talking about?" Sammy asked.

Lester furrowed his brow. He was still quite inebriated. Was the girl confused, or just fucking with them, or something else?

Lester followed up. "He ain't dead. What are you saying?"

"Oh, Darryl's dead all right. You shot him right in the armpit. He started bleeding from his mouth. We went to the school parking lot and he passed out. I tried to wake him up, but I'm pretty sure he's gone."

A cold sensation started to fill Lester's gut. *This woman can't be for real*, he thought to himself. *She's a crackhead and she has no idea what she's saying.*

Damon spoke up. "You expect us to believe that you just left him dead in that Chevy? That shit's crazy."

"Well, I didn't want to get in no trouble," the woman replied. "We was all messed up and stuff, you know."

The boys shared a concerned glance. Lester could not gauge whether anything that was coming out of her mouth was real or a drug-induced fantasy. He refused to believe that he had killed that dumbass cracker.

"Let's get the fuck out of here," he told Damon. They drove off.

The yellow sun eased into the sky on Christmas morning. Lester awoke with a brutal hangover. The proceedings of the prior day and night were spotty. He remembered most of what had transpired, but the details replayed in his mind with gaps and hiccups, as if he were watching an old VHS tape that had been left out in the heat for too long. Midmorning, he pulled on some jeans and shoved his .22 in his pocket—the same gun that he had fired into Darryl's car. For a fleeting moment, he considered ditching the weapon. Then again, there was no way that Darryl was dead. It was inconceivable. Lester hadn't intended to kill the dude. He just wanted to scare him off and protect Sammy from getting jacked. Surely that cracked out chick had no idea what she was talking about. Darryl probably just passed out from getting high, woke up later in the day, and then drove home.

Lester walked over to meet his crew. Sammy and Damon were there, and so was Kevin, a small-time hustler from the neighborhood who sometimes stopped by to see what was up. Lester didn't particularly like or trust Kevin. He never seemed to say what he meant.

"Yo, dawg," Kevin said to Lester. "The police were askin' about you boys."

Lester's stomach churned. "What police?"

"I dunno, man. The regular police. I was at the store by the school and they started throwin' me questions about some white boy who got killed."

"What white boy?" Lester asked aggressively.

Kevin looked nervous. "I have no idea. They found him by the school. That's all I know!"

"What'd you tell them?"

"I didn't tell them shit! I don't know shit, y'know. But they said it probably has to do with the Wells, and they wanted me to give them information. I kept my mouth shut, of course."

Kevin surely knew who was responsible for the prior day's shooting. News like that spread like wildfire in the neighborhood. Lester had a feeling that Kevin revealed more to the cops than he was willing to admit. But it wasn't worth the time to interrogate him further. The slippery bastard would probably go to his grave denying that he ratted Lester out.

Lester laid low for the rest of the day. Every once in a while, he popped out to see what was happening and get some face time. He couldn't go into hiding, or the whole community and, as a consequence, the cops would get suspicious. At one point, he drove over to the store to pick up some groceries for the Christmas dinner that his sisters were putting together. On the way back home, a police cruiser pulled up next to him and honked.

The sound made Lester's heart rattle against his sternum. The cop in the passenger seat indicated for Lester to roll down his window. Lester hesitated for a split-second as his mind raced to evaluate the situation. He figured the cops would be out of their car with guns drawn if they were onto him. Something else was going on here. Nonetheless, Lester gripped the steering wheel tightly and got ready to hit the gas if things went south.

"You from Spanish Wells?" the cop asked.

"Yeah, what's up?" Lester replied as coolly as possible.

"We're looking for a guy named Lester. You know him?"

Lester felt sweat beginning to bubble on his forehead. He struggled to maintain a poker face while panic racked his body.

He stuttered, "Um . . . I heard of a dude named Lester . . . But I don't really know him."

The cop eyed Lester suspiciously, then turned and said something to his partner in the passenger seat. He turned back to Lester.

"You sure you don't know him?" His tone was accusatory.

"Yeah," said Lester. "I've only seen him around."

"Well, do me a favor—if you run into someone who knows Lester, have him pass along the message that the police need to talk to him."

"Okay. I'll do that."

The light turned green and the cruiser pulled away. Lester patted his jeans to make sure he hadn't pissed himself.

Christmas dinner was not the lighthearted revelry that it normally was at the Young household. Lester could barely contribute to the tableside conversation. As his sisters dished out sweet potatoes and greens, and as his father and stepmother laughed and joked, Lester hunched quietly, trying to disguise his paranoia. He repeatedly eyed the front door, expecting a half dozen policemen to come knocking at any moment.

"What's wrong with you, boy?" Lester Sr. asked. "You just going to stare at that turkey?"

Lester Jr. replied catatonically. "Uh, there's something wrong with my stomach. I'm sorry. I just can't eat much."

Lester Sr. narrowed his eyes and appraised his son.

The next morning, Lester and his father drove together to the Port Royal Club for work. As usual, the radio was tuned to the AM news station. A female reporter was speaking.

> *News this morning of a homicide in the Spanish Wells neighborhood of Hilton Head. Police are reporting that a twenty-nine-year-old Bluffton man was shot to death during a drug deal gone bad. His body was discovered in the parking lot of Hilton Head Elementary School on Christmas Eve. According to police, a witness is cooperating with the investigation and warrants have been issued for two suspects. Anyone who may have information related to the incident should call the Beaufort County Sheriff's Office.*

Lester's eyes went wide. His father reached over and turned down the volume of the news report.

"Do you know anything about this?" Lester Sr. asked, concern percolating in his voice.

Lester Jr. could barely respond. "I . . . I haven't heard . . . anything," he garbled.

They drove the remainder of the way to Port Royal in silence.

Lester knew that this would be the day it all caught up with him. He figured the police would show up at the club and arrest him right in front of his dad and the rest of the staff and golfers. That would have been a disaster. So, midmorning Lester told his father that he was still feeling ill and needed to take the rest of the day off. He called his sister Tracy to pick him up.

When he got in the car, Tracy sensed immediately that something was off.

"What is wrong with you, Brother? You've been acting weird since yesterday."

"I don't want to talk about it," rasped Lester. And then, after a long pause, "I need to see mom. Take me to the cemetery."

Tracy did not need to inquire further. She drove him to the gravesite and waited in the car while he knelt and prayed at their mother's headstone.

When they returned home, Lester called Jamal in Virginia and told Jamal that he would be skipping town and heading that way. Tracy overheard the call and began pleading with Lester.

"People are saying you killed that man, Brother. Did you kill that man?"

Lester did not reply, and he didn't have to. His oldest sister was the hardest to deceive. She could read him like a book.

"You need to face the music," she insisted, sobbing. "You have to account for what you have done. You can't run away!"

"I can't stay here, Tracy. I just can't. I have to go."

"But we'll never see you again!"

Watching the tears run down his sister's cheeks, Lester felt like death. His chickens had come home to roost, and they were threatening to peck the Young family to pieces. But, Lester knew that if the police nabbed him, he was done for. He'd seen other guys get clipped for murder. He'd face life imprisonment, most likely; even the death penalty was possible. In that moment, Lester looked out the window to see his father's big, silver Ford pulling up the driveway. Following close behind were two squad cars, which creaked to a stop on the street. Lester thought about making a run for it out the back door, but he knew he wouldn't get far. Also, he didn't want to go down like a coward in front of his family.

Lester Sr. walked in the front door, his face drawn and ashen.

"Tell me it's not true, boy," he begged of his son. "Tell me it's not true."

"Dad, I had nothing to do with it!"

The officers entered the home, as Lester continued to plead. Tracy, weeping openly, wrapped her arms around her father and hid her face as the policemen turned Lester around, cuffed him, and marched him out the front door.

Lester was booked and sent to Beaufort County Jail pending trial. The state appointed him a public defender. Lester had wanted to hire Mr. Vance, but the attorney insisted on twenty grand up front and another ten later. Lester had a portion of that amount hidden back at his house, but he couldn't dare ask one of his family members to dig it out. It was packed together with thousands of dollars of crack. Lester asked one of his homies to retrieve the dope, sell it, and bring all the cash to him. But, in the end, the dude stiffed him on a good portion of the money. Either way, it would not have been enough.

The trial, four months after Lester's arrest, was rather uneventful. Darryl's female companion, Kevin the dubious local hustler, and even Lee took the stand for the prosecution. To a degree, Lester felt betrayed by this. Yet he knew the reality of the situation. The police surely were holding something over Lee's head—maybe a drug trafficking charge, or an accessory charge. He must have been compelled to come clean in court or be sent packing to prison alongside Lester.

The trial lasted only two days. Lester did not testify in his own defense, and no one took the stand on his behalf. None of the state's witnesses testified to seeing Lester actually shoot the weapon, but it was an open-and-shut case for the jury. They quickly returned a verdict of guilty to the judge, who read it aloud as Lester's family sat behind him and wept.

The judge then immediately proceeded with the sentencing procedures. Lester's attorney attempted to influence the determination of the court by describing the redeeming features of the defendant's life—his close relationships with his family, his work at the Port Royal Club, his plans to complete a GED. However, the judge appeared slightly bored by the appeal. He promptly sentenced Lester to life in prison with the possibility of parole after twenty years.

"Do you have anything to say for yourself, Mr. Young?" the judge inquired to conclude the trial.

Lester was bitter, enraged. Bile percolated in his gut. He raised his right fist—a defiant black power salute—and declared, "I'm gonna do me." The bailiff then escorted Lester from the courtroom.

After a few weeks at a Department of Corrections evaluation facility, Lester was remanded to the Allendale Correctional Institution in Fairfax, South Carolina. It is a medium-security prison, ninety minutes northwest of Hilton Head. Lester struggled to hide his nerves during the transport to Allendale. The bus, like the evaluation facility, was filled with hard-looking dudes from all over the state—men who had been sentenced for all manners of serious crimes. And so it became clear to Lester that the street rep he had built on Hilton Head Island would do very little for him moving forward. In fact, a handful of the guys on the bus were already openly threatening to kill Lester as soon as they arrived at the prison. These guys were from Charleston. Apparently, Charleston and Beaufort inmates had a bitter ongoing rivalry in the prison.

Once within the walls of Allendale, Lester made it his first order of business to find a weapon. Not only were the Charleston thugs breathing down his neck, but he had heard countless stories about how hardcore prisoners make a sport out of preying on newbies. In particular, Lester knew that if he wasn't vigilant, he could end up getting raped by one of the so-called "bootie bandits." A correctional officer told Lester that there were a number of inmates who were O-Heads from the island or were aligned with the O-Heads. These were the guys that could show Lester the ropes and provide him with necessary protection. He was then directed to his dorm room, where he was relieved to learn that his roommate was an agreeable guy named Roger who had been in Lester's high school class for a time. Halfway through sophomore year, Roger stopped showing up to school. Nobody knew where he went. Turns out, he was serving five to ten years for armed robbery.

Roger was not the only familiar face. Once Lester got a chance to spend some time in the yard, he tracked down the O-Heads. They usually hung out on some benches near the basketball court. One of the men spotted Lester and approached him with open arms and a big smile. It was Big Homie, the Spanish Wells drug dealer from whom Lester had purchased his very first dealer pack.

"Man, is it good to see you," Lester said, offering a solid handshake.

"You, too, my brother. You look nervous. Don't be. We'll get you squared away in here."

"Cool, man. That's good to hear. But I need to find a knife, dude. Where can I get my hands on a shank? I got some cats from Charleston lookin' to bum-rush me already."

Big Homie smiled, and there was an aura of peace in his eyes that Lester had never noticed back on Muddy Creek. "You don't need no shank right now, my friend. Don't worry about that just yet. Those boys are just letting' off steam, I'm sure. Plus, the fellas and I have your back in here. Stick with us and you'll be right as rain."

Lester was grateful to have a support system at Allendale. However, the learning curve was still exceptionally steep. As Big Homie further explained, and as Lester learned firsthand, everybody in prison had an angle. They were looking to take advantage of you, or to rob you, or to stab you, or to rape you. And, backup or no backup, the prisoner who wasn't on his toes at all times was an easy target. Some of the poor souls in prison were so meek and powerless that they became the sexual slaves of bigger, stronger deviants. Given the choice between sucking a man's dick and getting shanked in the liver, the sexual slaves chose the former. It was sad to see, and there was surprisingly little that the COs could do about it.

Not long after Lester was admitted to Allendale, a scrawny young man from rural South Carolina showed up. His name was Nick. It was obvious from his slight build and from the sheepish way that he strolled around the yard that this unfortunate boy was going to be an easy target. But, it got worse. He was assigned to share a dorm room with a gangster they called Hi-Top, who was probably the most notorious rapist in the entire facility. It was as if the prison system was setting up that little bumpkin to get violated.

It took almost no time, too. Within a few days, there came shouting and screaming from Nick's dorm room. A crowd of prisoners ran over to see what was going on. Hi-Top had jammed the door shut by wedging toothbrushes into the hinges. He was attacking Nick. Four COs came running over. They tried desperately to shoulder open the door to the room, but it would not budge. And, with the crowd watching through the window of the door, Hi-Top proceeded to ruthlessly beat Nick, then bend the poor kid over his bunk and viciously rape him.

When Hi-Top finished, he left Nick blubbering in a heap on the floor. He then plucked the toothbrushes from the hinges and casually opened the door. The COs had their pepper spray drawn, ready to blast Hi-Top if he made a move. Instead, the big thug stretched, yawned, and quipped, "I guess you'll be taking me to solitary now." They did.

The first year in the big house was rough for Lester. He was constantly tense and looking over his shoulder. He witnessed several hardcore beatdowns and multiple stabbings, which inspired him to spend time learning how to box and how to handle himself in hand-to-hand combat. He ultimately got his hands on a makeshift blade and carried it with him whenever he could. One of the O-Heads taught Lester how to attack and defend himself in a knife fight. It was like a perverted version of samurai training. He learned that the only safe way to take a shower was to wear underwear and running shoes for traction and to keep his knife strapped to the inside of his arm. Even still, Lester, like most guys, made sure to have two of his allies stand lookout while he washed.

And then there were prison economics. Allendale, like many correctional facilities, was a hybrid barter-cash marketplace. There were exchange rates for everything from socks to *Hustler* magazines, from gummy bears to cigars. The pricing varied from day to day. Also, to Lester's surprise, there was a thriving drug market in the prison. There were inmates who were making a solid living as dope dealers, earning money they could then spend on sundries, or contraband, or even legal services. Lester occasionally walked past a dorm room where someone was openly counting out thousands of dollars on his bunk.

Lester, at this time, was motivated to appeal his conviction. Sure, he was guilty, hands down, but he did not believe that he had the spiritual fortitude to survive a life sentence in this hellhole, much less a few years. Moreover, Lester felt justified in his belief that his own lifetime of incarceration would do nothing to bring Darryl back. Yet the legal angle required a good deal of money, which Lester did not have when he first entered prison. So, once again, he got in on the drug game and began slinging dope. The customers were not as abundant as they were back on the island, but the product sold at absurdly high margins. Lester found that he could turn over a slab of crack for $1,000 in prison versus $150 on the street.

Drugs made their way into the prison in all sorts of ways. Visitors would sneak in with them crammed in their anuses. Correctional officers looking for something to top off their meager paychecks served as secret couriers. People on the outside would literally throw the dope into the prison. This last method involved a highly coordinated effort. There were multiple lookouts who would monitor the progress of the officers patrolling the facility perimeters. There were other guys who shouted instructions. And there was a network of handlers who would pass the goods between each other until they were safely stowed away. The suppliers on the outside typically would cut open a football and pack it full of crack and marijuana. The more brazen ones simply filled duffel bags with contraband. And when the signal came that the perimeter patrol was safely out of sight, a half-dozen guys would sprint out of the nearby woods and lob the packages over the barbed-wire fences into the yard. It was actually comical to watch.

After hustling for just a few months, Lester made enough money to hire attorneys to challenge his conviction multiple times. However, he did not leave it in the hands of the lawyers. Lester learned from Big Homie that the best defense was a good offense. In other words, an inmate hoping to obtain freedom through the appeals process had to learn the law for himself. This meant spending time in the prison library, and consulting with "jailhouse lawyers"—convicts who had studied so much during their incarceration that their knowledge sometimes exceeded that of the professional civilian attorneys who serviced the prison population. Unfortunately, Lester's literacy level presented an obstacle. When he entered the facility at nineteen years old, he had the reading ability of a middle schooler. The first time he opened a legal tome, it was as if he were deciphering ancient Sumerian. Nonetheless, Lester persevered and, with time, became an avid reader, well-versed in jurisprudence.

What Lester learned from the books and the jailhouse lawyers was not especially encouraging. Only about 3 percent of convicts who received similar life sentences were ever granted parole. Generally, there was not much of an incentive for parole boards to put murderers back on the street, especially when, as in Lester's case, the victim's surviving family members were actively opposed to it. Also, he learned, many guys who were locked up in a madhouse like Allendale went crazy, killed themselves, or simply lost their sense of humanity by the time their twenty-year parole hearing came around. The question wasn't simply: Would he be granted parole? It was also: Would he survive, intact, to the day that he could stand before the parole board?

As Lester's funds were sapped by fruitless legal efforts, his situation became increasingly dire. Only a few years into his sentence, he found himself facing an ongoing existential crisis. Each day he woke up wondering if he could make it through to the next. In addition to the everyday suffering, inhumanities, and threats that inmates faced at Allendale, prison-wide lockdowns were common. If there was a brawl or a major drug bust, or some other kind of gross violation, the hard-nosed warden would order that the prisoners be confined to their dorm rooms around the clock. And these accommodations were anything but comfortable. The rooms were about the size of a walk-in closet, furnished with only two steel bunkbeds, an open toilet, and a sink. Where Lester laid his head was mere feet away from where his bunkmate would piss and shit. As a consolation, what coursed through their digestive systems during these extended confinements was insubstantial. For breakfast, lunch, and dinner, the COs would shove a plate through the door slot containing only two pieces of bread and two pieces of baloney. Prisoners were not even allowed to leave their rooms for showers or family visits. Lockdowns like this would last days, even weeks.

Lester feared that he would devolve into a soulless animal like so many of the long-term, violent felons who populated Allendale. He numbed himself with marijuana and jailhouse wine, and passed the time mindlessly flipping through porn magazines. With eighteen years to go before his first parole hearing—one that was almost certain to result in a denial—Lester was fading.

Big Homie came to the rescue. One day, he stopped by for a visit, taking a seat on the bunk next to Lester, who was high and drunk and all but catatonic with depression.

"Let's have a talk, brother," Big Homie suggested.

"What's there to talk about?" Lester replied.

This made Big Homie chuckle. "Well, we're alive, aren't we? That's more than a lot of people can say."

Lester didn't appreciate the attempt at humor.

"Let's talk about who we are and what this place is," Big Homie continued.

"This place is a hellhole."

"Sure. That's how a lot of cats see it. It's hell on earth, where bad motherfuckers and unlucky bastards and poor dudes who don't know any better get sent to rot away so that everybody else can sleep at night and enjoy their barbecues and go get a cone at the Tastee Freez."

"That's the truth," Lester intoned.

"That's *a* truth," the older man shot back. "And maybe that's how it's supposed to be. But it's not the *only* truth."

Big Homie looked at a small stack of books piled next to the bunk. He picked one out and began to flip through it before speaking further.

"My family had a dog when I was a child. It was an ugly old mutt that somebody had abandoned, but we loved him, and he was loyal like all dogs are. We named him Rusty, because that's what he looked like— an old, rusty mess. At first, we kept him in a wire crate. We couldn't let him run around the house and get into things and shit everywhere before he was trained properly. So when we slept, or when nobody was around, we locked him up in that cage. And he hated it. For weeks, he howled and whined as if we were torturing the poor bastard."

Big Homie stopped on a certain page of the book he had selected and took a moment to read a few sentences silently.

He continued. "As time went on, and Rusty learned how to behave, we no longer locked the kennel. We allowed him to roam as he saw fit. But, you know what? He learned to love that cage. For him it became a sanctuary, a place where he could rest and be safe, and find peace."

Lester had started to pay attention to what his friend was saying. And, of course, he began to pick up on the metaphor. Big Homie closed the book and stepped over in front of Lester.

"It's an interesting thing, how these things tend to work, Lester. No matter where you are, or what happens to you, reality is not just something that you find—it's something that you create."

"That's easier said than done, man," Lester pointed out mournfully.

"Now that's the kind of thing that a weak man says. And, I've known you a time now, and I'm pretty sure that you are not a weak man." Big Homie smiled and looked into Lester's eyes. Lester nodded slowly. "All that shit you did on the outside, that we both did— the hustling and the fighting and the lying—that's what landed you *in* here. Do you think that any of that is going to get you *out* of here?"

Lester wanted to speak, but the words caught in his throat. He shook his head "no."

"Then the time has come to make a choice, son. And it's clear as day that you can't wait any longer. Decide what reality you are going to create, and do whatever it takes to create it. There ain't no half-assing it. Choose your path and be true to it. Be real."

With that, Big Homie appraised Lester for a long moment. Lester was sullen and deep in thought. The older man gently jabbed him on the shoulder and headed for the door. But, just before he stepped out, he turned back to Lester and held up the book that he had selected.

"This is a good read, right here."

He tossed the book so that it landed on the bunk next to Lester. Then he strode out of the dorm and down the hall.

Lester thought for a while. He looked around his cell, at the scuffed cinder-block walls, and the foul toilet, and the ratty blanket that covered his bunk. Then he picked up the book. It was one that he had first acquired while in county lock-up awaiting his murder trial: *The Autobiography of Malcom X*. A black Muslim named Ali had given it to him. That was almost three years ago. He flipped to the first page and began reading.

Guided by Big Homie's ongoing moral example, and inspired by the story of the imprisoned Malcolm X's transformation from a street hustler to a spiritual, worldly intellect, Lester slowly started turning his life around. Though he had long ago repudiated God and had forsaken his Christian upbringing, he began to study the teachings of Islam—as Malcolm X did—and to adhere to its tenets of purity and surrender. Lester stopped dealing drugs and forced himself to disengage from the miscreant underbelly of the penal system. He eschewed prison wine and marijuana and pornography and instead committed himself to prayerful reflection, and to learning, and to expressing his thoughts and philosophies in a daily diary. He read voraciously, especially digging into stories of transcendental spiritual leaders and historical figures. In particular, Lester found solace in *Long Walk to Freedom*, the autobiography of Nelson Mandela, in which the great civil rights leader described the emotional challenges and opportunities he encountered during twenty-seven years of incarceration in South Africa.

Lester took an active role within Allendale's Muslim community. Within just a few years he became the imam—the religious leader—of the prison. As such, he was able to impact the lives of scores of fellow inmates, working with them to understand and follow the righteous path exemplified by Muhammad, and to channel their energies into worthwhile pursuits.

In 1995, Lester was given the opportunity to volunteer in a hospice program at Allendale. Each week he spent time providing emotional support to terminally ill inmates housed there. Notably, there were high rates of tuberculosis and AIDS throughout the South Carolina correctional system during this period. Many of the afflicted patients had no one to comfort them, no one to be there as their lives drew to a close. Lester eventually found himself at the bedside of a nineteen-year-old AIDS patient from Walterboro. The boy's name was Kendall, and by the time Lester encountered him, he had just a few weeks to live. Lester spent as much time as he could conversing with Kendall, providing him with water and medication, reading to him, and, when the boy cried, holding his hand.

Lester learned that he and Kendall had had almost identical experiences as young, violent crack dealers. They both had spent years hustling and cavorting without care or concern for anyone around them. Shortly after his incarceration, Kendall was informed that he had contracted HIV from one of the dozens and dozens of women that he encountered on the streets of Walterboro. Now, here he was, just a few years later, crying into a prison-issue pillow as his body wasted away.

Lester was bowled over by the realization that he had inexplicably escaped a similar demise. As a wannabe gangster on the streets of Spanish Wells, he was just as reckless and as promiscuous as Kendall had been, if not more so. But, for some reason, God had spared Lester this horrible fate and had given him the opportunity to rehabilitate himself. As Lester sat at the bedside, holding Kendall's hand and watching the emaciated teen gasp his final breath, he made a solemn promise that this second chance at life would not be squandered.

In 1996, the conditions at Allendale grew even more oppressive. South Carolina had installed a new director of the prison system who believed in severe regulations and draconian punishments. In response, Lester and other prison leaders organized a protest whereby the inmates who had labor and maintenance responsibilities within the facility would refuse to work. However, a handful of inmates declined to participate, which resulted in a violent dispute among some of the men. The conflict engulfed the cellblock and erupted into a full-fledged riot. Correctional officers responded but were beaten back by inmates. Prisoners began to tear up the dorm rooms and smash fixtures and start fires. The COs used shotguns to fire plastic pellets and beanbags at the prisoners, but the men defended themselves by creating barricades with their bunks and mattresses. A riot response team was called in from Columbia to assist in quelling the violence. Finally, after three hours of rage and destruction, order was restored.

The prison director ordered a complete lockdown of the facility. As usual, the men were restricted to their dorm rooms at all times. However, this lockdown was different from the others in that it lasted a full ninety days. After just a few weeks, many of the inmates were on the verge of nervous breakdowns. Lester did what he could to brave the solitude. However, he too found it virtually unbearable. Surviving on the very meager prison rations, and occasionally fasting as part of his religious devotion, Lester grew increasingly weak. He spent many of the days of the lockdown prostrate in bed. The physical and psychological torment of the experience stoked his anxieties about his future and amplified his regrets about past digressions. The lockdown became a battle between Lester and his own mind.

Toward the end of the three months, Lester experienced a powerful, lucid dream. In it, he awoke in the middle of the night, in his childhood bedroom. Outside his window the world was dark, except for the gleaming orb of the moon above the forest. Lester stood up and walked silently into the living room. His mother—youthful, and full of life, and at peace—sat in her chair, knitting. Seeing her, Lester was overcome with emotion. He called out to her desperately. *Momma! Momma! I love you, Momma!* She raised her head and looked toward him blankly, as if he were invisible. Lester felt as if his heart was about to burst.

Lester . . .

It was Lester Sr.'s voice this time, resonating somewhere behind Lester. Lester turned to respond, and unexpectedly found himself in the parking lot of Hilton Head Island High School. It was chilly and grim and abandoned, except for his towering father, who stood shrouded in the amber light of a sodium lamp, which shone from atop a tall post. Eyeing his son, Lester Sr. raised an arm slowly and pointed. Lester Jr. turned his head to view a white Chevrolet Malibu. He recognized it immediately, and felt his stomach tighten. Slowly he glided toward the vehicle, trembling at the thought of what he would see through the window. When he reached it, he peered inside. And it was empty.

Lester returned his gaze to his father. But the man standing there was no longer Lester Sr. It was someone else, some*thing* else—an indecipherable presence that exuded a throbbing, invisible energy. Lester strained to appraise the apparition, but its features would not come into focus. Nonetheless, Lester came to realize with certainty that it was God, the blessed one Himself, who stood before him.

Lester began to sob uncontrollably. All of the pain, and shame, and guilt that had, for years, taken residence so deeply inside of his soul now poured over him like a hot bath. Lester approached and collapsed to his knees at the feet of God. His tears poured onto the asphalt of the parking lot as he implored his divine savior to forgive him of his sins. *I am worthless*, Lester rasped. *I am a vile sinner. I am nothing. I beg you to help me. I beg you to save me.* Lester howled with anguish. *I will forever devote myself to righteousness and redemption. I will devote myself to honoring You!*

The light from the sodium lamp suddenly extinguished. Lester looked up, and found himself kneeling in the dirt alongside Muddy Creek Road. The neighborhood was completely dark and hollow, except for a barrel fire that crackled nearby. The white Chevrolet was parked on the street before him. Lester stared at it and wiped the wetness from his cheeks. The driver's door creaked open, and Darryl emerged, alive and well. Lester began to cry again, scalding tears pouring down his face. He felt as if sorrow would envelope his body until the day he died. Darryl approached slowly, the barrel fire lighting his path. He stopped directly in front of Lester. For a long moment, they looked into each other's eyes, deeply—the victim and his murderer reunited in a frozen moment. Lester blinked, and suddenly his mother was standing there, exactly where Darryl had been. She wore a pale nightgown that trembled in the gentle, evening breeze. She stared down at him with an expressive mix of both love and heartbreak. Then his mother reached out and gently placed her warm palm on top of Lester's head.

On May 15, 2014, a rainy day in South Carolina, more than twenty-three years after he was arrested for murder, Lester Young Jr. walked out through the main gates of the Kershaw Correctional Institution, a medium-security facility to which he had been transferred some years prior. Lester, now forty-three years old, was, at long last, a free man. At his second parole hearing he had been given barely two minutes to describe his hospice work, his role as a spiritual leader, his creation of a therapeutic educational program for inmates, his unceasing pursuit of knowledge and self-awareness, and how all of those things had prepared him for a productive return to society. The members of the parole board, who listened quietly during the presentation, unexpect-edly and unceremoniously approved Lester's release.

As Lester stepped into the world, he paused and looked down at his feet. To be standing outside of the prison walls without his ankles shackled together was surreal and oddly disconcerting. He took a moment to reflect on Darryl, God rest his soul. He knew that a fleet-ing, careless, ignorant act not only took the life of an innocent man, but also devastated that man's family. This was an existential burden that would, forever, press heavily on Lester's shoulders. Yet, he hoped that if Darryl were looking down on this moment, he would be com-forted, if only slightly, by the knowledge that his passing ultimately led to the spiritual reawakening of a lost young man, the rebirth of a condemned soul.

Lester's wife, Barakah, awaited him outside of the prison, raindrops spotting her hijab. Her smile was warm and radiant and chased away the wave of apprehension that her husband was experiencing after over two decades in lockup. The two had been introduced through a mutual friend and, following a few years of correspondence and regu-lar visits, married in 2007. They kissed and embraced for a very long time before driving away.

Today, Lester and Barakah live in West Columbia, South Carolina. Barakah is a state-certified pharmacy technician. Lester works as a machine operator for Tyson Chicken and, on the side, runs a small power-washing business. Shortly after his release, Lester founded a nonprofit organization called Path 2 Redemption. Its mission is to reduce the prison recidivism rate by providing an emotional and spiri-tual support system for ex-offenders.

The Spanish Wells Boys have long since gone their separate ways. Jamal moved back to Hilton Head, but suffers from various chronic health issues and struggles to make ends meet. Damon is a junkie, strung out on crack. He has a son who was recently charged with murder in a drug-related incident. Sammy is serving twenty-five years in federal prison for drug trafficking.

Lester and Barakah often spend time with Lester Sr., now retired, and Lester's three sisters, who all continue to reside on Hilton Head Island. In 2015, Barakah gave birth to a baby girl. They call her Kaleeyah, an African name which means "the most shining bright one." She has chubby cheeks, and great, big eyes, and a whole life yet to live.

CHAPTER 2

THE DRIFTER

John Frizzle

When John Frizzle was an elementary schoolboy, during the early and mid-1970s, he spent several weeks each summer at the home of his paternal grandparents. They, Wilbur and Dot, lived in Marysville, a bedroom community just south of John's hometown, Port Huron, in a region known as the "Thumb" of Michigan. The Thumb is a bulbous jut of land that gestures toward the heart of Lake Huron, which, in turn, carves out the eastern border of the state. Contoured on its western front by the giant, teardrop-shaped Lake Michigan, Michigan, then, takes the form of a left-handed oven mitt. Port Huron is the easternmost plat of land in the state, where, if you can imagine, a topographical knuckle might protrude from the Thumb.

Port Huron, the seat of St. Clair County, is a working-class, largely industrial city of approximately thirty thousand residents. Most of the residents are white, with a smattering of African Americans and Latinos. The economy features paper mills, and factories, and tourism-related enterprises, and automotive companies. Thomas Edison, one of John's personal heroes, experienced some of his upbringing there. That aside, Port Huron is not particularly out of the ordinary for the American Rust Belt. The city is about as Michigan as Michigan gets.

Port Huron also has the distinction of being located at the very southern point of Lake Huron, where its fresh waters funnel into the St. Clair River. Across that river is Ontario, Canada, specifically a village called Point Edward and a small city called Sarnia. This geography—a special place on the international border, nestled at the crux of a Great Lake—has always been a source of pride and fascination for John and is the reason he so enjoyed his estival stays with his grandparents.

Wilbur and Dot's home was a short walk to Veterans' Memorial Park, a stretch of lawn on the western shore of the St. Clair. From there, John would attentively watch on as a never-ending procession of titanic lake and sea freighters lumbered past. The ships, with cargo holds full of minerals, industrial resources, and assorted trade goods, each bore on its stern a flag indicating its country of origin. John's grandparents owned a book that listed and illustrated the flags of the world for John to reference. Many ships, of course, were American and Canadian, but, every so often, a more exotic vessel would sail past. John would excitedly flip through the book for the matching banner. He spotted French ships, Norwegian ships, German ships, and even Japanese and Liberian and Soviet vessels that had made their way into the bosom of North America via the Saint Lawrence Seaway. Upon returning home in the evening, John would pull the heavy world atlas off Grandpa's shelf and examine maps of these foreign ports of call.

The USSR, John noticed, was especially far away. He had often overheard his grandparents discussing an ongoing Cold War with this sprawling, distant empire. At eight or nine years old, John was not exactly aware of all that the phrase "Cold War" entailed, but he did find it strange that the enemy's boats were cruising Michigan's waterways.

The summer of 1975 was an especially memorable one for John. On August 1, reports surfaced that longtime Teamsters union president and powerful mafia figure Jimmy Hoffa had gone missing. He was last seen at a restaurant in upscale Bloomfield Township, about an hour drive to the southwest of Port Huron. The story was huge news where John lived, and indeed, headline stuff around all of Michigan, where thousands of men and women in various industries, including the auto and freight industries, were members of the Teamsters. John noticed that his father, Gary, paid especially close attention to the nightly news around that time. He was a non-union general contractor and craftsman who often competed directly with the Teamsters for construction and renovation work. In the days that followed Hoffa's disappearance, Gary and his associates talked about it frequently. In John's young mind, they exuded a reticent, conspiratorial tone that contrasted with the wild sensationalism of the news broadcasts and the speculative gossip of folks at the diners and grocery stores around town. It made John wonder whether his father was somehow involved in the incident. Gary, after all, ran with a fairly dicey crowd. During John's childhood, one of his father's friends was shotgunned to death. Another was sentenced to life in the big house for murder. In retrospect, it is most certainly not the case that Gary was involved in the Hoffa abduction. But John's imagination, once triggered, had a tendency to run hog-wild.

One day, in that same year, John saw the legendary freighter the SS *Edmund Fitzgerald* float past Marysville. He was dumbfounded by its size. For a time the largest ship on the Great Lakes, she measured over seven hundred feet from stern to bow and could transport more than twenty-six thousand tons of iron ore in a single haul. John waved enthusiastically at a handful of the sailors who had appeared topside in the sunshine. He dreamed of being one of them, a fearless crewman on a majestic ship. His thrill on that day, however, was superseded by shock when, in November, the papers announced that the ship had disappeared in the deep waters of Lake Superior amidst hurricane-force gales and four-story swells of roiling, icy water. The bodies of the twenty-nine crew members were never recovered.

John imagined what it must have been like for the crewmen: to have been thrust by a wave or some other great force off the ship and into the midst of a violent body of water the size of a sea. He wondered whether, if he were in that position, he would have been able to stay afloat, to keep himself from freezing, and to somehow ride the frigid currents back to shore. Yet, despite the horror of the incident, and despite his deep affinity for the vessel, John did not grieve her loss. The tragedy, certainly, was an eye-opening event and generated a lingering element of morbid curiosity, but the boy did not express what could be described as an adverse emotional reaction. Actually, as a youngster, and, indeed, throughout his whole life, John Frizzle quite rarely allowed an emotional reaction to surface.

Barely a month after the sinking of the *Fitzgerald*, the front page of the *Times Herald* of Port Huron declared:

POLICE FEAR MISSING CLERK WAS VICTIM OF FOUL PLAY

Twenty-one-year-old Valerie Lee Mills had inexplicably disappeared during her late-night shift at the Howard Johnson's Motor Lodge on Pine Grove Avenue. After an intense, five-day search, Mills's naked corpse was found discarded in a snow-shrouded field twenty miles north of Port Huron. She had been raped, strangled, and shot five times.

John followed along with heightened curiosity as a multi-department task force was assembled to investigate the murder. The *Times Herald* established a "Secret Tip Reward Fund" that ulti-mately exceeded $18,000. Soon, a man came forward with pertinent information. His brother, Robert Taylor, had made a suspicious visit to the home of another brother on the evening of Mills's disappearance. Robert had had a .30-caliber bullet lodged in his foot and required assistance in tending to the wound. Police investigated, and in late January, arrested the thirty-one-year-old and charged him with murder.

The jury trial that ensued was a sensation that rippled across regional newspaper headlines. Taylor was a handsome, former high school football captain, a married father of three who held down a supervisory position at the Ford auto plant in nearby Utica. He pled not guilty, but his flimsy alibi and spotty testimony were picked apart by the prosecution. In October of 1976, the jury convicted Taylor of first-degree murder. He was sentenced to life in prison without the possibility of parole.

Though the particulars of the crime and the subsequent proceed-ings had John on the edge of his seat, the real intrigue did not manifest for another eight months. On June 5, 1977, Robert Taylor, donning a correctional officer's uniform, sauntered out of the front door of Southern Michigan Prison and disappeared without a trace.

As police and prison officials scrambled, John, now eleven years old, began to fantasize about joining the hunt. He surmised that Taylor had stowed away on one of the freighters steaming into Canada or had hitched a ride in a northbound big rig. He began to concoct an earnest strategy for tracking the dangerous fugitive. He'd steal a shotgun from one of the neighbors and stuff a backpack with peanut butter sandwiches, scouting gear, and a few folds of cash. Then he'd pedal his bike down to the docks and sneak aboard a freighter headed for Duluth. From there, John would disembark and hitch his way along the Canadian border, bouncing from town to town, from gas station to motel, interrogating the clerks, and the proprietors and the waitresses just like Columbo did in that nifty detective show. Finally, he would walk into a greasy spoon somewhere, maybe in rural Alberta or Saskatchewan, and there, reading a newspaper over a coffee and a plate of steak and eggs, would be Robert Taylor himself. John would steel himself and stroll stealthily up to the notorious killer. He'd press the muzzle of his shotgun into the back of the man's neck, and announce with a gritty drawl, "The gig is up, Taylor."

Thoughts of the pursuit thrilled young John. He grew to believe, deeply and confidently, that he could actually execute his plan. He would be the hero of Port Huron, an American crime-fighting legend—a real-life Dirty Harry. Then autumn blew into Port Huron, and, along with it, the first day of sixth grade. John soon forgot all about the manhunt.

In early January 1978, Robert Taylor held up a Seattle massage parlor and attempted to rape one of the two women working there. The other woman on duty was able to wrestle the gun away and deposit two .22-caliber rounds into Taylor's stomach. Taylor was apprehended while seeking medical treatment at a local hospital. At an apartment Taylor had been renting in Seattle, detectives discovered credit cards belonging to a third woman who had previously gone missing from a nearby boutique. That woman was never found.

Taylor was convicted forthwith of the Seattle robbery and assault. Shortly thereafter he was stabbed to death by a fellow inmate at Washington State Penitentiary in Walla Walla.

A life on the waters beckoned to John throughout his youth. By freshman year of high school, he made the decision to join the US Navy. He craved adventure, and he knew that paging through back copies of *National Geographic* and tracing trade routes in the old atlas would not provide nearly the fulfillment that he could derive from sailing the seas to distant lands. Moreover, John never felt drawn to, or especially qualified for, a future in anything other than the military. He was, in most things, average or below, an expert underachiever. He squeaked by in school, properly applying himself only in a few mechanical vocational courses that required minimal mathematics. John enjoyed hunting, and archery, and scouting, along with various other casual outdoor recreational activities, but showed no promise in any particular athletic pursuit. And, to be blunt, he was inept with the ladies. Through high school, the closest he ever came to a romantic conquest was when a friend of a friend invited him to the eighth-grade prom at nearby Central Middle School. That night, John remembers, was notable only for its supreme awkwardness.

Later in life, John concluded that his sense of social maladjustment as a youth, his sense of "otherness," was not just a figment of his imagination. He had virtually no regular friendships nor a crew to run with in the neighborhood. Despite John's well-proportioned stature and piercing eyes, most girls viewed him as an odd bird, or simply ignored him outright. Some of the guys at school harassed John, including a few in particular who relentlessly taunted him during the daily bus trip to the vocational training center. And so, as a high schooler, John was frustrated. Aside from throwing punches or retreating into a hermitic shell, he did not have an effective method for dealing with the maliciousness and disregard he experienced during that period of his life. John arrived at the conclusion that he simply did not belong. He really *was* a different animal.

John came to blame his parents for his problems, at least in part. Both were high school dropouts who had rarely ventured outside of the Port Huron region throughout their lives. His mother, Shirley, was the daughter of an abusive, alcoholic father. Primarily a homemaker, she was an affable but strong-willed woman who refused to let others disparage her or her family. John has never forgotten one childhood incident in which an aggrieved neighbor lady appeared on the porch one afternoon. He never learned the nature of the dispute, but the interaction culminated in little Shirley dragging the rather sizable woman to the ground and smacking her repeatedly upside the head.

John's father, Gary, was no shrinking violet either. He was compact and sturdy and deceptively powerful due to his daily toil on construction sites. He had a viselike handshake and a gruff persona to match. Though business was unpredictable during the 1970s, especially surrounding the 1973 and 1979 oil crises, over time Gary was able to build a fairly successful contracting business, with a number of laborers in his employ. Yet he was a heavy drinker, and the booze fanned the flames of what seemed to be an inherent belligerence. This characteristic, along with his acute nearsightedness, earned Gary the nickname "Fuzzy." After a six-pack or so, he was inclined to go looking for trouble, often engaging in fisticuffs with local guys who did not show him the requisite level of respect. In order to fight, he would have to remove his spectacles, thereby rendering himself nearly blind. Gary's pugilism was not the most precise, but once he wrapped his rugged arms around his foe, the combat was usually short-lived.

Violence also found its way into the Frizzle household. During John's childhood, his mother and father often engaged in belligerent disputes. Screaming matches typically erupted in his parents' bedroom, then spilled into the living room—where John and his younger brothers, Troy and Ken, often watched cartoons and baseball on television.

Shirley would shriek at and smack Gary. He would tackle her to the couch, pin her arms back, and bark angrily about some issue or another. Occasionally he yanked her hair and slapped her in the face. There were a few times when John considered grabbing a frying pan and braining his father.

Gary, as one might expect, was no stranger to the law. He did some time as a younger man for paying people with forged checks. He also had some dings on his record for driving under the influence and for carrying a concealed firearm without a permit. Gary mostly dealt in cash and paid his men under the table, so he packed a pistol every time he left the house.

But, overall, John's father was a durable and relatively competent man. John, not so much. The boy was goofy, and not particularly focused. He walked around with his head in the clouds, so to speak, a characteristic that his father neither related to nor appreciated. Gary was never satisfied with John, and, to some degree, may have been ashamed of the boy. He occasionally snapped at John for laughing or shrieking "like a girl." He would come down hard on John for even the slightest of screw-ups at school or around the house. He was relentlessly critical and dismissive of the boy's carpentry and handyman skills. When he needed a new apprentice, he opted to bring on one of his nephews rather than offer the role to John.

The Frizzle family relocated frequently, a trend that compounded John's struggles as a social outsider. Gary was frequently buying, renovating, and reselling small homes in the Port Huron region. He did this so often, in fact, that by the time John graduated high school, the family had occupied eleven different homes. Sometimes they moved into a house before construction was half-complete. This migratory, roughhewn way of life was destabilizing. John felt like a drifter, and, for nearly all of his life, in one way or another, he would be one.

At the start of his senior year of high school, John enlisted in the Navy via a delayed-entry program. Boot camp at the Naval Station in Great Lakes, Illinois, began shortly after graduation. At the outset, John envisioned a long career of daring international conquests and esteemed service to the country that he loved so well. He was eager to develop valuable skills and knowledge, to achieve a certain degree of glory, and to finally show his father his true worth as a man. However, his performance left much to be desired. He bungled his way through boot camp, struggling to muster a modicum of drive or self-discipline.

From Great Lakes, John was ordered to "A School" at Memphis Air Station for another few months of specialized training. He would prepare for work as an aviation structural mechanic, a technician who services and repairs the bodies of aircraft. There, in Tennessee, fairly removed from his home turf, John began to sow some wild oats. For the first time, he started drinking. He frequented bars on Beale Street in Memphis, hunting for excitement and loose ladies. And, with practice, John's tact with the opposite sex began to improve marginally. He was not quite scoring, but at least some of the girls he approached paid attention to him, or even agreed to play a game of pool when he offered to put up the quarters.

At age nineteen, John was more than ready to surrender his virginity. He became fixated on sex. All of the other guys at A School boasted of exhilarating romantic triumphs. And so, every female that John encountered—the cashier at the convenience store, the redhead at the laundromat, the busty girl at the Air Station who worked on Seasprite helicopters—became a romantic intrigue. But, time and time again, John's inroads turned out to be dead ends. The women could obviously sense his strangeness. They could smell it. *These women are like damn bloodhounds!* John would think.

On one rare occasion, a few of the other naval trainees invited John to join them for a night on the town. They went to a bustling pub and music venue on Beale Street called Silky O'Sullivan's. Late in the evening, they were approached by an exceptionally friendly gal in an impressively scant outfit. After a brief negotiation, she agreed to join the party and relocate with the four boys to a seedy motel around the corner.

It wasn't until someone turned on the lights in the motel room that John got his first good look at their female companion. She was about five or ten years older than the boys, and, as blue-collar working girls go, not half-bad-looking under her layered, nocturnal makeup. Her name, the one she offered, was Lizzy. She had agreed to a group special: forty dollars per man.

While one of the sailors tuned the clock radio to a local rock-and-roll station, another shouted, "Johnny Boy first! The virgin gets priority!" Loud guffaws filled the room, and Lizzy cackled, revealing her not-quite-white, gapped teeth. John was nervous as hell but just drunk enough to overcome his inhibitions. He dropped his jeans to his ankles and awkwardly climbed atop Lizzy, who had quite professionally tossed her panties and heels into a corner of the room. John grinded his pelvis against the prostitute's warm crotch while his mates shouted raunchy encouragements. Three or four thrusts later, the event reach its climax. The sailors roared with approval and clinked their beers. John, half-embarrassed, half-satisfied, scrambled off of Lizzy, who rolled her eyes and picked at a cuticle.

Upon completion of A School training, the graduates were given the opportunity to apply for an ongoing service placement. These "billets" were delegated in order of performance ranking. John—it came as no surprise—was second from the bottom of that list. He was assigned to Naval Station North Island (NASNI) just outside of San Diego. The work wouldn't be thrilling, but at least he was headed to sunny Southern California.

John had two weeks of leave before he was required to report for duty. He spent a good deal of this time imbibing heavily at a bikini bar near the Memphis Air Station known as the Anchor Lounge. The establishment served only beer, but thirsty bachelors like John were allowed to bring in their own harder stuff. One evening, John arrived with two fifths of vodka and a half-gallon of orange juice. Within a half hour he guzzled almost all of it. He summarily blacked out.

John briefly came to in a Navy hospital as two medics were forcing a plastic tube down his throat. He passed out again and did not regain consciousness until the following morning when a doctor entered the room to check his vitals.

"You're lucky it wasn't worse," the doctor remarked as he inflated a blood pressure cuff. "I've seen folks end up in intensive care with that amount of alcohol running through their veins. You must have a cast-iron stomach."

John did a double-take. *A cast-iron stomach?!* The doctor had just confirmed that John could really handle his booze! Perhaps, he even had an exceptional constitution. That meant—no matter what else about John was off-kilter or weak or underdeveloped—he was at least partly, if just in this unique way, a real man. Though the bikini bar incident may have been a troublesome harbinger, the possibility that he was developing a drinking problem like his father or his mother's father was overshadowed by this encouraging medical assessment.

John spent two days recouping in the hospital. On the second day, two unfamiliar young marines visited him. They introduced themselves as Stuart and Greg, and explained that they had come to his aid after he blacked out at the Anchor Lounge. John, in a sloppy state, had attempted to crawl onto the stripper stage, but was booted off by an irritated dancer. He collapsed to the filthy club floor and passed out. Stuart and Greg then dragged the inert sailor to their Jeep and transported him back to the Air Station. During the ride, John sprayed vomit all over the interior of the vehicle. Disgusted, they schlepped John's limp body into the barracks, and dumped him on his bunk. Later, the night watchman found John in a pool of puke on the floor and summoned an ambulance.

Stuart and Greg wanted John to come over to the Marine barracks and clean out the Jeep upon his release from the hospital. John apologized profusely and agreed to sanitize the vehicle. That last part, however, was an expertly delivered lie. As soon as John was discharged, he collected his personal effects and headed to the airport.

Upon arriving at San Diego International Airport, John hailed a taxi. It carried him down the Harbor Freeway, past the Embarcadero and downtown. He rolled his window down and indulged in the crisp, salty breeze that washed in from the bay. It was December 1984, a time of year that would have been arctic and punishing back in Port Huron. Here, however, the sun was beaming and the temperature was hovering in the mid-sixties. John had to peel off his wool sweater because his back and armpits were starting to drip.

The taxi crossed into Coronado and left John at a gate on the eastern edge of the naval station. An on-duty sailor greeted him and escorted him through the North Island base, pointing out the notable features and important buildings. As they walked, John noticed helicopters hovering in the distance, a mile or so out over the Pacific.

"What's going on over there?" he asked his escort.

"Oh, those are the SEALs. For training, they toss those guys out of a chopper and make them swim back to base with all of their gear."

John raised his eyebrows. "Man, I'm glad that I'm just a lowly mechanic!"

For the foreseeable future, John would be based here at NASNI. His first obligation was to complete FRAMP—the Fleet Replacement Aviation Maintenance Program. He would spend a few months learning to service and repair S-3A Vikings, small surveillance jets whose primary purpose, at that time, was to track Soviet submarines. The regimen wasn't horribly oppressive, but the seemingly endless series of tutorials was a far cry from the glory and adventure that had seduced him into enlisting.

John was happy to make the acquaintance of a sailor from Long Beach named Jeff, who, coincidentally, had also completed A School in Memphis. Jeff's peculiar, hippie style appealed to John, and made him feel less of an outsider. Perhaps the most unusual thing about Jeff was that he drove around in a beat-up old Cadillac hearse. John thought it was cool as hell. The two spent several weekends cruising Broadway Avenue in that macabre wagon, passing a flask of Mad Dog malt liquor back and forth and catcalling after any remotely cute girl that crossed their path. They'd blast heavy metal music, letting it pour out of the windows onto the streets of the Gaslamp Quarter.

Jeff, in fact, had a fascination with the occult. He introduced John to some rather hardcore Satanic rock bands, and the two occasionally discussed the power and purpose of the dark prince within the realm of modern religion. John, at this time, was in rebellion mode. He had grown disaffected with organized Christianity, which he regarded as archaic and irrelevant. After meeting Jeff, he began identifying as a Satanist. John was not particularly devoted to the gospel of Lucifer, but he felt that an affiliation with the dark side gave him an edgy, dangerous mystique. Declare that you are a devil worshiper and people tend to take notice.

One night, the guys drove the hearse up to Oceanside and parked right next to the strand. The odd spectacle drew a crowd of young people. Jeff produced a cooler full of Mad Dog and beer, and the gathering quickly evolved into a full-on beach party. Sometime before sunup, as the eastern horizon was just beginning to bleach, a fully-clothed John drunkenly sauntered into the surf. A gaggle of young ladies pointed and laughed as he waded into deeper and deeper waters. The waves, icy in the late winter, were breaking hard and knocking John off of his feet. His jeans and tennis shoes made it difficult to swim, but he ultimately paddled out far enough that the rough surf was behind him. For a time, he floated languidly on his back and gazed toward the alabaster moon. He wondered whether the ocean current would wash him out to sea. One of his uncles had drowned in a riptide some years back. *Maybe it's okay if I drown*, he thought.

A few weekends later, Jeff introduced John to Tijuana, Mexico, a seedy tourist destination just south of the border. Jeff claimed that the purpose of the trip, in addition to sampling the lusty delights that the town had to offer, was to have the seats of the hearse re-upholstered.

But he winked as he said that, and John got the sense that his friend might have been moonlighting as a drug smuggler. The two cracked bottles of beer and ambled their way down Avenida Revolución, a tawdry lineup of dirty bars and dirtier strip clubs. Blinking blue-and-pink neon signs illuminated the littered street. Jeff guided John to a doorway underneath a placard that read "Bambi Club."

"Beautiful girls, no cover," a portly Mexican man at the entrance announced.

"Free is the right price," John replied.

The main room of the club was dark and brimming with enthusiastic male patrons. Naked and mostly naked women shimmied on stages, sauntered along the bar tops, and cavorted giddily. John and Jeff claimed a table off to the side. In no time, an attractive Guatemalan with dyed red hair was draped across John's lap. She seemed to know few English words other than "fuck," "suck," and "twenty dollars." John, however, was not concerned with her linguistic prowess.

The woman took John by the hand and led him to a neighboring motel. It was decrepit. John decided not to turn on the lights because he was sure he would witness cockroaches scurrying up the walls. The woman bent over the bed, and pulled down her leopard print underwear. To his relief, John lasted considerably longer than he had with Lizzy back in Memphis.

John was immediately hooked on Tijuana. The prostitutes at Bambi's became very familiar with the lanky Michigan boy who showed up by himself almost every weekend. A few of them even invited John to spend the night at their homes when he was too smashed to find his way back north. John enjoyed the attention but occasionally wondered whether these women were honestly infatuated or were simply working angles. In the end, he decided that he did not care what the truth was. It felt good, and it seemed real, and these were the best, most intimate relationships he had ever had with members of the fairer sex.

In January of 1986, John deployed for a six-month West Pacific and Indian Ocean cruise. No more drilling—it was time for him and his NASNI colleagues to take their place on the world stage. They were transported via DC-9 jet to Alameda, then ferried to the USS *Enterprise*. Commissioned in 1961, it was the longest naval vessel ever constructed and the first nuclear-powered aircraft carrier. She had been in service twenty-three years by the time John first set foot on her. For John's cruise, the *Enterprise* would serve as the backbone of a battle group that featured two destroyers, two frigates, two cruisers, one submarine, and one supply ship.

As the *Enterprise* was herded across the San Francisco Bay by tugboats, John experienced the sensation that his life was about to change completely. He was topside as the carrier passed beneath the breathtaking Golden Gate Bridge and chugged into the shimmering blue of the Pacific Ocean. At long last, John would traverse wild oceans and touchdown in faraway ports. He was primed to test his mettle—to discover exactly what he was made of and who he was meant to be. *Get ready, world*, John thought. *Here I come.*

The charge of the USS *Enterprise* was to take the place of the USS *Coral Sea* in the Mediterranean off the shore of Libya. American forces, under the direction of President Reagan, had been keeping a very close eye on the country's revolutionary leader, Colonel Muammar Gaddafi, who was known to encourage and support terrorist efforts against western targets. Libya was implicated in the deadly December 27, 1985 attacks on international airports in Rome and Vienna. On April 5 of the following year—two months into John's deployment—Libyan agents bombed a Berlin discotheque. Two hundred and twenty-nine people were injured and three were killed, including a US serviceman. Ten days later, the US Navy, Air Force, and Marines blitzed Libya with a twelve-minute aerial attack, during which they dropped sixty tons of ordinance. The attack, however, had limited impact on Gaddafi's power and stance toward the West. He declared himself the victor of the engagement, and denounced Reagan as an "Israeli dog."

From positions in the Mediterranean, American naval forces had been testing Libyan defenses, making incursions into the Gulf of Sidra, near Benghazi. John wholeheartedly supported the effort. He believed that Gaddafi posed a grave threat to American values and hegemony. As the carrier steamed westward, and as tensions escalated in the region, John grew eager to play a role in deposing the Libyan autocrat.

As a structural mechanic, John operated primarily in the hangar bay, below the flight deck. The aluminum bodies of the aircraft were vulnerable to the salty spray of the ocean, so corrosion control was an ongoing concern and John's primary charge. He would spend hours upon hours breathing into a sweaty respirator and applying a special-ized epoxy onto the tarnished wings and underbellies of the Vikings. It was mindless, thankless work that required the skills of a trained monkey. Just a few weeks out to sea, John began to wonder how he would survive the drudgery.

Fortunately, the *Enterprise* made numerous port stops, which helped with morale. It docked off of Honolulu, the Philippines, Singapore, and Pakistan, hopscotching its way toward the Mediterranean. The ship conducted patrols in the Gulf of Oman and traversed the Red Sea before weaving its way up the narrow Suez Canal. It was the first nuclear aircraft carrier to pass through this man-made waterway, and, indeed, barely fit.

As the *Enterprise* toured the Mediterranean region, John had the opportunity to visit Rome, Paris, and Vatican City, among other notable tourist destinations—enjoyable diversions that appealed to his fascination with antiquity. But, during the long stretches between port stops, when he did little other than spray rust inhibitor and sleep, John grew restless and resentful. He felt as if he had committed a good portion of his life to the Navy, had completed all sorts of training and education, only to be pigeonholed as a glorified handyman. With the completion of each monotonous shift in the hangar bay, his fixation on this existential dilemma amplified. He shuffled back to his rack each night weary and ready to rip his hair out.

It began as a mental exercise during the quiet moments before lights out. John would contemplate ways to make a more consequential contribution to American military goals despite his lowly position within the naval hierarchy. At first he thought about how he might work hard to distinguish himself and thereby rise in the ranks. However, he quickly dismissed this notion. Diligence was never his strong suit. To date, he had never impressed a superior enough to earn an advancement of any kind, within the Navy or elsewhere. Furthermore, John did not have that kind of patience. To climb to an officer rank that carried any sort of influence would take years, decades even. Poor John could not imagine where he would be in life six months down the road, much less craft a long-term career strategy.

John shifted his tack. His move would have to be dramatic and immediate—something that would send shockwaves throughout the Navy, across the world even. His thoughts returned to public enemy number one: Colonel Muammar Gaddafi. One night, while staring at the ceiling of his rack, listening to jet wheels thump and screech on the flight deck one level above, John had a moment of clarity. His heart began to thump in his chest. The solution was both obvious and grandiose. He would singlehandedly track down and assassinate the Libyan leader.

This line of thinking evolved into a consuming, day-after-day obsession. The narrative began to unspool within John's imagination. He would trek into Northern Africa, blend in with the local population, evade enemy agents. When the time was right, he would sneak into Gaddafi's palace, quietly terminate a few unsuspecting guards, and, like a shadow, make his way to the Colonel's bedroom. There he would find Gaddafi slumbering peacefully, perhaps draped with the naked bodies of two or three nubile concubines. John would steel himself and stroll up to the infamous revolutionary. He'd press the point of a bowie knife into the Colonel's chin, and announce with a gritty drawl, "The gig is up, Gadaffi."

Envisioning this bold act of vigilantism, John experienced a visceral giddiness that reminded him of when, as a child, he schemed to hunt down the fugitive Robert Taylor. But the Gaddafi plan felt much more tangible, more real—the burning desire to execute the strategy, more potent. John was old enough, man enough, and, he believed, competent enough to follow through on this gambit, however ambitious. If he succeeded, there was no doubt that he would go down in history as an American military hero.

The risks of the plan, John knew, were significant. He could, of course, be killed in the process. If not, discovery of the action—even the mere conspiracy to take this sort of action—would result in severe discipline, likely a court-martial. Also, there was a decent chance that the Navy would pursue John once they discovered that he was AWOL. This meant that John could not simply slip away during one of the port stops. He would have to throw the hounds off his scent. It became evident that he would have to fake his own death.

John decided that the most effective way to abscond would be to abandon the carrier while at sea. No one in his right mind would do that. If John turned up missing while the ship was steaming through the depths of the Mediterranean, there would be no reasonable conclusion other than that he had fallen overboard and perished. However, exiting a moving nuclear aircraft carrier is no walk in the park. The flight deck is sixty feet above sea level, nearly double the height of an Olympic diving platform. John could kill himself by plunging into the water at the wrong angle, or, once overboard, get pulled beneath the carrier by a current. Moreover, John was not sure he possessed the physical strength or endurance necessary to swim miles to shore. He might have to endure hypothermia, or severe sunburn, or dehydration. Also, he would have to make his move without being noticed by any of his fellow crewman.

One night, at two, while the majority of the crew slumbered, John snuck out of his rack and headed down to the hangar deck. From there, a door opened out onto the stern of the ship. This gave John access to a steel service ladder that extended straight down the back of the vessel. John gripped the handrails and began descending toward the water level, some thirty feet below. The sea was placid, and a thick cloud cover shrouded the moon. As John progressed, he came closer and closer to the frothy trail of sea water churned up by the ship's massive propellers. The wake was ivory white against the blackness of the sea and the starless, charcoal sky. It was all that John could see, the only source of illumination that provided him with any semblance of spatial awareness. He reached the tail of the ladder, just a few feet above the seawater, and there paused to contemplate his options. If he were to use this ladder as a method to abandon the ship, he most certainly would have to do so when they were anchored. There was far too great a risk that he would get swept under by the wake, maybe even somehow sucked into the propeller blades. Yet, as he gazed down at the bubbling trail of seawater and felt the low thrum of the carrier resonate in his chest, John was mesmerized. The rhythmic pulse of the propellers and the steady wash of the waves against the steel hull were siren songs beckoning. He felt a peculiar, almost irresistible desire to leap into the water right at that moment—to release and fall backward into the salty embrace of the Mediterranean. For what felt like an eternity, he stared into the hypnotic whirlpool spinning just below his feet. Then, his heart palpitating, his extremities tingling, John climbed back up.

John crawled back into his rack that night feeling conflicted. He was exhilarated by the prospect of his impending escapade, but also frightened. Hanging precariously from the back of the *Enterprise*, John had no longer felt as if he were in complete control of the situation. It was as if the two halves of his brain—the rational and the irrational—were at war with each other, or, if not yet engaged, then rattling their sabers. He began to worry that his quixotic sense of adventure was obscuring a more perilous reality. Was his scheme as insane as it was brash? Did he have a sound grasp of what it all entailed? Was he ignoring a subconscious death wish? John lay awake until sunrise trying to make sense of it all.

The following day, after completing his shift in the hangar bay, John sought out his executive officer in his office.

"Sir, I considered throwing myself overboard last night," he blurted upon entering.

The XO, a rigid Norwegian from North Dakota with the surname of Hansen, looked up from his paperwork with narrowed eyes. "What the hell are you saying to me, Frizzle? I'm not in the mood to be trifled with."

John immediately second-guessed the decision to come here. He stared at his feet as he continued with his confession. "Not, uh, trifling with you, sir. Last night, I woke up in the middle of the night, and . . ." He paused, not wanting to reveal the true nature of his conspiracy. "And I could not stop thinking about climbing up to the flight deck and taking a header into the sea. I think there might be something wrong with me."

Hansen eyed John carefully, then set down his work and stood up from his desk. He came around to get a close look at his subordinate's face.

"What's going on with you, Frizzle? This is a serious thing you are telling me. You know that, right?"

"Yes, sir. It's just . . . I don't know what my issues are. I'm telling you this because I'm not sure that I can stop myself next time."

The XO wrinkled his chin and thought about this for a moment. Then he turned to his desk and scribbled onto a small tab of paper. He folded the note and put it into John's hand.

"Take this to sick bay. See Dr. Watts. Tell him what you told me. I want an update afterward."

John stared down at the note, wondering if he had opened a Pandora's box that would be very, very hard to close again.

The following evening, despite his reservations, John did as he was instructed. But, with more distance between the incident and the present moment, John had begun to feel that his existential crisis was not such a crisis after all. He downplayed the concern, explaining to

Dr. Watts that he had experienced only a fleeting sense of hopelessness that now seemed to be fading. Nonetheless, Watts, a humorless clinician, ordered John to stay off of the flight deck for his own safety.

John's fixation on the Gaddafi ploy waxed anew. And when, little more than a week later, the *Enterprise* anchored off of Sicily, he decided that the time was ripe. He spent a day refining his escape plan, which would require a two-mile swim to shore. If John took his time and did not wear himself out right away, he could complete that part of his journey in a single night. However, there were a couple of additional obstacles remaining. When the carrier was stationary, it was also at its most vulnerable. Typically, a whale boat was dispatched to monitor the ship's perimeter throughout the night. Also, John still had not determined a suitable way to go overboard. He felt that the stern service ladder was too out-in-the-open.

By nightfall, John had come up with an alternative. One of the aircraft elevators—a hydraulic platform that transported jets from the hangar deck up to the flight deck—was locked in place at the flight deck. The shaft of this elevator opened to the sea on the starboard side of the carrier. Hanging over the side of the carrier, near the elevator, was a small motorboat known as the "captain's gig." It was lashed via a thick mooring rope to an iron cleat. John determined that he could use the rope to climb down to the base of the shaft and then drop the final ten feet into the water from there.

Once again, John waited until the middle of the night to make his move. He equipped himself with two hundred dollars cash, a switchblade, and two large, plastic trash bags, which he planned to inflate for flotation. Sailors were each assigned a "float coat," which they were required to wear while on the flight deck. However, John realized that he had to abandon that essential item in order to make it seem as if he had died from a tumble overboard. While the rest of the vessel slept, he snuck out of his rack and crept along a gangway to the elevator. He took hold of the mooring rope and carefully shimmied down a steel guide column. That column was covered in slimy graphite grease—a lubricant for the elevator. By the time John reached the bottom of the shaft and stepped out onto a ledge overhanging the water, he was covered in the noxious stuff.

John collected himself and peered out toward the horizon. The lights of Naval Air Station Sigonella flickered like so many distant candles. He spotted the whale boat with its flashing beacons slowly trolling toward the bow of the carrier. John crouched and prepared to drop into the water. However, just before he made his move, his mind began to race. There were sharks in those waters, he suddenly realized. Why had he not thought of this before? Perhaps they would leave him be as long as he was not thrashing or bleeding. But what if he was wrong about that? John noticed, too, that the stern of the carrier was drifting out toward the open Mediterranean, not toward shore. This meant that the current was flowing in the wrong direction! Even if he swam vigorously for hours, it was more likely that he would get swept out to sea than reach dry land. And, just like that, John arrived at the sobering awareness that he was jammed between a rock and a hard place. If he jumped in, one way or another, he would almost certainly die. His hunt for Gaddafi would have to remain on ice until another opportunity arose. Only God knew when that would happen.

John grabbed hold of the rope and attempted to climb back up. However, because his hands and clothes were slathered in greasy lubricant, he could not get a proper grip nor find purchase with his feet. He could hardly ascend five feet, much less the forty feet that he had to climb to get back to the deck where his rack was located. John was stuck, and hopelessly so.

He remained perched on that overhang for over four hours, shivering in the brisk pre-dawn air. Finally, at about six, during one of their routine passes, the sentries on the whale boat spotted John. For a time, they kept their distance and observed John through binoculars. Given the severity of the security breach represented by John's actions, these men would have been within their rights to shoot the suspicious subject clinging to the side of the carrier and then ask questions later.

They took a more diplomatic approach and radioed to the carrier bridge. Within minutes voices came from above. John looked up to see a group of crewmen peering down at him. Among them, notably, was John's XO, Hansen.

"Frizzle, what in the hell are you doing?" Hansen hollered.

"I don't know," John replied sheepishly. "I'm stuck!"

Satisfied that John was not a saboteur, the patrolmen motored over to a position on the side of the carrier, just below John's ledge. John lowered himself onto the deck of the whale boat. Then the patrolmen escorted him back onto the carrier to account for his bizarre behavior.

The Master of Arms, a stout, ruddy-faced man, barked questions at John and demanded prompt answers. John claimed that someone had pushed him off the flight deck into the water below, and that he had been able to pull himself back up onto the elevator ledge. His clothes, however, though greasy, were conspicuously dry. The Master of Arms informed John that his actions constituted a serious crime, and that he would be investigated for sabotage, and potentially face a court-martial.

"Or you can tell the truth, and we can try to help you," the Master of Arms continued. "I spoke with your XO. He told me that you thought about killing yourself last week, that you were going to throw yourself overboard. Is that what you were up to this morning?"

John did not like that his neuroses were becoming common knowledge. However, he recognized that the Master of Arms was throwing him a lifeline, and that affirming this dubious narrative could get him out of hot water. The truth—that he was attempting to go AWOL, to trek to northern Africa and assassinate Gaddafi—would have had far more disastrous consequences. He owned up to the suicidal thoughts.

John was helicoptered to Sigonella for processing and then flown to Naples, Italy, for assessment and treatment. John spent ten days, including the Fourth of July, 1986, in a barracks there. He was given free rein to come and go as he pleased—odd, considering his recent erratic behavior. He briefly considered skipping town. Soon, however,

the attending psychiatrist filed a report diagnosing John with a person-
ality disorder and recommending an honorable psychiatric discharge.

John was shuttled via C141 transport plane across the Atlantic
Ocean, back to Great Lakes Naval Station. As the craft approached
the runway, he realized with considerable pride and a sense of irony
that he had succeeded in circumnavigating the globe. It may not have
occurred how John had envisioned it, but the journey still felt like a
noteworthy achievement.

Now twenty-one years old, John was committed to a psychiatric
ward in the hospital at Great Lakes. Inexplicably, a psychiatrist there
quickly overruled the Naples specialist and deemed John fit for duty.
After a few days, John was transferred to a transient barracks to await
deployment orders. During this hiatus he was assigned various menial
tasks around the base, including mopping floors, transporting garbage,
and cleaning the surprisingly unsanitary ladies' head.

John quickly grew frustrated. Precious days were wasting. That vile
snake Gaddafi was still out there, taunting the young sailor with every
boastful public statement and military encroachment. John could not
imagine surrendering his ambition to follow through with the assas-
sination. In fact, until the Libyan strongman was killed in 2011, that
dream never fully faded from John's mind.

John concluded that it was time to go AWOL. However, all of his
belongings, including his cash, were still aboard the USS *Enterprise*,
somewhere in the Mediterranean. He decided to raid some of the personal lockers in his barracks. They were cheaply made of pressboard,
and the doors readily popped off their hinges. But the spoils were
meager. After twenty minutes of pillaging, John walked away with only
five dollars cash, a navy ring, and a pair of medical scissors. *Screw it*,
John thought. He pocketed the items and headed outside to hail a taxi.

John's destination was Rush Street, near a popular triangle of ritzy
restaurants and nightclubs in Chicago. The driver, a burly, Hispanic
ex-marine, agreed to a twenty-dollar flat rate.

"Sounds good," said John. "I'll pay you when we get there."

Forty minutes later, the taxi pulled up in front of bustling Gibson's Steakhouse. The driver asked for his fare. Prepared for this moment, John brandished the medical scissors and held them to the driver's throat.

"I don't think so, fella," John hissed. "I'm not paying you. You're paying me."

The driver smacked the scissors away and jumped out of the cab. He yanked the rear door open, dragged the shocked sailor from his seat, and threw him violently onto the pavement. The scissors flew out of John's hands and skidded into traffic. The driver knelt on John's belly and grabbed him by the shirt collar.

"You're gonna give me that twenty bucks or you're gonna give me your ID, right fucking now. Otherwise I bash your skull in." Passersby in sport coats and cocktail dresses paused to casually observe the spectacle. Smothered, John dug his driver's license out of his pocket and handed it over. The taxi driver looked at it carefully and then stood up.

"If I ever see you again, John Frizzle, I'll kill you."

John scampered to his feet, snatched up his pair of scissors, and fled down the avenue.

He spent most of the night wandering by himself. He strolled between the high-rises and brick row houses of Streeterville, crossed over to the lakeshore, and killed an hour exploring Navy Pier. There, he came across a few old-timers fishing and drinking beer from a cooler. John thought about robbing them, but was not feeling as bold as he had before the public shaming on Rush Street.

He headed toward downtown. On the way, he cut through a parking lot, casing a few of the vehicles as he went. To his surprise, when he lifted the handle on a shiny red Corvette, the driver's door popped open. John quickly jumped into the front seat and began rummaging through the glove compartment. He found a leather wallet. Flipping it open, he was deflated to discover no cash inside. However, there was a shiny silver medallion in one of the flaps. It was a Chicago policeman's badge. *Holy shit!* John slipped the wallet into his pocket, hopped out of the Corvette, and jogged off into the night.

It was closing time as John made his way toward the Loop. Bouncers were hollering at drunkards and guiding tipsy bachelorettes out onto the sidewalks. He came to a twenty-four-hour McDonald's, and bought a fifty-cent cup of coffee. He loitered for a while out front, sipping the hot beverage, brainstorming ways to put the policeman's badge to good use. Across the street, a Yellow Cab pulled into a gas station. The driver emerged and began pumping.

Inspiration struck. John crossed the street, ambled up to the taxi driver, and flashed the silver badge. Summoning his most authoritative voice he announced, "Chicago PD. I need to commandeer your vehicle."

"What are you talking about?" the taxi driver, an older man, snapped in reply.

"Sir, I don't have time to explain. Give me the keys." John held out his open hand.

"I don't think so!" The man turned on his heel and walked over to a payphone. John followed him, persisting with the charade. The man picked up the receiver and dialed 9-1-1. Seeing this, John fled.

A few minutes later two squad cars rolled to a stop right next to John. Four policemen emerged with their hands grazing their holsters. John wanted to run, but they had him surrounded before he could even get into gear. One of the men directed John to place his hands on the hood of one of the police cars. He vigorously frisked John and, in the process, discovered both the wallet and the pair of scissors.

"Where'd you find this badge?"

"I found it on the ground outside the McDonald's," John replied as convincingly as possible.

"Sure you did, you fucking punk." The cop cuffed John and tossed him into the rear seat of the police car.

John spent a week in Cook County Jail—one of America's more notorious penal institutions—before his father was able to drive down from Michigan and bail him out. They returned to Port Huron.

John's parents wanted an explanation not only for why John was arrested, but also for what he was doing back stateside. Before he called them, they thought he was still on his Navy cruise, halfway around the world. John concocted some flimsy explanations for his current predicament, but his parents clearly were not falling for it. During the days that followed, their demeanor toward him shifted noticeably. The pride and hope they had exuded upon his enlistment seemed to have completely evaporated, replaced by suspicion and thinly veiled apprehensiveness. They behaved toward John now as if he were a loose cannon that would unleash at the slightest provocation.

Gary and Shirley convinced John to take a train back to Great Lakes and face the consequences for his unauthorized absence. There, John was summoned to a captain's mast—a non-judicial naval hearing. He was sentenced to fourteen days in a restricted barracks with janitorial duties.

John pushed his broom and ruminated on Gaddafi. Clearly, he was not making progress. In fact, with each setback he was, quite literally, getting further and further away from his target. He worried that, sooner than later, the window of opportunity would close for good. John thought about the ancient Carthaginian general Hannibal, who achieved greatness as a war hero in the third century BC. Had Hannibal sacked Rome during the Second Punic War, the great Roman Empire may never have risen and flourished. John wondered what might happen if he never followed through on his gambit, if Gaddafi were allowed to persist. Would the world bear witness to the rise of a powerful, oppressive Arabic empire? Surely, something had to be done—a preemptive strike that would cut the Libyans off at the knees. And, despite the false starts and fuck-ups that had hamstrung him to date, John was still convinced that he was the man—the Hannibal—for the job.

A few weeks later, John appeared before a Chicago judge, who issued him a one-year suspended sentence for impersonating an officer. John returned to base, relieved not to be doing time. To celebrate, he went AWOL again.

He took a Greyhound bus back to Port Huron. The plan was to quietly abscond with a cache of weapons—a hunting bow, some knives, his father's T-bolt rifle—a set of tools that would come in handy during the manhunt. When he reached his family's home, John snuck to the rear of the property and climbed up into a hunting blind that was positioned in the crown of an oak tree. As he sized up the situation, his thirteen-year-old brother Troy trudged up the driveway with a .22 rifle over his shoulder. Troy noticed movement in the tree and shouted to the house.

"Hey, Mom! Someone's up in the tree blind!"

"What are you talking about, Troy?" Mrs. Frizzle hollered in response.

Troy raised his rifle and aimed it at the hunting blind. John held his breath.

"I think it's John! Should I shoot him?"

Mrs. Frizzle emerged and, hands on hips, peered up into the tree. "John, what the hell are you doing up there?"

"Nothing, Ma!" John shouted back. Then he climbed down and hugged her.

Gary and Shirley were unindulgent this time. They ignored his protests and put him on an Amtrak to Chicago the next day. John secretly tucked a large hunting knife into his duffle back before departing. Great Lakes, however, was not on the itinerary. Arriving in Chicago, he walked over to the Greyhound station and bought a cross-country ticket.

A few days later, on a Friday evening, the bus rolled into a San Diego depot. John emerged into the familiar warmth with a smile on his face. It was refreshing to be back in his home away from home. He shouldered his bag and hustled over to the North Island Credit Union to retrieve a few hundred dollars that he had on account. By the time he arrived, the facility was closed for the weekend. This was a problem: John had less than five dollars in his pockets, no one to ask for help, and nowhere to stay.

John spent the night meandering throughout the city, before coming across a vagrant camp downtown near where the railroad crossed West Broadway. Dirty tents were set up across a vacant, weedy lot. There were shopping carts full of clothes, and rumpled tarps stretched across the ground, and even a couch and a few stained mattresses. *I guess I'll be homeless for the weekend,* John decided. He walked over and introduced himself to a few of the squatters. They were only mildly welcoming, eyeing him suspiciously and whispering to each other when he was out of earshot. Nonetheless, the small patch of ground he claimed was comfortable, kind of, and the price was right. He took comfort in knowing that he could always pull out the hunting knife if someone tried to mess with him.

John decided to remain at the camp even after he had retrieved his savings the following Monday. He made the acquaintance of an older guy named Bill who lived in a rusted-out old sedan and who seemed to be the top dog at the camp. Together they scavenged for leftovers behind local restaurants and panhandled amidst the swarms of drunken college kids who crowded into the Gaslamp District. One day, John and Bill decided to take the trolley down to Tijuana. John hoped to reconnect with a few of the old flames at the Bambi Club, and Bill wanted to carry out some sort of arbitrage grift that involved exchanging dollars for pesos, and then swapping them again elsewhere for a healthy profit. The plan, as Bill explained it, sounded slick enough to John. Once they arrived at Bambi's, Bill took two hundred bucks from John and told him to sit tight. The older man never returned. Late that night, drunk and pissed off, John decided to head back up to the railroad camp.

When he arrived, he discovered that all of his belongings, including the hunting knife, had been looted. Fearing that the perpetrator, perhaps Bill, might stab him in his sleep, John left the camp and checked into a homeless shelter for the night. In the morning, he concluded that homelessness was not his thing. He was not making any progress on Gaddafi, and, with empty pockets, had little hope of finding his way across the ocean, or even into the next county. With a loan from a cousin who lived in California, John purchased a plane ticket home.

Back at Great Lakes, John faced another captain's mast and was levied another mild punishment. Then he was temporarily reassigned to Cecil Field in Jacksonville, Florida. From there, John's superiors explained, he would be shipped overseas to service a jet squadron based on the USS *John F. Kennedy*. At this point, even John was shocked by the decisions about his service allocations. At minimum, he deserved to be discharged. There was also a reasonable case that he should be locked up for AWOL violations. Instead, they were sending him right back to the scene of his original crime—to a carrier in the Mediterranean!

That deployment never came to fruition. In Jacksonville, John's drinking grew increasingly careless and severe. He faced two additional captain's masts: one for avoiding work duties, and one for drunk and disorderly behavior. Then, during the festivities surrounding a Navy-sponsored fun-run, John experienced his second bout of alcohol poisoning. He guzzled a case of Coors Light and a quart of peppermint schnapps. He woke up in the hospital at the Naval Air Station in Jacksonville.

The Navy brass finally came to their senses. When John was released from the hospital, he was ordered to remain under restriction pending discharge proceedings. He was to be given an "other-than-honorable" characterization, a generous judgment considering the atrocity that had been his brief military career. In a matter of weeks John would pack his things, walk of the base, and move on in life as if his Navy stint had never happened. However, staying in one place for that period of time posed an insurmountable challenge. Something was not right in John's head. And, by this time, even he, in his deluded state, was aware of it.

One night, alone and agitated, John painted the words "GOD HELP!" in sprawling block letters across a wall of his bunk room. The characters were ominous, and black, and the center of the "O" was smeared thick with a bloody, crimson gloss. John snatched one of his roommate's car keys, along with a .25-caliber pistol that another roommate kept hidden behind a ceiling tile. He found the 1984 Ford Thunderbird in the parking lot, then drove off the base and away from Jacksonville.

John gunned it south down I-95 along the Intracoastal Waterway. He was not quite so carefree as he had been during previous AWOL escapes. As he buzzed past St. Augustine and Daytona Beach, there was an undertone of manic desperation. The plan, as always, was to find his way to Libya, but, this time, he aspired to take a boat back to the Mediterranean. Perhaps he'd be able to find work aboard a freighter headed to Europe. He even toyed with the idea of stealing a ship, or pirating one and taking the crew hostage.

John made it to West Palm Beach before his gas tank began flirting with empty. Once again, he had no money. This time, however, he was packing a firearm. Under the cover of night, John rolled into a quiet residential neighborhood and eased into a secluded parking spot. He tucked the gun into his waistband and walked a few blocks to a nearby filling station. He cased the joint and was relieved to observe only one person on the premises, a young Cuban guy working the cash register. John entered, approached the counter, and pointed his pistol at the man's forehead. With little hesitation, the cashier handed over the contents of the register—four hundred dollars. John stuffed it into his pocket and bolted.

His getaway, however, was not as clean as he had hoped. The Cuban man soon emerged from the gas station with a pistol of his own in hand. John sprinted into the darkness as fast as his cowboy boots would allow. He scurried up a narrow avenue and then dove into the bushes between two houses. Once his pursuer passed by, John doubled back to where he had parked the Thunderbird and stealthily drove off.

John headed to the Palm Beach Airport. With just a military ID and no passport he could not book a ticket overseas, so he purchased a ticket for a flight headed to Houston. He recalled that his father had an old friend named Leonard Schmidt who had moved there from Port Huron. Leonard was a shady character, the kind of dude who hissed when he spoke. He had most certainly been involved in criminal enterprises in Port Huron. If anyone would be willing to help John find a way out of the country, it would be this guy.

John imagined hijacking the jet as it pressed westward across the Gulf of Mexico. He had thought long and hard about trying to sneak his pistol through security, tucking it deep inside one of his steel-toe boots so as to hide it from the X-ray scanners. Then, he would simply have to bust into the cockpit and press the muzzle of his pistol to the back of one of the pilot's heads. If they gave him a hard time, he'd shoot one of them in the leg. Alas, there went John's wild imagination again. Unarmed, there was nothing he could do, and, beyond that, he knew that the domestic airliner probably did not have sufficient fuel to make it to Europe. If they had to make a pit stop somewhere, he would be cornered.

Upon arriving at the Houston airport John found a phonebook and flipped through it. There wasn't a single Leonard Schmidt listed. *Shit*. The old-timer must have either altered his identity or moved away. Another dead end.

John hung around the airport for three days. He snoozed on chairs and benches, and every once in a while went outside for a breather or a snack. Finally, he came up with a new plan. He would join a local Catholic volunteer group, one which carried out missionary work overseas. Somehow he'd obtain the necessary credentials to travel, and then it was just a matter of blending in with the crowd until he could make his move. He left the airport and hitchhiked to a church in Humble, Texas.

An affable, white-haired Irish priest greeted John and invited him into the rectory. He listened as John spoke about his recent interest in becoming a missionary. Without thinking, John went on to divulge his troubles with the Navy and admit to the armed robbery in West Palm Beach. His brain knew that such confessions, even to a clergyman, were a bad gamble, but his heart and conscience were contorted and yearning for absolution. The priest agreed to find John a place to stay for the night so long as John was willing to turn himself in the following morning. He drove John to a nearby motel and paid for a room.

In the morning, John reported to the Navy reserve station in Houston. Aware that John was AWOL, but in the dark about the armed robbery, an officer at the station arranged for John to take a commercial flight back to Jacksonville. Quite unbelievably, he drove John to the airport and released him on his own recognizance.

During the flight, John had second thoughts about turning himself in. Sooner or later, the Navy would learn about the gas station score, and then the whole situation would escalate significantly. He could deal with a few weeks in the brig for an AWOL violation, but armed robbery in Florida would merit a much stiffer, and much lengthier punishment. John resolved to go on the lam again after landing in Jacksonville. That plan was quashed, however, when he emerged into the terminal and was greeted by a well-armed fugitive retrieval team.

John was detained at the Naval Air Station in Jacksonville for ninety days until his court-martial. He was found guilty of destruction of government property, auto theft, and AWOL violations. He received a one-year sentence at a naval brig in Charleston, South Carolina. Additionally, and at long last, John would be dishonorably discharged.

Doing the time was not terribly difficult for John. He stayed out of trouble and found constructive ways to occupy himself. He spent countless afternoons reading about world history and flipping through sporting goods catalogs. Despite his incarceration, the Navy continued to deposit eight hundred dollars per month into John's bank account. He used this money to order camping gear and weapons—in particular, two high-powered, pistol-grip crossbows, which were shipped to his parents' home.

One day, John came across a fellow inmate praying over some rosary beads. He inquired about the practice, and the man explained that it was part of his Catholic faith. This interaction, brief as it was, was rather consequential in John's life. He had come to realize that, undoubtedly, he had strayed from the righteous path. His fumbling and stumbling and erratic rebelliousness had not liberated him, but rather had placed him in a cage. John began attending brig mass, paying close attention to the lengthy homilies that the priests delivered. He also began reading books about the lives of the saints. He wanted to learn about how these men devoted their lives to faith, and how they stayed the course despite myriad temptations and tribulations. *Perhaps my problems are a matter of education,* John thought. *If I simply study the righteous path and unlock its secrets, I can sort my life out.* Of course, redemption would not be so simple.

Upon completion of his stint in Charleston, John was transferred to Palm Beach County Jail. He spent three months there awaiting trial, and, during that time, was baptized. He could have faced life in prison for the armed robbery, but the public defender was able to arrange a plea deal that dropped the charge to "robbery with a weapon." John was levied two-and-a-half years at a low-security prison camp in Caryville, in the panhandle of Florida.

Eight months later, having earned credit for good behavior, John was released. He flew back to Port Huron. It was August 1988, and he had just turned twenty-three years old. This homecoming, ironically, occurred shortly after his original naval service commitment would have ended. As a result, most people around town assumed that John had simply finished his tour in the Navy and was now moving on with his life. The Frizzle family did what they could to obscure the truth from friends and neighbors. For a while, even John's younger brothers were not fully aware of all that had transpired.

John went to work for his father's construction business. He had no other apparent job opportunities, and, given his criminal record and military discharge, would have qualified for very few had he pursued them. His best hope would be to develop some skills as a contractor—earning back some of his father's respect in the process—and then, when the time was right, move on to bigger and better things. Gary Frizzle was neither licensed nor insured, so he did most of his jobs under the table and transacted in cash only. As a result, the guys that he employed, who worked alongside John, were not the most dignified characters. Generally, they were uneducated roughnecks with checkered pasts. John referred to them as a "pirate crew." And, to a considerable degree, he fit right in.

Most days after work the crew would hit up a local watering hole. John began drinking more heavily than he had ever before. Sometimes, one of the pirate boys would get so wound up that the bar owner would ask the crew to move on to another establishment. On those nights, they might head across the river into Sarnia, maybe patronize a strip club or two. John's father, it turned out, enjoyed this pastime as much as anyone. And, while this shared interest gave John a perverted sense of connection to his father, it also gnawed at him on a deeper level. He recoiled at watching Gary stuff dollar bills into the underpants of lascivious young ladies when poor Shirley was at home making dinner and keeping house.

John resolved to make a major change in his life, and soon. If he wasn't proactive, he'd end up ripping out old bath tiles and applying spackle for the next two decades. The clock was ticking, loudly. John had fucked up royally in the Navy. There was no two ways about it. Now he had to find a way to compensate for that—an honorable act that would overshadow his past failures. There was always Gaddafi. But, as interminably tempting as that pursuit was, John realized that, in the short term, he should set his sights on a more attainable, more proximal target. He began to take a long, hard look at the culture and people of his own hometown.

Having developed a worldlier perspective during his travels with the Navy, John began to see the social ills and economic disparities within Port Huron more clearly. In the five years that he was gone, it appeared, the town had changed noticeably, and for the worse. He was especially affected by the poverty and rampant drug use in the southern part of Port Huron, an area called South Park. John decided that there must be something he could do, some action he could take to prevent the ongoing decline of the community. Success here would surely earn him a few much-needed feathers in his cap. After some deliberation, he decided that he would go after local criminals—the big ones. He would hunt down the shadowy kingpins who pulled the strings of the Port Huron narcotics trade.

In the spring of 1989, John bought a used 1977 Mercury Grand Marquis—an expansive sedan, with square features and an imposing silver grill. It had a jet-black paint job. When John cruised around town he felt as if he really were a bona fide vigilante crime fighter, a bizarro Batman. Late at night, he would load the trunk with his crossbows, then slowly navigate through South Park, prowling for miscreants. John came across a drug dealer here and there. However, he felt that taking out a low-level pusher would have negligible impact on the overall criminal infrastructure. Another lackey would soon show up to take the dead one's place.

In the meantime, John's parents were growing increasingly concerned about him. John was making a decent wage working for his father, but he was constantly broke and asking for handouts. He stayed out all hours of the night, and reports came from the neighbors that he was behaving suspiciously and spending time in seedy neighborhoods. Also, John was ever more disruptive and unreliable at work, sometimes engaging in ballistic arguments with his father. Gary and Shirley had suspected that John dabbled in marijuana, but now they worried that he was getting into harder stuff. They repeatedly tried to engage him about what he was going through, but to no avail. Their trust faded. With time, John's parents grew to dread his intentions.

The breaking point came when John revealed that he was writing a book about world history from the perspective of Satan. He read a macabre excerpt of his writing to his mother, one which appeared to herald the devil's omnipotence. Shortly thereafter, John's parents informed him that he had to move out of the house. They agreed to set him up in a motel for a few weeks until he found his own place.

John never identified or confronted a significant player in the Port Huron criminal community. For a time, he considered targeting a local attorney, who was known for dealing cocaine on the side. He hoped this man might be a critical link in the narcotic food chain. But after a few days of evaluation, John determined that the guy was a schlub and not worth the effort.

Simply no one matched up to Gaddafi. John came to feel that there was a persistent cosmic influence nudging him in the direction of Libya. It was time to make one more go of it. He considered a risky plan to rob some of the local drug dealers, and to use those funds to finance his travels. However, he soon identified an easier target, one that had been sitting in plain view the whole time: his father. Gary typically kept around $50,000 in cash on hand, some of which he carried in thick rolls in his pockets. The rest he stored in a combination safe in the house. John's new scheme was to stage a phony robbery and make off with his father's savings and weapons. However, as his relationship with Gary continued to disintegrate, and as John grew increasingly frustrated and bitter about his living situation, and as his mind continued to concoct increasingly demented thought patterns, the plan evolved into something more sinister.

John came to the determination that his father must have had a large life insurance policy. He had no evidence of this, and, indeed, had never even heard his parents discuss anything of the sort. Yet he was sure that the policy existed. Furthermore, the payoff from that policy would be a lot more than $50,000 (another unfounded speculation). He decided that, when the time was right, he would murder his father, collect the benefits, and leave Port Huron for good.

On April 18, 1989, John did not show up to the job site, the second day in a row that he had skipped work without notifying Gary. The plan was to sneak into the house, collect his father's weapons, and wait for the old man to return home from work. John spent most of the day drinking beer and cruising around town in his black Grand Marquis, before driving over to a bikini bar called Bisco's Inn, in the nearby Emmett Township. He had a thing for a dancer there named Trixie. In fact, a few weeks earlier she had agreed to let him drive her home. They had spent a few minutes making out in his car.

Trixie greeted John warmly and gave him a five-dollar lap dance. While grinding on his thigh, she suddenly said, "Tell your dad, thanks for yesterday."

"Thanks for what?" John asked.

"Oh, he drove me home from work," she replied, turning around to give John a good view of her backside. "That was nice of him."

John saw red. What was his father doing escorting strippers around town? Had his dad fucked Trixie? And, if so, was she the only sex worker he had indulged in? It disturbed John that he and his father might both have fooled around with Trixie. But, more importantly, *Dad was married to Mom!* He was supposed to be a loyal husband!

"What's wrong, Johnny?" Trixie asked sweetly.

"Aw, nothin'. Nothin' at all." John paused for a moment to think. "Why don't you come away with me?"

"Come away where, baby?"

"Well, I'm gonna go over to Europe for a bit. I'm coming into some money. It would be nice if you came with me."

Trixie smiled, then planted a peck on John's cheek. "That could be fun. How much money are you talking about?"

"Plenty. More than enough."

Trixie stood up and continued to dance. Then, over her shoulder, she suggested, "When you have the money, why don't you let me know and then I'll decide?"

"That's what I'll do," John replied, sipping deeply from a bottle of cheap lager.

An hour and several beers later, a fairly inebriated John drove to his family's home, and parked down the street. He grabbed one of his crossbows out of the trunk of the Grand Marquis, then snuck into the house through the sliding door in the rear. He could hear the shower—his brother Ken washing off after a long day at work. John made his way to his parents' bedroom. He rummaged through the closet, and found his father's .30-30 lever-action rifle—a powerful hunting weapon. He sat down on the bed and loaded it. Then he tiptoed down the hallway to Troy's bedroom. He retrieved his youngest brother's shotgun, and carried the armful of weapons into the kitchen, setting the guns near the back door. That's when John realized what had to be done. To solve all of his problems, and to collect the entirety of the life insurance benefit, he would have to murder not just his father, but his entire family.

John cocked the crossbow and loaded it with a bolt. He took a position opposite the bathroom, aimed the weapon, and waited for his brother to emerge. After a few minutes, Ken, dripping, a bath towel around his waist, opened the door.

"John, what the fuck are you doing?!" he shouted, and then slammed the door shut.

John tried to open the door, but his brother had already locked it.

"Ken," John announced, "I want you to get into the bathtub." John knew he would have to clean up the aftermath. He wanted as much of the blood as possible to drain away.

Ken screamed for help. John kicked the door hard, and the veneer cracked. He kicked again and a small hole broke open. He dropped to his knees and began ripping the door apart, tearing pieces away from the hole to make it large enough for the crossbow. Ken shrieked and bellowed. John peered through the hole and saw that Ken was cowering in the corner of the bathroom. He angled the crossbow to target his brother's chest.

Suddenly, John's mother appeared at the end of the hallway. She screeched, "John, oh my God! What are you doing?"

John stood up and pointed the crossbow at her. She backed up and then ran out the back door. She began yelling at Troy, whom she had just picked up from track practice, telling him to get back in the car. John hurried to the kitchen, picked up the rifle, and strode after her. The Cadillac was parked in the driveway, very close to John's position. Shirley started the car. John raised the rifle to his hip, leveled it, and squeezed the trigger.

Bang!

The report of the shot was booming and sharp, a slap to the face that startled John and heightened his senses. The bullet pierced the windshield near the steering wheel. The Cadillac, shifted into drive, now slowly rolled toward John. Troy reached across his mother's lap, threw the car into park, and jumped out of the passenger seat, screaming.

John dropped the rifle and picked up the crossbow. Troy cowered on the opposite side the Cadillac. John began chasing his brother around the vehicle. He then jumped up onto the trunk of the car in order to draw an unobstructed bead on the boy. Troy sprang away and sprinted toward the far wall of the house. John aimed the crossbow— a clean, clear shot. He squeezed the trigger. Click. The bolt did not loose. The safety was on.

Troy disappeared into the back yard. John lowered the weapon.

John jogged back inside and scooped up the rest of his arsenal. He walked out the front door and headed up the driveway. As he passed the Cadillac, he peered through the window. Blood was sprayed all over the driver's seat. Shirley was sprawled across the bench, her blond hair soaked crimson. John noticed that she was moving slightly, perhaps trying to reach for something. For a moment, he considered calling 9-1-1. Instead he hurried over to his car, threw the weapons into the trunk, and drove off.

John collected his belongings from his motel room, then drove back to see Trixie. Although he did not succeed in seizing any of his father's cash, he was going to convince the dancer to come with him. He'd tell her that they had to leave right that instant.

Arriving at Bisco's, John spied his father's pickup truck in the parking lot. Sensing an opportunity, he parked in an inconspicuous area, reloaded and cocked the crossbow, and waited. About a half-hour later, Gary emerged. John opened his driver door and stood up, hiding the crossbow from view.

"Where were you today, John?" Gary asked, surprised to see his son.

"Oh, nowhere. Drivin' around," John replied, his index finger on the trigger of his weapon.

Gary narrowed his eyes and stared at his son for a long moment. "You comin' back to work tomorrow?"

John came very close to putting a bolt through his father's heart right then and there. However, he decided that the parking lot was too visible an area. Bikini bar patrons were coming and going. John would surely be identified. Also, there was almost no point in killing his father any more. There was no money in it. Furthermore, when Gary returned home in a few minutes he would discover that his world had been destroyed. That would be enough pain for one day.

"Work tomorrow?" John responded after a hesitation. "Maybe."

Gary appraised John for a few more moments, then hopped into his pickup and drove away.

Watching his father go, John decided that it was probably time to skip town. In his black Grand Marquis, he fled west on I-94, first bypassing Detroit, then Ann Arbor. He did not have a well-formed plan. He was operating on autopilot. After a few hours of driving, he came upon a rest stop and slept.

Waking up, John began to comprehend the grave truth of the crime he had perpetrated. *He had murdered his mother—the loving woman who had so generously supported him throughout life.* He thought back on the event and the hours and days that preceded it, but he could not piece together exactly what had been going on in his mind. In retrospect, the robbery and life insurance scheme was hopeless from the start. Now a fugitive, he had nothing to show for assaulting his younger brothers and putting a bullet in his innocent mother's head. Why had he become convinced that killing his family was necessary in the first place? His mother had never done a thing to him that would have merited such violence. Had dabbling in Satanism left him suscep- tible to possession by a demonic spirit? Had his soul been corrupted? John's head felt as if it were about to boil as he sped through Central Michigan.

John considered returning to Tijuana and holing up there, but instead decided to head for Canada. It would be faster, and the sooner he left the country the better. Crossing the border would give him some running room and possibly an extradition buffer. He continued on I-94 through Chicago, and then northwest through the patchwork of dairy farms that carpet Wisconsin. He did not break again until he arrived in Duluth, Minnesota. International Falls, where he would cross into Canada, was some three hours north on the international line, but it was time for a breather. Also, John needed money. Duluth would be a good place to unload his car. He would take a bus from there, leaving little trail, then disappear into Canada for good.

John considered spending some time in the wilderness once he crossed the border. Among his possessions were a tent, a backpack, a scout cooking kit, and a rifle. Perhaps he had everything he needed to get by for a few weeks or longer, if he was crafty enough—a big if. Maybe that's how old Robert Taylor eluded the authorities way back in 1975, roughing it for a while. John found it morbidly ironic that his childhood fascination with the murderous Taylor was, in some ways, pertinent to his current predicament.

A used car dealer handed over a hundred bucks for the Grand Marquis. John booked a cheap bed at the Seaway Motel, a grimy lodg- ing option for longshoremen and merchant sailors, right next to the docks at Rice's Point. After checking in, John went next door to Curly's Bar and shot some pool. Having been too frenzied to check the news, he began to wonder whether word of the murder had reached these parts. None of the patrons, however, seemed to pay John any sort of special attention.

The following day, John took a Greyhound to International Falls. From the center of town, he walked over to the international bridge that spans Rainy River into Canada. There was a border patrol station set up in the middle of the bridge. Crossing here, clearly, was not an option, and attempting to swim across would be quite stupid. The only reasonable option, it now appeared, would be to hitchhike his way west along Highway 11 until he found a safe spot to cross on foot. John decided to sleep on it.

In the isolated gloom of his motel room, John's mind, again, felt like it was malfunctioning. How had it come to this? Everything that had transpired was so damn haphazard, so poorly conceived. He was stricken with alternative waves of extreme remorse about what he had done to his mother, and acute fear about what would happen if he were apprehended. Visions and sounds of the incident played on a loop in his mind—the terror on Ken's face when he was cornered in the bathroom, the resonant blast of his father's rifle, Troy's screams as John pursued him around the Cadillac, the blood pouring from his mother's head. John felt like he could not relate to the person he was just three days earlier. It was as if the person who had perpetrated that attack were a fictional version of John, a marauding monster from a horror film that John had temporarily embodied but could not understand or control.

After a turbulent, restless night, John resolved to return to Port Huron and surrender to the police. He threw a bag of personal effects over his shoulder and began walking out of town, along Route 53. A man in a pickup truck offered John a ride and drove him all the way to Duluth. John would later learn that his generous driver was an off-duty policeman from Ely, Minnesota.

John returned to the Seaway Motel that night. He approached the front desk and requested a room. The clerk, who, two nights before, was welcoming and conversational, seemed to have grown tepid and inhospitable in the meantime. A few other tired fellas sat in the lobby, watching the Detroit Tigers play the Minnesota Twins on the television set. John decided to join them for a few innings before retiring. They eyed John warily. *What's going on here?* John thought. *Do these guys know something, or am I just paranoid?* He kept his focus on the television and tried to appear unaffected by the foreboding atmosphere. In a moment, there came the sound of footsteps on the staircase behind him. He turned around to see two burly men in overcoats descending into the lobby. The clerk motioned toward John, and one of the men nodded. John returned his gaze to the baseball game while his mind and heart raced. These men were surely law enforcement agents, probably plain-clothes detectives. John readied himself. This was the make-or-break moment: he could dart out the door and hightail it up the street, or he could take his lumps like a man.

Before John could make up his mind, the two gumshoes took a position directly in front of him, their shoulders broad, their countenances grave.

The taller one spoke up. "Are you John Frizzle?"

"Yes, sir," John replied steadily.

The man flashed his badge. "Stand up for me, please."

John did.

"I want you to put your hands up against that wall and spread your legs."

John complied.

The other man grabbed John's wrists and twisted them behind his back. Then he locked them together with handcuffs. "You are under arrest for the attempted murder of Shirley Anne Frizzle."

For a moment, John thought he misheard the detective. *Attempted murder?* Judging from the volume of gore splattered onto the headrest of the Cadillac, John had been certain that his mother was a goner.

"She . . . she's alive?" he stammered.

The taller detective sighed. "Yes, she's alive."

John was processed and detained in Duluth. On May 12, he was flown across Lake Michigan, back to Port Huron in a twin-engine Beechcraft. There he was charged with three counts of assault with intent to commit murder, and one count of felony possession of a weapon. He was locked up in the St. Clair County Jail, where he would stay for fifteen months pending trial.

A public defender was assigned to John's case. The county prosecutor offered a plea deal that would have reduced two of the charges to felonious assault. However, the charge related to the shooting of his mother would have remained unchanged, meaning that John would face up to life in prison regardless of whether he accepted the offer. John decided that he would leave it in God's hands and go to trial.

A few weeks after his arrest, John was allowed a phone call with his father, who described, in hideous detail, the extent of John's mother's injuries. Because the bullet first connected with the windshield of the Cadillac, its trajectory to his mother's head was not clean. The bullet caused a serious entry wound above her right eyebrow, and, askew as it proceeded, inflicted catastrophic trauma to her brain. Exiting, it blew a large hole in the rear of her skull. The ejected bone matter smashed through the rear window of the vehicle, leaving a plate-sized hole. The bullet itself was found within the vehicle.

John's mother lay gravely injured for nearly four hours after law enforcement arrived at the scene of the shooting. John's whereabouts were unknown. There was concern that he might have been hiding in the home or in a hunting blind on the property, waiting to pick officers off as they responded to the incident. Also, there was suspicious movement within the Cadillac. The automatic locks were triggered a few times. The police were not sure that Shirley was alone in the vehicle, and were compelled to proceed with extreme caution. At around 1 A.M. that evening, Shirley, somehow regained consciousness, sounded the horn, and then tumbled out of the passenger side of the vehicle.

"John," his father pleaded, "we, as a family, need to know why you perpetrated this horrible act."

John thought for a long moment. He racked his brain, dug through his tangled synapses, hoping to uncover a shred of reason that might underlie his madness. The effort was fruitless.

"I don't know, Dad," he finally replied. "I really don't know." And, this time, John was telling the truth.

The trial lasted for four days and was covered extensively in the *Times Herald* of Port Huron as well as in other regional newspapers. John pled not guilty by reason of diminished capacity. Shirley, though severely debilitated, testified against her son. A piece of glass had lodged in one of her eyes, rendering her mostly blind. Due to brain damage, she had lost the use of her right arm and could only walk with assistance. Struggling to form words, Shirley indicated under cross-examination that she had limited recollection of the night of the shooting. Her appearance served as a gruesome exhibition more than an evidentiary testimony. This enraged John. He struggled to contain his anger at the exploitative prosecutors, at his dad for permitting this hideous charade, and at himself for stupidly turning down the plea deals. Proceeding with a trial, John came to realize, heaped unnecessary anguish upon his family members, and delayed the emotional healing process.

John, nonetheless, took the stand in his own defense. He made it clear that he had had no intention of attacking his mother or brothers before arriving at the house—that his actions reflected a completely irrational frenzy and loss of self-control. But, at the same time, he did not sugarcoat the facts. He spoke earnestly, describing the steps that he had taken upon arriving at the family home and encountering his brother Ken. In laying bare the awful truth, John hoped that members of the jury would recognize just how delusional he was on that fateful evening, and perhaps come to the conclusion that he needed psychiatric treatment rather than a lifetime in a penal facility.

On Friday, June 20, 1990, the jury, deliberating for only six hours, found John guilty on all counts. He was levied three concurrent twenty-five- to fifty-year sentences for the attempted murders, and an additional two-year sentence for the felony weapons charge. The day of the sentencing, John met with a jail psychologist, who asked the convict to explain how he was feeling about the crime and its outcome. For the first and perhaps only time in his adult life, John broke down and sobbed.

John was remanded to Jackson State Prison, Michigan's oldest facility, and, at that point, the largest walled prison in the world. It was an intimidating fortress, but time in the naval brig and in the Florida prison system had readied him for this longer sentence. After a brief adjustment period, John got down to the business of analyzing his circumstances and the chain of events that landed him there. The sterility of the facility, the dearth of worldly distractions, the long stretches of idleness, all served to amplify his capacity for introspection. In time, John arrived at some stark, unsettling conclusions. First and foremost, he realized, the source of many, if not all of his troubles, was his obsessive inclination to take matters into his own hands when faced with a dilemma. Whether it was going AWOL, or committing robbery, or even, ultimately, attacking his family, John had viewed his foolhardy actions as necessary and justifiable steps to right a perceived wrong in his life or in the world. Staring down a quarter-century in a cage, he now began to accept that the bigger problem was not the rest of humanity, but, in all likelihood, himself. He came to understand that a resolution would come about only through self-awareness and perpetual self-discipline. He committed himself to bringing his destructive thought patterns and erratic impulses under control.

Yet, the circumstances of John's incarceration were not as stable as he had hoped. He was transferred between correctional facilities a total of seventeen times, each venue presenting new social dynamics, norms, and frustrations. In general, however, because John did not cause problems, and because he found constructive outlets for his energies, he was assigned to prisons that were progressively lower in security level. His freedom to develop himself and explore intellectual curiosities broadened. At one institution, he got involved in the Vietnam Veterans of America group, at another he participated in a dog rehabilitation program. Later, he worked as an assistant to a prison counselor, and, in such capacity, facilitated educational programs about addiction and domestic violence.

John remained heavily involved in his Catholic faith throughout his imprisonment, attending mass and volunteering for services. He derived inspiration, in particular, from St. Francis of Assisi, a high-born Catholic convert and proselytizer. As a young man, Francis had abandoned his pursuits of fortune and fame, and, in their place, devoted his life to spreading the message of Jesus. John was also encouraged by the remarkable narrative of Karla Faye Tucker, a woman who was sentenced to death for a gruesome murder. While on death row she became a Christian missionary, preaching to her fellow inmates and using media appearances as opportunities to spread the gospel. As the months and years in captivity ticked by, John held out hope that he, too, might undergo such a redemptive transformation.

In 1996, news came that John's mother had been killed. By that time, she had made notable gains in physical and mental rehabilitation, and was, in some ways, self-sufficient. But, as she crossed a street to meet Gary at the local donut shop, she was mowed down by a drunk driver. The news devastated John. Despite the senseless attack he had perpetrated, he still loved his mother deeply and wanted the best for her. Some people have a hard time believing John when he makes this claim. They argue that it is not possible to love someone you have attempted to murder. However, John knows in his heart that his violent, deranged actions were not representative of his truest feelings for his mother or younger brothers.

Regardless, John has always struggled with the knowledge that he was the source of the physical and emotional suffering Shirley experienced in her final years. He also recognized that alcohol played a supporting role in this suffering, and so chose to remain sober for the entire duration of his incarceration. John eschews alcohol to this day.

After Shirley's death, John went approximately nine years without a single visitor. Fortunately, in 2006, he was approved for participation in a pen pal program for incarcerated Catholics. He began communicating regularly with a woman named Michelle, who resided in Kalamazoo. Although the program featured safeguards to prevent inmates from involving themselves financially or romantically with their pen pals, the two developed a relationship. Michelle began making visits to John. In 2007, they were married.

The last stop of John's twenty-three-year tour of the Michigan penal system was at the Ojibway Correctional Facility in the Upper Peninsula of the state, not far from Minnesota. In a way, he had come full circle: while incarcerated there, John often passed the time by watching news broadcasts from Duluth—the very city where he had been arrested back in 1989.

John was granted parole at his first hearing and released on September 27, 2011. He left with ten dollars, a foot locker full of toiletries, and a small bag of clothes. A prison official dropped him at the Greyhound Station. While John waited for the bus, he purchased a gumball. He prayed over it for a moment, and then popped it in his mouth. *This gumball is symbolic of my freedom*, he thought with a mix of sincerity and levity.

John traveled to Grand Rapids to move in with Michelle, who had recently relocated there. He relished his freedom, but reentry presented a new set of problems, in particular some complicated sexual neuroses. He had not had intercourse in over two decades, and had abstained from masturbation for the last twelve years of his sentence. However, on the outside, temptations were irresistible. Beautiful women were everywhere. John would get aroused by something as benign as the click of a woman's high heels. Then he discovered internet porn and became addicted to it.

Eighteen months after John's release, Michelle became pregnant. The celebration was short-lived, however, because, not long thereafter, she learned of John's sexual obsessiveness and was appalled by it. The two worked on the issue and attended couples therapy, but the situation saw minimal improvement. In July 2014, one year after the birth of their daughter, Michelle filed for divorce.

The family continued to cohabitate for another few months until John revealed that he was struggling with some destabilizing emotions that he feared might negatively impact Michelle and their daughter. John admitted himself to a mental hospital. This was the first time in his life that he had ever been properly treated for psychiatric issues. A doctor prescribed him two medications for anxiety and mood issues, one of which is an antipsychotic. As his condition improved, John felt compelled to wonder what might have happened had someone in the Navy made a real effort to provide him with the appropriate treatment. In retrospect, it was not only clear that his situation necessitated a concerted intervention, but that his actions, at times, were a clarion call for help. Why were they so apt to disregard his erratic behavior, and to keep returning him to active service? Why did they let it go so far? Was it a bureaucratic cock-up? Or did it reflect a graver cultural deficiency in the Navy? John feels that his crimes could have been preempted had someone in a position of authority taken heed of the warning signs. For a long time he harbored resentment over this issue.

After leaving the hospital, John took up residence at Mel Trotter Ministries, a homeless shelter in Grand Rapids. There, he worked to repair his life and to rebuild it upon a foundation of Catholic values. He became an essential contributor to the religious programs at the shelter, tending to his fellow residents, and helped establish an anger management curriculum. Finally, in the summer of 2017, six years after his release, John secured employment as a driver for a medical transport company. He chauffeurs needy patients, many of whom are senior citizens with cancer and other acute illnesses, from their homes to clinics and hospitals around the Grand Rapids area. It is his first paying job since 1989. He has since transferred out of the shelter and into his own apartment.

John's father passed on six months after his son's release from prison. John attended the memorial service. The two had spoken on the phone over the years, but, per Gary's request, never reconnected in person. John has resurrected a relationship with Troy. Ken, however, remains estranged.

In Grand Rapids, the summers are warm and humid. Recreational boats crawl up the river, past the Gerald R. Ford Presidential Museum, and the downtown business district, and the verdant Canal Park. At fifty-two years old, John Frizzle—the drifter, the ex-convict, the father—has started over. His days of impulsive behavior and selfish pursuits and criminality are long past, or so he believes. The plan is to continue working on behalf of people in need, in the pursuit of collective, righteous goals. He wants, one day, to be recognized as an upstanding member of society, an example for others who have committed similar crimes, a testament to the power of self-belief. He hopes that people will witness his optimistic spirit, and his good works, and his unwavering faith, and recognize that an evil deed does not, with certainty, an evil person make. Every man is worth more than his worst act, John insists. Every man is redeemable.

CHAPTER 3

THE DEVIL'S BARGAIN

Marvin Gomez

On November 15, 1844, a dark-horse candidate by the name of James Knox Polk was elected president of the United States of America. A fervent proponent of the concept of "manifest destiny"—a belief in the divinely ordained right of the American nation to expand fully across North America—he presided over the 1845 annexation of the Republic of Texas, which had declared independence from Mexico in the spring of 1836. This territory subsumed the eastern bulk of present-day Texas and disputed swaths of land that included pieces of present-day Oklahoma, Kansas, Colorado, and Wyoming, as well as the eastern half of New Mexico.

The maneuver greatly increased tensions between the United States and Mexico, which had never recognized Texan independence. War broke out between the two nations in the spring of 1846. The United States prevailed in a rather lopsided affair, its forces ultimately marching to and occupying Mexico City. On February 2, 1848, the Treaty of Guadalupe Hidalgo was signed, ending the conflict and defining the land transfer known as the Mexican Cession. Under this agreement, Mexico surrendered over a half-million square miles of territory to the United States. It was the third-largest American acquisition of territory in history, after the Louisiana and Alaska Purchases.

The dwindling Rio Grande, which marks the eastern border of the Mexican Cession and the western border of the Texas Annexation, runs north to south through the center of Albuquerque, the largest city in New Mexico and the hometown of forty-two-year-old Marvin Gomez. Marvin's ancestors have resided in this region for generations, stretching back to the period before it was granted statehood in 1912, before the Mexican Cession, even before the 1821 Mexican declaration of independence from Spain. Marvin, consequently, like some 340,000 other New Mexico residents, can be considered a "Hispano," a descendant of early Spanish settlers in the region, some of whom began arriving at the advent of the seventeenth century.

In response to inquiries about his ethnicity, Marvin identifies himself as "Hispanic."

"Does that mean you are Mexican? Honduran? Colombian?" one might ask.

"No," Marvin would reply. "As far as I know, I don't have family in Mexico or any of those countries. My family has always been here in New Mexico. I'm Hispanic. That's it."

Nor does he view his ancestors as immigrants in the way that most Americans might define an immigrant. They were in New Mexico *before* the United States owned New Mexico. In a way, America immigrated into Marvin's country, not the other way around.

Marvin's grandfather fought for the United States in World War II. At the time of his conscription he owned a considerable amount of land near Pecos, in the north-central part of the state.

"There are people in this country who want me to go back to my homeland," Marvin would point out. "They don't understand that I am already *in* my homeland."

And, so, in a way, ethnically speaking, Marvin is an American curiosity—not quite indigenous (though there may have been intermixing during his family's history in the Americas), but perhaps more akin to native peoples than to the typical European or Latin American migrant to this country. During a period—the first year of the Trump administration—when there is a sharp spotlight on issues of nativism, nationalism, and the existential threat posed by the "other," Marvin Gomez finds himself somewhat untethered: confident in his Americanness, but not wholly certain where he fits within this ubiquitous, contentious sociopolitical debate.

What complicates Marvin's place in society further is the fact that he is a convicted violent felon.

On Sunday, October 1, 2006, after a day and a half on the lam, Marvin was arrested by a tactical Albuquerque police unit and imprisoned at the Bernalillo County Metropolitan Detention Center. He was charged with first-degree murder, aggravated assault, and tampering with evidence for his actions related to the shooting death of a local musician the previous Friday night. This was Marvin's first trip to the big house, and so he was proportionately apprehensive. The Bernalillo jail, he knew, typically corralled scores of violent criminals, most awaiting trial, most active members of gangs. After all, Albuquerque had no shortage of gangs back then: 18th Streeters, TCK, Los Padillas, Westsiders, and Bandidos, to name a very few. Marvin, a generally law-abiding citizen, had never rolled with a crew like that and was not looking forward to the interactions and inquisitions he was sure to experience behind bars.

A correctional officer led Marvin into a sally port—a controlled vestibule—where he would wait while someone processed his intake paperwork. Marvin felt cold sweat percolate on his forehead as the officer left the room and secured the door with a clank. He wiped away the moisture with the back of his sleeve and took a seat on a bench.

At the far end of the room was a reinforced door with a window that looked into the E-6 pod, a high-security unit that housed the most hardcore, seasoned offenders in the jail. Shortly, there was a sharp bang on the door and, from the other side, a young Latino man with a neck tattoo peered through the window.

"Hey!" the inmate shouted, his voice muffled by the door. "What you doin' here?"

Marvin was not sure what the protocol was. He considered ignoring the man, but knew that might not be the best way to ingratiate himself with one of his future cohabitants. The man rapped the window with his knuckles.

"Yo, *ese*! I asked you a fuckin' question!"

Marvin cleared his throat and announced, "I . . . I shot someone."

"A woman?" the man inquired with a bark.

"No. A man."

"You a rapist?"

"Am I what?"

"You heard me! I asked if you was a rapist!" The man was growing increasingly agitated.

Marvin replied, "I've never raped anyone, dude."

"Well, you lucky, then. If you a rapist, you won't make it a day in E-6."

"Well . . . I'm not. Okay?"

The man thought for a moment, then, "You fight?"

"Do I fight?"

"Yeah, man. You box?"

"What do you mean?"

"I mean this here is a gladiator pod. You gonna have to fight up in here, whether you like it or not."

Marvin did not like the sound of that. Sure, he'd been in his share of dustups, but nothing worth bragging about. He wanted to create as few ripples as possible before getting bailed out, assuming bail was not denied.

"I'm not gonna fight, bro."

"Did I ask if you was gonna fight?!" the man snapped back sharply. "I didn't ask you, son. I told you. You are gonna fight in this here pod, homes. That's a fact."

The man stared coldly at Marvin for a moment, then abruptly disappeared from the window.

An hour or two went by before an officer entered the sally port and escorted Marvin into the E-6 pod. "Enjoy your stay," the officer remarked before exiting.

Various prisoners hurried up to Marvin and badgered him. They wanted to know why he was locked up and, more importantly, what gang he ran with.

"I'm not in a gang," he told them. "I just keep to myself."

Eventually, an exceptionally bulky and thoroughly inked inmate made his way over. Some of the other guys stepped to the side, in the way that hyenas might make room for a lion. The man looked Marvin up and down carefully before speaking.

"You a *Burqueño*?" He was using a slang term that refers to Albuquerque natives.

"Yes," Marvin answered. "Born and raised here."

"What part?"

"Cypress Circle."

"Hmm." The imposing man narrowed his eyes. "Nice part of town."

"I guess so," Marvin replied. Cypress Circle was a bit better than some of the surrounding areas, but it was working-class and, in the scheme of things, not *that* nice.

"What's your name?"

"Marvin. And you?"

"I'm Sagger from Westgate."

Marvin raised his eyebrows. He had heard that name before. It summoned the recollection of an incident that occurred right around high school graduation, some thirteen years earlier. While cruising around town with a friend, Marvin was hailed by a few local girls.

"Sagger!" one shouted to him. "What are you doing?"

"Who's Sagger?" Marvin replied.

The girls approached his car window and peered inside.

"Oh, we thought you were Sagger from Westgate," one said.

"Who's that?"

"You don't know who Sagger is?" they chuckled, departing. "Well, he ain't you, that's for sure."

Marvin later asked around and learned that the girls had mistaken him for a rather notorious gang leader. And now, here he was, face-to-face with that dangerous man. Marvin decided to relay the anecdote about the girls. It made Sagger laugh.

"They thought you were me? You ain't half as handsome. But, I guess you're all right, then," Sagger concluded, patting Marvin on the shoulder before walking away. Marvin sighed with relief. He seemed to have made an ally of the biggest dog in the pound.

Marvin's bail was set at a quarter of a million dollars. He hired a shrewd and seasoned private defense attorney named Ray Twohig, who appealed successfully for a reduction to $100,000. This amount was more palatable, but still necessitated the engagement of a bail bondsman, who charged a nonrefundable fee equal to 10 percent of the bail, or $10,000. Marvin, in his career, had managed to scrimp and save about $20,000. Surrendering half of that was a bitter pill, but it was the difference between rotting in a jail cell and living a somewhat normal life during the months (or longer) that led up to his criminal trial. In addition, Twohig required a $10,000 retainer. Marvin instructed his sister Rosella to empty his checking and savings and distribute the cash accordingly.

Marvin was released on pretrial supervision, allowing him to return home and get on with his life while the legal process advanced. Only, it was not so simple. At the time of the shooting, he was employed by the New Mexico Educators Federal Credit Union as a facilities manager, where he oversaw the mechanical systems, security protocols, and general upkeep of a dozen or so branches throughout the state. It was a secure, relatively lucrative position, and Marvin had no intention of abandoning it. However, upon learning of his arrest, the credit union immediately terminated his employment. They assured Marvin that he would be able to return to his old position if he were acquitted of the charges, but that offered little solace. Marvin would potentially have no income for the duration of his legal defense.

This financial jam was out of the ordinary for Marvin. Since the age of twelve, he had been an assiduous member of the workforce. His first job was selling newspapers out in front of the local grocery store. The pay was paltry, but at least he could afford to buy one of his favorite comic books every once in a while. At the age of thirteen, he took on an under-the-table gig as an errand boy at the Dunkin' Donuts where his mother worked. He continued to earn wages throughout high school, even quitting the football team so that he could work more hours at a Little Caesars Pizza store.

After high school, Marvin was hired to a position on the floor of the local Motorola factory. Back then, in the late nineties, the tech giant manufactured pagers by the truckload. Marvin was on an assembly team. At the same time, he began evaluating longer-term career paths. For a while he wanted to become a pharmacy technician. The compensation was attractive and the hours and quality of life were desirable. However, because of these features, there were few such jobs available, as well as a waiting list to get into the pertinent program at the local community college. Marvin shifted his focus. He spent some time earning a certification as an HVAC and refrigeration technician, then went on to pursue and complete an associate's degree in mechanical technologies.

These qualifications generated broader employment opportunities in the Albuquerque area. Marvin left Motorola for a more lucrative apprenticeship with Wagner Mechanical, a well-established regional HVAC, plumbing, and electrical contractor. During his five years there, he further augmented his technical résumé, obtaining a journeyman boilermaker license, a refrigerator contractor license, and a journeyman gasfitter license. But the industry, he found, was feast or famine. As an hourly employee, he sometimes went weeks with shortened workdays and insubstantial income. It was, therefore, a relief, when he came across an open facilities maintenance position with Emcore, a rapidly growing communications technology firm. Marvin joined the division that manufactured photovoltaic cells for satellites. Its operations involved high-tech equipment and sophisticated clean rooms that required diligent monitoring and maintenance. There were complicated electrical networks, and temperature control protocols, and chemical waste systems, and a myriad of pumps and pipes and switches and conduits that demanded round-the-clock attention.

Marvin had a hand in overseeing all of this, monitoring the infrastructure and maintaining precise environmental conditions from a laptop in his office. It was a demanding, high-stress role, but Marvin thrived. He was fascinated by the complexity of it all, and enjoyed being on a team that performed a mission-critical function. Furthermore, the position was cushy. This was during the so-called "dot-com bubble" of the late nineties. Emcore, for a time, was awash in cash. The salary was juicy, the benefits were abundant, and the swanky corporate parties featured champagne fountains and bottomless shrimp cocktail.

In 2001 the bubble popped and the gilded age came to an end. Emcore, as susceptible to the downturn as many of its peers, began laying off personnel in droves. During the restructuring, an engineering job opened in the tier just above Marvin's. Whoever filled that spot would be immune from the downsizing. Marvin had the second-longest tenure in the department, and was generally regarded as its most reliable, highly skilled technician. His employment reviews had always been glowing, and so he expected to be a strong candidate for promotion.

Unexpectedly, the job was given to a lower-level employee, a young white man who did not have anywhere near the expertise or training that Marvin and several of the other maintenance personnel had. Marvin was not even interviewed for the job and, apparently, had never been in the running. Shortly thereafter, as part of another wave of layoffs, his employment was terminated.

Though Marvin had never been one to play the victim, he could not help but infer that the process was discriminatory. He and his colleagues discussed the situation at length and could make neither heads nor tails of the hiring decision. Most, even the white guys, had expected that Marvin would be promoted, and shared their condolences when the decision was announced.

This was the first time in Marvin's life that he sensed he might be subject to institutional racism. It just was not a common theme in his part of the world. Hispanics in New Mexico have long represented a significant fraction of the state population. According to the 2000 census, 42 percent of the population identified as having a Hispanic or Latino background. By 2010, that number had risen to over 46 percent. Marvin was raised in an almost entirely Hispanic community, surrounded by other Hispanic communities, and had not, in school or in the working place, previously felt maligned or targeted because of his ethnicity.

Now, however, something seemed off. Marvin was not the only one to suspect it. His friends and family, even some of his colleagues, suggested that he communicate his concerns to the Emcore human resources department. He considered it for a time, but ultimately chose to depart from the company without incident. He had the skills to find employment elsewhere and didn't feel like making a stink. Emcore had been good to him for the most part, and, even if he did have a legitimate case, he did not have the spirit to follow through with an administrative appeal.

The experience stuck with Marvin well after the dust settled. He grew sensitive to incidents that, previously, may not have drawn his attention. Late in his tenure at Emcore, he moved to a more affluent neighborhood of Albuquerque, in a section of town known as the Northeast Heights. Although the house that he rented, as well as the general environs, were nicer and more aesthetically pleasing than any of his previous living situations, the transition presented a bit of a culture shock. Almost all of his neighbors were white, and, soon after settling in, Marvin began experiencing friction with some of them. One repeatedly called the landlord to complain about Marvin's nocturnal activities. The strange thing was that Marvin worked the graveyard shift at Emcore four nights a week, so he was normally away from the house until sunrise. Other than that, he tended to be a bit of a loner. He never had parties, rarely had guests other than an occasional lady friend, and did little that would have disturbed a reasonable neighbor. Nonetheless, the complaints kept coming, and Marvin frequently was forced to defend himself against unfounded allegations.

Marvin often walked his dog, a German shepherd mix named Sierra, in the early morning when he returned home from work, and then again in the afternoons. Sometimes he crossed paths with a neighbor who lived a few houses down. There was nothing unusual in the appearance of the man: he looked to be a middle-aged professional of some sort, perhaps a banker or lawyer like many of the local residents. However, he often ogled Marvin strangely, as if the newcomer were out of place strolling down the sidewalk.

Then, one day, as Marvin picked up after his dog, he glanced up to see the man standing in his doorway, glaring angrily.

"We all know what you are doing," the man announced steadily.

Marvin looked back over his shoulder because, at first, he did not know who the man was addressing. However, there was no one else in the vicinity.

The man continued to stare daggers.

"What are you talking about?" a befuddled Marvin replied.

"I said, 'We all know what you are doing'!" The man spoke with a booming tone this time, clearly enunciating each word as if English were unintelligible for Marvin.

Marvin narrowed his eyes, irritated by the demeanor of the man and the rather enigmatic allegation he seemed to be making.

"Okay," Marvin replied. "Whatever." He resumed his walk down the sidewalk with Sierra. The man tracked Marvin with his gaze, then, finally, retreated into his home and shut the door.

Over the next few days, Marvin ruminated about the incident. He was not sure of precisely what the mysterious man's beef was, but clearly the comment was meant to insinuate some sort of nefarious behavior. Perhaps he thought that the out-of-place Latino was dealing drugs, or ran with a gang, or both. Whatever the suspicion, clearly—as implied by the man's use of "we"—the neighbors had been talking behind Marvin's back.

What they did not know was that Marvin had never in his life abused drugs and only a few times had puffed a joint. He considered himself a straightedge homebody. Whatever the angry man was alleging was completely unsubstantiated, and, therefore, in Marvin's view—a view colored, perhaps sharpened, by his distasteful ouster from Emcore—was most likely bigoted or racist in nature. The more he thought about it, the more inclined he was to conclude that the "we" the man identified did not just refer to other people in the neighborhood, it referred specifically to the other *white people* in the neighborhood. And so, although the interaction was brief, and, in the scheme of things, somewhat insignificant, Marvin had a hard time moving past the disrespect the comment connoted or the hurt that it caused.

The next week, Marvin returned home in the evening to a distressing situation. As he approached the gate to his backyard, where he often left his dog during the days, he heard an unfamiliar bark and whine. He looked over the gate to see that there was a strange, large canine penned up with Sierra. It was scratching at the fence in a panic, desperate to escape the enclosure. As Marvin opened the gate, the dog bared its teeth and snarled. Without collar or tags, it appeared to be a stray. Sierra was cowering in another corner of the yard. Marvin stepped out of the way and the mystery dog sprinted out, disappearing down the street.

Marvin concluded that there was no way that the dog could have gotten into the yard of its own accord and then somehow latched the gate behind itself. Clearly someone had placed it there. But who? And why? Marvin immediately suspected that smug asshole who had yelled at him the previous week, but it could have been any of the allied neighbors. What really enraged him, though, was the thought that whoever brought the big, mean hound over may have wanted it to attack, even kill, Sierra. *There is a sadistic motherfucker out there,* Marvin thought. *These people have no reason to dislike me, but they're trying to run me out of the neighborhood!*

Marvin never found his place in Northeast Heights in the way he had back in Cypress Circle. He did his best to keep to himself and attract minimal attention. The following year he moved across town.

Despite these few hiccups, things were going quite well for Marvin as he rounded thirty years of age. He was making a good living, which afforded him a nice apartment, two cars, and a fairly padded bank account. He decided that, after years of grinding it out, it was time to let his hair down a bit. He began going out on the town more, drinking from time to time, inviting nice young ladies out to trendy new restaurants. Also during this era, he and a few friends made a habit of patronizing the local Hooters restaurant to watch football and basketball on the weekends. It was a great place to catch a game: big TVs everywhere, a lively atmosphere, bubbly waitresses serving up big mugs of beer. Over time, Marvin got to know most of the staff and management there. In fact, they all liked him so much that they eventually offered him a job as the doorman and bouncer. Marvin was not much of a tough guy or a roughneck, but he was big and even-keeled and well-respected by most people he met. He didn't need the extra job, but, outside of Hooters, few fun social opportunities arose. He agreed to cover some of the Friday and Saturday shifts, and did so until the weekend of the shooting.

After his arrest, and after being cut loose by the Credit Union, Marvin went into crisis mode. Twohig estimated that a full defense would cost upward of $40,000—a problem because Marvin had already emptied his coffers. Moreover, aside from this case-related burden, he had bills to pay and a life to live that required funding, if modest. His father and sister chipped in a bit, but most of Marvin's friends and family had nothing to contribute to the cause. Marvin moved back in with his father, took out a $10,000 personal loan from the credit union, and began digging through the help-wanted ads.

The problem Marvin quickly encountered was that almost every job he set his sights on required a criminal background check, which can include arrest records in addition to information about convictions. That was essentially a nonstarter. Although the United States Equal Opportunity Employment Commission (EEOC) prohibits employers from using background checks to disproportionately reject candidates according to criteria addressed in Title VII of the Civil Rights Act of 1964—race, color, religion, sex, and national origin— private employers have considerable leeway in making hiring decisions based on criminal status. State and local statues may further restrict employer discretion in this regard, but violations of such statutes are difficult to prove and require the aggrieved party to take legal action, a potentially costly and time-consuming endeavor.

For Marvin, the employment situation was dire until he finally came across a posting for a maintenance job with the Albuquerque Parks and Recreation Department. It would be low-pay grunt work— picking up trash in the parks, cleaning up the medians along city streets, weeding—the kind of unskilled toil that, just a few weeks earlier, he would have considered far below his pay-grade. However, there was no mention of a background check in the ad, nor discussion of one during the interview process. Marvin was hired without a hitch. He thanked his lucky stars.

A few months later, Marvin was able to transfer into a higher-level maintenance position with the Albuquerque BioPark, a facility that consisted of both a zoo and an aquarium. Again, the human resources department did not run a background check. Or, perhaps, whatever report they procured did not highlight Marvin's pending case. Either way, he kept his head down and his mouth shut.

The job provided a dose of stability, but did very little for Marvin's emotional condition. He found himself in a state of depressive limbo. Prior to his arrest, he had been diligently working toward a set of long-terms goals—the purchase of a house, an upgrade of his vehicle, the starting of a family. But all of that was now not only on hold, but likely squandered indefinitely. When he wasn't working, he isolated himself at home. Occasionally a friend or family member invited him to a barbecue or a birthday party, but those outings were all but impossible to enjoy. Whenever Marvin smiled, a voice in his head would whisper: *What are you grinning at? There is nothing to be happy about.* When he laughed, the voice would admonish him: *How can you giggle like a child when your life hangs in the balance?* Moreover, Marvin could not even begin to think about romantic liaisons. He did not have funds to go on dates, much less the enthusiasm. Until his criminal case got sorted out, for better or worse, he was stuck on an existential treadmill, expending effort, struggling and sweating, but going nowhere. He would remain on that treadmill, as it turned out, for approximately two years.

Some six months into the pretrial process, the prosecutor, as expected, offered a plea deal. Marvin's charge would be reduced to voluntary manslaughter with a seven-year prison term. Twohig explained that, factoring in good time, Marvin would likely spend only four years behind bars if he accepted the offer. This was a vast improvement on the second-degree murder beef he was originally facing, which would be served up with fifteen years of hard time. On the other hand, Marvin was firmly convinced that the actions he took on the night of the homicide constituted self-defense. At the moment he pulled the trigger, he was in fear of being attacked and wounded, or possibly killed.

Generally speaking, in the United States the commission of violence in the act of self-defense is acceptable if such an act is necessary to defend against the immediate threat of unlawful violence. However, as with many principles in criminal law, the concept is interpreted and applied in disparate and complex ways from state to state and municipality to municipality. Traditionally, in the United States, behavior in such situations has been regulated by a "duty to retreat," which is the legal requirement that an individual must attempt to escape a threatening situation prior to using violent or deadly force in response. The exception to this rule is a four-hundred-year-old English concept known as the "castle doctrine," which permits an individual to employ deadly force without a duty to retreat in the case of a home invasion. In most United States jurisdictions, some variation on the castle doctrine has been adhered to.

However, over the past dozen years, the right to self-defense has been augmented via both legislative action and judicial interpretation. Beginning with Florida in 2005, more than thirty American states have passed laws that explicitly eliminate the duty to retreat in instances of self-defense, effectively permitting the defender to react violently without first seeking to avoid the confrontation. Beyond that, a number of states have, in practice, adopted "stand-your-ground" principles despite a lack of legislation that explicitly addresses the issue.

Since its inception, there has been acrimonious ideological discord over the social costs and benefits of stand-your-ground laws. Proponents—the National Rifle Association (NRA) notably among them—contend that they are advocating a reasonable right that is necessary for the safety and peace of mind of law-abiding citizens. Detractors point to the moral hazard of the concept, and argue that these laws will encourage reckless vigilantism. Furthermore, many prosecutors are dismayed by the inherent disadvantages they face in prosecuting cases in which a resulting homicide was not justified. Effectively, the prosecution must prove, beyond a reasonable doubt, that the shooter was *not* acting in self-defense, when, in most cases, there is only one living witness: the shooter himself.

Debate on these issues reached a fever pitch in 2012 after the shooting death of a Florida teen named Trayvon Martin. The shooter, twenty-eight-year-old George Zimmerman, was the neighborhood watch coordinator for his gated community in the town of Sanford. He spotted Martin walking down the street, called 9-1-1 to report his suspicions, and then pursued the boy on foot. These actions culminated in a physical altercation, during which Zimmerman shot Martin to death.

The legality of Zimmerman's behavior was hotly contested in both the media and the legal community. As it turned out, Martin was staying with his father's fiancée at her home in the community, and was simply returning from a trip to the local 7-Eleven when the incident transpired. He was not acting criminally when he was first noticed by

Zimmerman, and may have even ran away from Zimmerman at some point prior to their violent interaction. Many observers have asserted that the homicide proceeded directly from Zimmerman's decision to investigate and follow Martin, and therefore could not possibly fall under the purview of Florida's stand-your-ground directive. Rancor, however, focused foremost on the racial circumstances of the homicide. Zimmerman is a mixed-race Hispanic. Martin was black, and, at the time, was wearing a hooded sweatshirt.

Zimmerman was initially released by police, who concluded that there was insufficient evidence to contradict the shooter's claim to self-defense under Florida law. However, Zimmerman was later charged by a special prosecutor for the state. In the summer of 2013, he was acquitted of all charges.

Defenders of Trayvon Martin argue passionately that he was the innocent victim of a fatal case of racial profiling, and that, had the roles been reversed, Trayvon would have likely been convicted. Indeed, some studies have found significant racial disparities in the adjudication of stand-your-ground defenses in the United States, although there does not appear to be expert consensus on the issue.

Unlike Florida, New Mexico is one of the states that has not enacted specific stand-your-ground legislation. However, its statutes and legal standards effectively offer the equivalent protections. New Mexico law deems homicide justifiable when an individual is defending his life, his family, or his property, or when an individual deems that a perpetrator is about to commit a felony or cause grave injury, or when an individual is acting lawfully to detain someone who has committed a felony, to suppress a riot, or to keep and preserve the peace.[6] Thus, the letter of the law, although it does not expressly eliminate the duty to retreat, allows for rather broad reasoning behind the use of force.

After discussing these parameters with Twohig, Marvin was adamant that the homicide he committed was justifiable. Nonetheless, in contemplating the existing plea deal, the attorney did not nudge

Marvin in either direction. Assuming that the deadly use of a firearm was, indeed, warranted under state law, and, assuming that the case was abundantly defensible, then to serve four to seven years for the act was unconscionable. At the same time, Twohig emphasized, there are no guarantees in criminal trials. Regardless of the solidity of one's defense, there are many moving parts: the judge's competency, the prosecutor's scruples, the jury's empathy, prejudices, and understanding of the law.

It was an agonizing decision for Marvin. He, like so many other American criminal defendants, was faced with a devil's bargain: either wave the white flag and endure a relatively small fraction of life in a cage, or put up a fight and risk decades of incarceration. Over the past thirty years, plea bargaining has eclipsed trial by jury as the primary system of criminal adjudication in the United States. Today, over 95 percent of non-dismissed criminal cases are resolved via closed-door negotiations between a government prosecutor and defense counsel—negotiations which are neither guided nor supervised by a judge. This number is up from just 19 percent of cases in 1980, an increase that some attribute to the establishment of mandatory sentencing guidelines.

While proponents argue that the rise of the plea bargain regime has been a beneficial, even necessary response to extreme legal costs, judicial inefficiencies, and federal and state court logjams, others criticize it for creating an imbalanced, constitutionally dubious environment in which the prosecution wields vast advantages over the defense. In most scenarios, prosecutors are largely unrestrained in determining the charges brought against the accused. That is, whether the defendant faces a manslaughter or murder charge, for example, is at the sole discretion of the prosecutor. Additionally, when a plea deal is first offered by a prosecutor, he or she may have had access to a robust tranche of information related to the case—police reports, witness interviews, forensic evidence, and other investigatory data—while the defense attorney's appraisal may be limited to a brief few conversations with his incarcerated client.

The defendant, and his attorney, can feel tremendous pressure to accept the most lenient offer from the prosecutor, which often occurs early in the process. Generally, if they choose to reject the offer, it is gone with the wind. Future plea deals, if presented, will be for higher-level charges featuring more severe punishment. Additionally, most criminal defendants who go to trial—perhaps more than two-thirds of them—are then convicted.[7] The urgency and heightened emotions of the situation may compromise the defendant's ability to rationally and comprehensively evaluate the defensibility of the case or the likelihood of acquittal. As a consequence of these handicaps, some innocent defendants feel compelled to plead guilty to a completely unsubstantiated charge. Although such situations may represent a relatively small percentage of guilty verdicts—between 2 and 8 percent according to some researchers—the actual number of American convicts imprisoned due to this sort of false plea may be in the tens of thousands.[8]

Marvin believed that he was compelled to protect himself when he fired his shotgun on that night in September. He was certain of it, and convinced that any rational person would incur, at minimum, a more-than-reasonable doubt about the legitimacy of the murder charge he faced. Marvin instructed Twohig to reject the plea deal.

The criminal trial took place at the Bernalillo County courthouse over the span of two weeks in August 2008. Judge Denise Barela-Shepherd presided. At first glance, she appeared to be a sharp, put-together official. She had been a district court judge since 2003. However, on the first day of the trial, Marvin sensed that she was not fully prepared for the proceedings. At the start of the day, she directed her bailiff to clear her schedule for the coming weeks, a move that Marvin expected to have been completed prior to the trial. It was as if she had expected the case to be resolved in a single day. Also, at times, though Marvin may have misinterpreted Barela-Shepherd's demeanor, she seemed uncertain of how to proceed. Occasionally she had to double-check statutes that Twohig and his associates had known forward and backward. Marvin felt that these missteps, though slight, did not bode well for the coming trial days.

The state's prosecutor was Theresa Whatley, an assistant district attorney who, at the time of trial, had occupied that position for around four years. She was a white woman with gentle features that belied an aggressiveness that emerged during the trial. From the get-go she seemed uncompromisingly determined to put Marvin behind bars. In the opening statement, she described him as a reckless violator—someone who happily took it upon himself to assume the role of judge, jury, and executioner. It was a damning, widely inaccurate description, in Marvin's view. *Another card stacked against me*, he fretted.

On the other hand, the jury selection process was relatively fair. Twohig and Whatley grappled over a pool of candidates in a somewhat tense proceeding during which they each presented a variety of peremptory and causal challenges. To Marvin's great surprise, one of the candidates was a former coworker at the credit union, a young woman named Stephanie. He felt very uncomfortable during her questioning, but Twohig later explained that this was a positive turn of events. Although Stephanie was disqualified, she had voiced a positive appraisal of Marvin in front of the other future jurors—in a way, serving as a preliminary character witness for the defense. When the dust settled and the final twelve members were impaneled, the demographics of the jury did not seem overly detrimental to the defense's aims. It was rather evenly split between Hispanics and whites, and between men and women.

Witnesses testified on both sides. Two of the victim's friends who had been present during the homicide offered their version of events, which starkly contrasted with the version that Marvin presented during his time on the stand. In particular, they refuted the defense's claim that the victim was wielding a knife. Marvin's sister Rosella and two of his friends who had pertinent perspectives on the case details took the stand for the defense. Rosella, in particular, had played a central role in the events that led up to the shooting and was able to

put forth a detailed, exonerating testimony. There were a variety of
character witnesses as well.

The prosecution called in a blood spatter expert and a ballistics
expert to reinforce its claims about exactly how the shooting transpired
and where Marvin and the victim were positioned at the moment the
gun went off. Marvin felt that their analyses were substantially inaccurate. Twohig, in rebuttal, called a martial arts expert who demonstrated how quickly the victim, who was allegedly armed with a knife,
could have advanced on Marvin.

Whatley, as expected, described the victim as a good-natured,
fun-loving, upstanding member of the Albuquerque community.
And, for all Marvin knew, that may have been the case aside from
their run-in. At the same time, she went to great lengths to impugn
Marvin's character. She showed photographs of dumbbells in his
apartment, seeming to imply that he was a muscle-bound, aggressive thug of sorts. She suggested that, as a bouncer at Hooters, he
surely knew how to defend himself with his hands and to diffuse
a potentially physical confrontation—skills that he opted not to
employ prior to firing his weapon. Marvin recalls that she made an
unfounded, almost comical assertion that Rosella may have planted
the knife that was discovered between the legs of the prostrate victim. But what Marvin found to be most insulting and atrocious were
Whatley's allegations regarding his stance toward women. The circumstances that led up to the shooting involved the victim's behavior
toward a group of women at an Albuquerque saloon. Marvin had
intervened physically on behalf of the women. Whatley insinuated
that, although Marvin wanted people to believe that he was a protec-
tor of women, he was, in reality, a perverted exploiter of the opposite
sex. Investigators had found a video camera in Marvin's apartment,
on which was stored an intimate video that he had made during a
rendezvous with one of his girlfriends. Though the tape was found
to be impermissible as evidence in the trial, Whatley referenced
its contents, inquiring, "Isn't it true that you videotaped women's

breasts and bottoms from your bedroom window when they're in the laundry?"

Marvin had no recollection of creating recordings of that sort, and was about to rebut, when his counsel objected vociferously. Incensed, Twohig went on to move for a mistrial on the grounds of prosecutorial misconduct, irrelevance, and improper cross-examination. Whatley defended her line of questioning, citing the right of the state to impeach the defendant's character. The court concluded that the state had a good faith basis for making the inquiry and, though no additional questioning in that direction would be allowed, denied the motion for a mistrial.

Another intriguing moment occurred when an Albuquerque police officer testified on behalf of the prosecution. After Marvin's arrest, this man had been tapped to conduct an analysis of some of the evidence that had been introduced into the case. Part of his testimony included an assessment of the distance between Marvin and his victim at the moment the gun went off. The policeman concluded (in line with the ballistics expert's analysis) that the two were approximately ten feet apart. The prosecution was using this distance estimation to assert that Marvin was not in immediate danger and had fired his gun without justification.

Twohig attacked during cross-examination. He called attention to a commonly cited policing doctrine known as the twenty-one-foot rule, which suggests that an officer of the law is within his rights to shoot if an armed offender is within twenty-one feet and advancing with malicious intent. This measurement is based on an estimation of how far an attacker might advance during the two seconds it takes an officer to draw, aim, and fire. Twohig knew that this particular officer had been in a similar situation much earlier in his career, and had shot an advancing offender. Twohig pointed out the irony, and suggested that the officer was employing an unfair double standard: the metric apparently served as justification for police actions, but not for those of a civilian who felt compelled to defend himself.

Though most of the circumstances of the homicide, in Marvin's view, pointed toward an open-and-shut case of self-defense, there was one major aspect that he recognized would seem incriminating. After the shooting, as the wounded man lay on the ground, Marvin got into his truck and fled. He and his twenty-year-old friend Jimmie, who was present for the incident, sped away from the scene in a desperate panic.

"I can't believe this!" Marvin kept shouting as he piloted his big Dodge Ram 1500 down dark Albuquerque streets. "Why did he come at me like that?"

Jimmie, stunned, replied, "I don't know, dude. I don't know."

Back at his apartment, Marvin parked the truck. The two jumped into Marvin's Jeep and drove to Jimmie's place, where the young man exited. Marvin took off again.

His phone rang. It was Rosella. Police and paramedics had shown up at the bar, and she was freaking out. Marvin explain what happened and told her that he was okay. However, he wasn't sure what he should do at that point. He had never been in this kind of hot water. His worst offense to date was a speeding ticket. He told Rosella that he had to make some calls to figure out what the best move was.

Marvin decided to go to his trusted friend Robert's house. Robert, who was also Jimmie's cousin, had invited Marvin to come over and lay low until they determined the best course of action. Marvin brought the shotgun along and stashed it there.

During the course of the evening, Marvin spoke to several of his family members. Rosella called him a few more times. She had gone to the hospital to check on the status of the victim. He was in critical condition after an emergency surgery.

"Pray for him," Rosella said to Marvin.

"I will," Marvin replied. "I didn't want this to happen."

"I know."

At six in the morning, Rosella phoned once more with tragic news. The man that Marvin shot had passed away. She began crying, as did Marvin.

The death made it official, Marvin realized. He might get charged with murder. He knew in his heart that his actions were justified, but he had no idea whether the police would see it that way. Running away, he realized, probably looked very bad. But he was absolutely freaking out! He was on autopilot, not thinking clearly about what he was supposed to do!

That afternoon, a Saturday, Marvin and Robert picked up Jimmie and drove to a local Red Roof Inn. Marvin was leaning toward surrendering to the police on Monday. He felt he needed to let things calm down over the weekend. However, at the same time, he was not confident that he had the courage to turn himself in. It was probably the most prudent course of action, but the thought of it was horrifying.

Ultimately, the decision was made for Marvin. The men spent the night at the hotel, and, Sunday morning, went to a nearby McDonald's for breakfast. Apparently, the police had been able to track Marvin to that neighborhood using cell phone data. One of the cops spotted the men returning to the hotel. Later that morning, there was a knock on the motel room door. Marvin, Robert, and Jimmie looked at each other with wide eyes. The police announced themselves. Marvin was stunned. He had convinced himself that he was safe for the time being. He opened the door to reveal several officers in tactical gear with weapons drawn. Behind them were additional patrolmen. They pushed into the room, ordered Marvin and his friends to the ground, then handcuffed them.

The details of the manhunt and arrest were recounted in court. Marvin felt dopey and ashamed as he listened. If only he could have kept a level head at the time of the shooting. He should have just waited for the police to arrive and explained the whole thing in rational terms. Hindsight, unfortunately, is 20/20.

Nonetheless, when both sides finally came to rest and the jury was released to begin deliberations, Marvin felt that things had gone reasonably well. Twohig, in his opinion, had performed admirably. He had conveyed Marvin's story clearly and compellingly, and had seized on several opportunities to rein in Whatley's contentious tactics and brazen attempts to sensationalize the facts. Furthermore, Marvin felt that his attorney developed a propitious rapport with the jury. Handsome, with a thick comb of a mustache and smooth oratory skills, Twohig was a kind of working man's Tom Selleck. His charm, Marvin hoped, would pay dividends.

The jury deliberated for three days, and, on a few occasions, reported to the court that it was deadlocked. A hung jury was a good thing, or so Marvin thought. It was not quite a "not guilty" verdict, but it was close. The longer the jury remained undecided, the more likely a mistrial would be declared. And, if that occurred, the prosecution would be between a rock and a hard place. Whatley had shown her whole hand during the trial; in the event of a redo, the defense would be even better prepared to fight back. Furthermore, a hung jury, while not an acquittal, indicates that the state's position might not be as convincing as it had believed. Consequently, the prosecution often decides not to pursue the charges further, or, alternatively, offers an even milder plea bargain. Marvin kept his fingers crossed and his chin up. His fate, at this point, was out of his hands, but, so far, things were looking fairly promising.

On the third day, however, just when it seemed that the jurors would fail to coalesce, they returned to the courtroom with a definitive verdict. Marvin was instructed to stand and face the jury for the moment of truth. He did his best to remain stoic, as advised by Twohig, but the oppressive anxiety of the moment caused him to swoon and sweat profusely. The bailiff passed the verdict envelope to Judge Barela-Shepherd, who solemnly unsealed it and read silently for a moment. Then she looked directly at Marvin and spoke aloud for all in the court to hear.

Guilty.

Guilty.

The jury had convicted Marvin of second-degree murder and tampering with evidence. Something exploded in Marvin's brain. It was as if someone had smashed him over the head with a crowbar, knocking him into a state of hazy semiconsciousness. He put his hands on the counsel table to steady himself. Barela-Shepherd continued to speak, but Marvin barely heard a word. After a moment, he looked to Twohig, whose countenance was grim and apologetic, then turned around to face his loved ones in the gallery benches. His mother, his father, his siblings, his friends—they were all sobbing openly.

Marvin was sent back to the Bernalillo County jail, where he would stay for approximately six months. Twohig suggested that they immediately begin an appeals process. He would bring on three additional lawyers and begin sifting through every piece of evidence that had been presented, every word that had been uttered at trial. It would cost $10,000, and, he warned, if there were a positive outcome, it would not happen overnight. He encouraged his client to settle in, spiritually and logistically, for the long haul.

Marvin was assigned to the F-8 pod, which, like E-6, contained a bevy of violent offenders. The Los Padillas gang, a local outfit headed by the powerful Padillas family, ran the show here. It was an unpleasant place to be. The facilities were stark, oppressive, and scant. The limited outdoor space was bordered by high concrete walls that afforded a view of nothing more than the sky directly overhead. Inmates were not allowed to interact with visitors face-to-face. Even though a loved one may have traveled a long distance to the jail, the prisoner was required to sit in a separate room and conduct the visit via teleconference.

Marvin was constantly checking his blind spots, expecting to be accosted by one of the many hustlers who were working angles on new blood. And, indeed, just a few weeks into his sentence, he ran into trouble. He had a cellmate, a strange white guy named Henry, who he generally did not get along with. The friction they experienced was compounded by the fact that the toilet in their cell repeatedly clogged. One day, as Marvin watched the communal television from the mezzanine walkway outside of the cell, Henry angrily confronted him about the plumbing situation. Marvin, tired of his roommate's complaints, snapped back. The disagreement rapidly escalated to the point that they were gripping each other by the shirt collars and shouting into each other's faces.

Noticing the fracas, one of the senior Los Padillas members came over and ordered Marvin and Henry to confine their belligerence to the inside of their cell. Fighting out in the open was a no-no. A small scrap could spread, incorporating additional participants, until it became a major disruption. When that happened, the entire pod would bear the wrath of the correctional officers. Furthermore, guys who fought in front of officers or security cameras were likely to be transferred into protective custody. Often, such a move was a strategic, deliberate action by a prisoner who felt threatened for one reason or another. It had a nickname; to employ this tactic was to "PC" oneself. The Los Padillas crew did not like when guys pulled this move. It meant one less inmate to take advantage of. Also, in most cases, the Los Padillas were the ones creating the threatening situation, and therefore were likely to feel some heat from the authorities in the aftermath.

Back in their cell, Henry and Marvin stared at each other.

"Do you want to do this?" Marvin asked.

Henry threw up his hands. "Naw, man. No point in gettin' busted up over a fuckin' shitter."

Then a voice came from the doorway. "What do you mean, you ain't gonna do it?"

Marvin looked to see two small Mexican men step into the cell. They were Los Padillas foot soldiers. One of them advanced aggressively, continuing to berate Marvin and Henry. "We fight in this pod. You know that shit. Gomez, you best smack that boy."

Damn, Marvin thought, *what is their obsession with fighting?* He responded evenly, "I'm not going to attack someone who doesn't want to fight."

The two little men glanced at each other and cackled.

"Well, unfortunately, that's not how this shit works," the other one said. "If you don't get it on with Henry here, then you're gonna have to fight the two of us."

Marvin rolled his eyes. This was ridiculous. There was no point to it. Plus, he was nearly as big as the two of them put together. He looked the men up and down, then raised his fists and replied, "All right, then."

The men attacked, throwing wild, stinging punches. Marvin retaliated with heavy swings of his arms. His fists connected on each of their faces a few times. One of the strikes cracked against a nose, which sprayed blood all over the floor. Despite their diminutive statures, the foot soldiers were more durable than they looked. They pressed the assault, backing Marvin into the corner of the cell. The violent thrashing and boxing continued until, suddenly, from elsewhere in the pod, a sharp whistle pierced the air. The two men promptly backed off. One of them grabbed a rag, and quickly swabbed up some blood from the floor. Then they exited the cell.

Confused, Marvin stepped outside and looked down onto the main floor. A correctional officer had entered the pod with a maintenance man who was carrying a bucket and a plumbing snake. The two trudged up the stairs to the mezzanine and approached Marvin's cell.

"You have the fucked-up can?" the CO asked.

"Yeah, right here," Marvin replied.

The maintenance man got to work on the toilet. Marvin went about his business as if he had not been part of a wild brawl just moments earlier.

After that, Marvin crossed paths with the two foot soldiers frequently, but they did not mess with him again. He had earned their respect, apparently. Sometimes, they would laugh and call him "Mexican Mike Tyson."

I'm not Mexican, Marvin would think to himself. *I'm Hispanic.*

While Twohig and his team continued their review of the case, Marvin was transferred to the Northeast New Mexico Detention Facility in Clayton. It was a privately run, medium-security facility, and a considerable upgrade from the county lockup. There were plenty of unsavory characters in Clayton, but Marvin rarely ran into trouble. It helped that, during yard time on the first day, he bumped into an old friend: Sagger from Westgate. The two rekindled their friendship, and the oversized gangster looked out for Marvin for the next thirty months.

A notable difference between state prison and county jail was that, at Clayton, street gangs did not run the show. Rather, the population was classified according to geographical origin. Inmates from Albuquerque (the *Burqueños*) comprised the largest and most powerful demographic block. There were also constituencies from Santa Fe, Las Vegas (the New Mexico town), Roswell, and Las Cruces. The pariahs of the prison were the guys from out of state who had committed crimes and been convicted in New Mexico: Texans, Arizonans, Mexican nationals (known pejoratively as *Paisas*), West Indians, and Central Americans. These groups represented a small proportion of the population and benefited least from the overall power structure. Members of each crew rallied around informally selected leaders, the "shot callers," and cooperated to maintain security and consolidate resources.

Surprisingly, there was limited racial tension within the facility in Marvin's experience. Most of the inmates were Hispanic, but blacks, whites, and Asians were also mixed in with the appropriate geographical faction. In some cases, allegiances were somewhat blurry. Many of the black guys, regardless of hometown, were Muslim, frequently prayed together, and coalesced around their religious identity. Similarly, many Latinos were Catholic, and so, despite municipal origin, interacted during mass and formed interfactional relationships. There was even a group of white guys who banded together to worship mythical Norse gods like Thor and Odin. Some prisoners razzed them for it, but the association was generally tolerated.

Sure, there were occasional violent conflicts among the inmates. Marvin once got into a fist fight with a Texan who had tormented a gay *Burqueño* about his sexuality. Marvin came to realize that prison was not that different from real life, except when tensions flared, walking away from the situation was neither logistically nor strategically a viable option. The key to staying out of trouble was level-headedness and strategic diplomacy.

At Clayton, Marvin went through the paces from day to day: eating, exercising, watching television, reading. He participated in some vocational classes and a computer course that covered Microsoft productivity software including Excel and PowerPoint. The instructor for the computer course, Miss Montoya, took a liking to Marvin and invited him to become a tutor for other inmates. He found this to be an enjoyable way to pass the time, and felt proud that he was having some sort of positive impact on the lives of his cohabitants.

Additionally, Marvin focused on his criminal appeal. Twohig was diligent in his work on the case and kept Marvin apprised of meaningful developments. However, the process, as expected, was a long, torturous slog. Occasionally, extended stretches of time passed without a substantial advancement, causing Marvin to grow exceedingly pessimistic about his future. As the weeks and months ticked past, he began to surrender to the idea that he would serve the entirety of his second-degree murder sentence and only emerge from captivity as a middle-aged man.

During this time, Twohig interviewed the jurors who had convicted Marvin. Although the information garnered from this process cannot be used to impeach the original outcome of a trial, it can be helpful to the defense in determining exactly what went wrong during the proceedings, and what new strategies it might employ in an appeal. A few of the jurors indicated that they voted to convict Marvin even though they had reservations about the state's case. Their reasoning went something like this: *I wasn't sure whether the defendant was explicitly guilty of the charge, but I felt it was more prudent to convict him than to risk the probability that a murderer would be released back onto the streets of Albuquerque.* In sum, although a criminal defendant in the United States must be found guilty "beyond a reasonable doubt," some of the jurors chose to convict Marvin *in spite* of their reasonable doubts.

In Marvin's opinion, it was a complete perversion of justice. He was not sure whom to blame. The jurors had been given written instructions about the conditions necessary for a guilty verdict, including whether, beyond a reasonable doubt, the defendant acted as a result of sufficient provocation. That is, if the circumstances of the crime caused Marvin to become so enraged or fearful that his ability to reason was compromised, then a second-degree conviction would not be warranted. Apparently, they did not fully understand those instructions.

At the same time, to this day, Marvin cannot help but wonder what would have transpired had a white man been the defendant and a Hispanic man the victim. He questions whether the result would have been the same. This doesn't necessarily mean that the jurors were purposefully or even consciously racist. However, at minimum, in his view, they may have acted on subconscious racial instinct, even the Hispanic jurors. Marvin surmises that those kinds of instincts—more so than malicious intent—are the foundation of institutional racism. Americans have been so conditioned to view Hispanics and blacks as perpetrators that we have a hard time impartially applying criminal justice, whether we like it or not. Nationwide, Latino men are more than twice as likely to be incarcerated as white men. Black men are almost six times as likely to be incarcerated as white men. Blacks and Latinos make up roughly 69 percent of the United States prison population despite accounting for only about 25 percent of our national population. [9]

Moreover, in retrospect, Marvin believes that institutional racism may have had an impact long before the jury returned their verdict. Had he been a white man and the victim a Hispanic, perhaps the police would not have charged him in the first place. It is possible that they would have perceived the incident to have been a legitimate shooting by a righteous citizen defending himself against an existential threat. Maybe Marvin's actions, too, were impacted by internalized racial perceptions. Had he felt more empowered as a citizen, more confident in his rights, more justified in standing his ground, he might have kept his head and not fled the scene. That choice may have made all the difference.

About two and a half years after the conviction, Twohig informed Marvin that the appeal was gaining traction. His team was, in particular, focusing on the allegations of sexual deviance—regarding purported surreptitious videotaping of women—that Prosecutor Whatley had made during the trial. Twohig maintained his belief that this line of questioning constituted a violation of a state regulation regarding the proprieties of cross-examination even though the judge denied his objection. He believed that the court erred in admitting this evidence and that, in appeal, a mistrial might be granted on the basis of prosecutorial misconduct.

The strategy bore fruit. On March 30, 2011, Judge Roderick Kennedy on the New Mexico Court of Appeals overturned the conviction of Marvin Gomez. Twohig called Marvin in prison and told him to pack his bags.

Although Marvin was to be released from prison, he was not technically a free man yet. The appellate court's decision to overturn the conviction was made "without prejudice." This meant that Marvin's case could be retried if the prosecutor deemed such action appropriate. However, that would not happen. Whatley returned to Twohig with another plea deal: voluntary manslaughter with a sentence of time served and three years of probation. In other words, if Marvin pled guilty to this new charge, he would not have to return to prison. Twohig presented the terms to Marvin, who accepted on the spot.

A bureaucratic snafu delayed Marvin's release. He was transferred from prison to the county jail back to prison. He spent three extra days behind bars because the corrections personnel were not on the

same page as the courts. During those hours, he obsessively worried
that something would change or that he would be killed in a freak,
last-minute incident. But finally, the moment arrived. Rosella picked
him up from the Central New Mexico Correctional Facility in Las
Lunas. They drove straight to her salon, and she gave Marvin a proper
haircut.

Upon release, Marvin moved back into his childhood home in
Albuquerque with his father. He has spent the last six years picking up the pieces and attempting to configure a viable and content
existence. His felony record does not make things easy. Although his
voting rights were restored upon completion of probation, he cannot
own a gun, does not qualify for certain professional licenses, has dif-
ficulty renting an apartment, and continues to encounter obstacles to
employment. Without the felony record, Marvin would qualify for a
plethora of good-paying positions throughout the metropolitan area.
However, he has been compelled to search for modest jobs that do
not hinge on a background check. In 2017, the New Mexico legisla-
ture passed a "ban the box" bill—legislation that prohibits employers
from inquiring about criminal records or screening based on criminal
history until the later phases of the interview process. It would have
made a world of difference for Marvin's economic prospects. Tough-
on-crime Governor Susana Martinez vetoed the bill.

Unlike some ex-cons, Marvin has been able to pay the bills and
keep moving forward. A few years back, he landed a part-time gig
with an electrical contracting business, retrofitting fluorescent lighting
systems in businesses and industrial buildings. However, most of that
work dried up when the government program that subsidized the projects was restructured. After that, he was hired to repair and maintain
water dispensation machines in grocery stores, such as Whole Foods,
throughout the Albuquerque region. This was a weekend-only job.
Later, the company offered Marvin a full-time position, but it was
three hours away in Santa Fe, and relocating was simply not feasible.

Also, Marvin learned that the hiring process involved a background check. He left the company not long thereafter.

In the last couple of years, much of Marvin's income has come from labor gigs that he sources via Craigslist: moving jobs, cleaning gigs, various assembly and repair projects. It's an unpredictable strategy, but in many cases the pay isn't half-bad and comes in the form of cash. He has scraped together a few extra bucks by finding miscellaneous items at yard sales and Goodwill stores and reselling them on eBay. Recently Marvin came across a facility maintenance position with a local manufacturer. The employer did not run a background check, and, impressed with Marvin's credentials, hired him on the spot.

Marvin does not feel bad for himself. At the end of the day, he has a roof over his head, a healthy constitution, and even a girlfriend. He has been with a sweet and supportive woman named Jade for the past couple of years. They frequently discuss getting married and go back and forth on the idea of having children. Marvin would like that, but only if he has the resources to maintain a happy household. Either way, there is one thing he is sure of: he will never leave Albuquerque.

In late September 2006, Marvin's nephew Sergio, Rosella's son, performed at a popular sports bar in Albuquerque. He was part of an eighties rock cover band that offered renditions of hits by Poison, Bon Jovi, Mötley Crüe, and the like. Marvin decided to attend and show his support. He brought Jimmie with him.

As the band rocked out, Marvin and Jimmie played some pool. But Marvin was distracted; there were a couple of men dancing wildly in front of the band, and it appeared that they were harassing some of the women who had gathered to watch. Among the women were some of the band members' mothers, including Rosella. One of the men, a forty-year-old white man named Kevin, seemed particularly aggressive. He was grabbing the women by the hand and trying to pull them onto the dance floor. When they refused he would flip them the bird.

Once or twice it seemed that he was directing the offensive gesture toward the women's private parts. At one point the photographer, a woman who had been hired to take photos of the band, turned around and snapped sharply at one of the men. She later claimed that he had groped her.

Marvin stopped playing pool and stared at the men, who appeared quite intoxicated. He was getting hot under the collar as the men continued to mess with the female patrons. Then, Kevin shimmied in the direction of Rosella. Marvin saw red. He'd be damned if he let that obnoxious guy harass his sister. He stomped over and grabbed Kevin by the neck, shoved him across the dance floor, and slammed him against the stage. The music clanked to a halt. Two bouncers quickly intervened and pulled the men apart.

Marvin then engaged in a heated discussion with the manager. He was livid about what had gone down.

"Are you going to kick those assholes out of the bar or what?"

"No," replied the manager. "But we'll watch them and make sure that they don't get out of line again."

"You better promise me that," said Marvin. "I don't want to have to step up to them again."

"I promise you that."

Marvin felt reassured, but was still bitter. If that guy so much as looked toward his sister, another brawl would break out. Marvin decided that it might be best if he just left. He told Rosella to call him if there was a problem, said his good-byes to some friends, then headed out to the parking lot with Jimmie.

They climbed into Marvin's truck and were about to leave when an SUV suddenly pulled in front of their path. The three men, including Kevin, got out of the vehicle and approached. Marvin wanted to drive off, but he was blocked in the rear by a tree and some bushes. There would be a confrontation.

Marvin suddenly remembered that he had a shotgun, a Winchester Defender, in the rear of the cab. He had gone target shooting earlier in the week and had not yet transferred the weapon back to the gun cabinet in his apartment. He reached back, grabbed the weapon, and stepped out of the truck.

Marvin showed the men the shotgun.

"I don't want any trouble," he announced.

The men continued to approach, with Kevin in the lead. Marvin thought he saw something glint in Kevin's hand: perhaps a knife? A screwdriver? He could not tell, but Kevin seemed to be advancing with malicious intent. Marvin racked the pump-action shotgun. He was about to fire in the air to scare his assailants away when Kevin suddenly lunged toward him. Marvin lowered the muzzle of the weapon and fired a round into Kevin's shoulder. Despite having only a moment to think, he made a conscious decision to target that part of Kevin's body. Marvin did not want to shoot him in the center of the chest or in the face and surely kill him. The echo of the blast rattled against the nearby buildings.

Kevin jerked backward and took a few stuttering steps in retreat, his eyes like saucers, his mouth agape.

"You shot me!" he rasped in disbelief. Then he collapsed to the ground.

The other men scampered away from the scene.

Breathing heavily, shaking, Marvin stared down at the man he had just shot.

A wisp of gray smoke rose into the black New Mexico sky and disappeared.

CHAPTER 4

A MAN FOR OTHERS

Alphonsus O'Connor

Chicago Police Officer Alphonsus O'Connor had a hard time syncing his biorhythms to the schedule of the so-called "midnight" shifts. And so, for the first ten months of his assignment to the 7th district, which mostly encapsulates a high-crime neighborhood called Englewood, he battled to keep his eyelids apart while on duty. Once or twice, even, he woke up with his forehead pressed against the cruiser window and a line of saliva dangling from his square Irish chin. Ultimately, Al figured out a regimen that worked. Rather than collapsing onto his bed pillow immediately after returning to his home midmorning, he'd stay up for a few hours after his shift and run errands or get things done around the house. Only when the clock struck noon would he hit the sack for six to eight hours.

In the evening, when most of the city was around the dinner table, Al would wake and head straight to the gym for a vigorous workout. The exercise would give his blood the momentum it needed to stay pumping for the evening. The exercise *and* a large cup of diesel coffee, that is. And so, as the witching hour drew near, the young patrolman would be running on all cylinders, ready for all comers, primed for another overnight ride.

Policing was in Al's blood. His mother's father, also named Alphonsus, with the equally Irish last name of Gilhooly, was a Chicago policeman. In fact, he had served as a bodyguard for the legendary Mayor Richard J. Daley, the unflinching democrat known as "The Boss," who had presided monolithically over the city during the sixties and seventies. With this pedigree, it was never out of the question that

young Al would one day don a blue uniform. Beyond that, several
of Al's close pals were on the same path. His high school friend Dan
O'Brien planned to follow the footsteps of his lieutenant father. The
father of Marty Walsh, who Al knew from the neighborhood, was also
a cop, and Marty would be, too. There were several more like that.

As far back as he could remember, Al's goal in life was to honor
the legacy of his forbears and of his homeland across the sea. Like
so many Irish immigrants to Chicago, he wanted to acquire some
property, build wealth, and sire a healthy and happy family. Just as
importantly, he hoped to make an enduring impact on the society
around him. Al had always wanted to grab the world by the lapels, give
it a good shake, and straighten things out. But, for a year or two after
graduating from Northern Illinois University, where he studied political science and public administration, he did not make much headway
in the direction of that mission. He had spent some time working in
the loading docks of the Merchandise Mart—a giant, landmark office
and showroom building on the north side of the Chicago River. He
had helped manage a few apartment buildings that his old man and
brother owned in gentrifying areas of the city. And he had bartended a
bit at a little Irish dive bar on the northwest side. Fortunately, in those
capacities, Al found plenty of time to kick back and contemplate his
future and his place in the world. His analysis repeatedly circled back
to the same conclusion: that he truly was cut from the same cloth as his
namesake grandfather, and that as a Chicago police officer he would be
able to achieve his aspirations and do right by his family. So, at twenty-
four, Al submitted an application to the police academy.

Sandra, Al's significant other, took a while to warm to the idea,
however. The two had been living together for nearly a year. She,
like Al, had grown up in Ireland, not far from where he was born.
Al's hometown was a modest hamlet called Augherskea, just outside
a slightly larger town named Dunshaughlin, some thirty kilometers
to the northwest of Dublin. During the economic downturn of the
1980s, Al's father, a butcher who had put all he had into real estate,

lost most everything. Exasperated, Al's mother rounded up young Al, his brother, and his three sisters and made the transatlantic journey that so many of their ancestors had made, to the Irish home-away-from-the-homeland: the Windy City.

Sandra, unlike Al, did not emigrate to America until she was in her twenties. She had been reared in a little town called Athboy, not very far or very different from Augherskea. Also, unlike Al, country folk from her parts generally did not hold law enforcement in the highest esteem. On the rare occasions that the *gardaí* showed up with their billy clubs, the townsfolk would hiss and shout and tell them to get the hell out and mind their own bloody business.

The first few times that Al mentioned his interest in the police force, Sandra responded with a fair bit of sourness.

"Isn't there nuttin' else ye can find yerself doin', luv?" she would ask in her thick, fresh-off-the-boat brogue.

But Al's enthusiasm was overwhelming and incessant. When he laid out the police academy application in front of her, she asked, "Are yiz a hundred percent sure dat dis is sumtin dat ye want ta do, Al?"

"Hell, yeah!" he replied without hesitation.

"Then I have ta give ye me blessin," she replied with a sigh and a wan smile. "Yer happiness is the most important ting."

And that was that.

After two years on the force, there was one aspect of the job that Al still had not mastered: promptness. He had a tendency to be scatter-brained, with the disposition of an excited puppy, or of a mad scientist on the verge of a new discovery. He was always trying to juggle too much at once. He would get ready for work, then decide to rearrange some tools in the basement, or clean behind the refrigerator, or search the Internet for some new real estate opportunity. Before you knew it, he'd be running behind.

On March 26, 2005, as the clock ticked toward midnight, Al scrambled out the front door of his red brick Georgian home on the northwest side of the city, massive travel mug of coffee in hand, and hopped into his black 1997 Oldsmobile Aurora. His destination, the Englewood station on the south side, was a good twenty-five minutes away. Al was supposed to report for duty in fifteen minutes. He jammed on the gas pedal.

As usual, Al's route was southbound on the I-90 Kennedy Expressway, continuing through the Jane Byrne Interchange near downtown Chicago onto the I-94 Dan Ryan. It was a little brisker than usual in Chicago that weekend, and the heater in his Olds was not the most efficient. But, despite his visible breath and the stress of his late start, Al was in high spirits. Things with Sandra, not always the smoothest, were quite healthy at the moment. He didn't have too much to complain about at work, now that he had adjusted to the hours. For a while he had been hoping to get assigned to a tactical operations team, whose role, primarily, was to issue and execute search warrants, and to tally as many arrests as possible. At first this sounded exciting, but then Al got wind of the downsides. The "tac" guys were under a lot of pressure to hit the arrest numbers that were expected of them, so they ended up locking people up for chintzy infractions such as urinating in an alleyway or drinking in public. He had second thoughts, and decided to stay put as a beat cop for the time being. For now, he was more or less content with his career, relatively speaking.

And, goddamn, he loved this big whale of a sedan. So quiet. So comfy. As he pushed seventy-five, passing beneath Roosevelt Road, just east of St. Ignatius College Prep, where he had attended high school, Al felt as if he were the captain of a big, speedy, impervious yacht with wheels.

Al's memories of high school were especially fond ones. It was at St. Ignatius that he first developed an understanding of what kind of man he was and aspired to become. Established by Jesuit priests in 1870, St. Ignatius is a historic and architecturally significant institution. Its main building, a distinctive, five-story brick city landmark, is one of only five edifices that survived the Great Chicago Fire of 1871.

The rear of the campus opens onto Taylor Street, the epicenter of Chicago's Little Italy. Although the area gentrified in the first decade of this millennium, back in the mid-nineties, when Al attended, there were public housing projects across Roosevelt Road and to the west of the school.

The demographic makeup of the St. Ignatius student body reflected the cultural patchwork of the geographical surroundings. The school drew students from every corner of Chicagoland: the historic Beverly neighborhood on the south side, posh Lincoln Park, the mostly white western suburbs, the high-rises along Lake Shore Drive, the working-class melting pots of the northwest and south sides, the wealthy north shore suburbs. Al commuted fifteen miles each way from his home in Edison Park. Hispanics, African Americans, Asians, and other minorities comprised more than one-third of the student population. And, despite the Catholic affiliation, there were more than a few Jews, Hindus, Buddhists, and Muslims who traversed the carpeted halls.

Students at St. Ignatius are taught the school motto on the first day of freshman year: "men and women for others." There is a heavy emphasis on community engagement, with various courses and extracurricular programs entailing social activism and volunteering. Al was never an exceptional academic, nor particularly devoted to his studies, but this spirit of altruism resonated with him. He volunteered in youth programs at the nearby Duncan YMCA, and spent time assisting and providing companionship to the blind patrons of the Illinois Visually Handicapped Institute. Later, in college, he briefly considered pursuing a degree of study that would have equipped him for a high-level administrative role in similar nonprofit organizations. Now, as he drove to the police station on this spring evening in 2005, Al was proud of the man he had become, and he felt that his experience at St. Ignatius deserved a fair share of the credit.

The dashboard clock showed 12:01 a.m. as Al exited 59th Street and careened westward toward the station. *It's officially Easter Sunday,*

Al thought to himself with some satisfaction. Irish Catholics had a particular affinity for the holiday. It was a welcome occasion to rally the troops and whip up some big dishes and drink a nice taste of whiskey. Sandra and he had some family and friends stopping by the house that afternoon, as a matter of fact. He looked forward to the festivities.

Al jabbed the power button on the stereo. The CD that he had been listening to constantly as of late started spinning—Guns N' Roses' *Appetite for Destruction*. Yes, the record was some eighteen years old, and, sure, it juxtaposed oddly with the spirit of a holiday commemorating the resurrection of the Christ, but the heavy rock album was working for Al lately. It pumped him up during his workouts and placed him in the right mindset for nine-hour shifts patting down drug dealers and responding to early-morning domestic violence calls. When Al guided his Olds to a red light at 59th Street and Normal Boulevard, he was singing along and banging out steering wheel drums to "Paradise City."

Al was tardier than usual. He worried that maybe, this time, Captain Tobin wouldn't be so understanding about it. There was no time to wait for the red to change, so he decided to slip around the two or three cars that were lined up in front of him and blow the light. At that hour of night, in this neighborhood, it was unlikely that anyone would care in the slightest.

However, just as Al began to creep toward the intersection, he spied a stocky man sprinting up the alleyway ahead on the left side of the street. It was dark, and the man was about fifty feet away, but Al could register that he was an African American of roughly 250 pounds. Also, there was an object in the man's right hand. Judging from the rigid way the man was swinging that arm, Al deduced that the object was undoubtedly a pistol. On edge, Al rolled forward slowly. The man emerged from the alley and hustled right across Al's path on 59th Street.

Holy moly, Al thought to himself, Axl Rose shrieking soulfully from the Aurora's speakers, *this might be my lucky break! I'll pop this*

*guy for unlawful use of a weapon. Then I'll have an excuse for being late,
plus a nice little arrest as a feather in my cap!* No sooner had Al finished
that thought when a squad car came shooting out of the alley with its
roof lights spinning, in hot pursuit of the armed offender. The car was
almost in front of Al's face before he even noticed it or heard its sirens
blaring because the rock and roll was cranked up so loud. He clicked
off the radio and the hair on the back of his neck stood on end.

Al didn't immediately recognize the vehicle. It was an SUV, but
with a different stripe and emblem on the side than the typical city
cruiser. Nonetheless, the word police was stamped across the doors in
bold. Al tracked the action as the pursuing vehicle shot across 59th
Street, and banged hard over the concrete curb on the north side of
the street. It screeched to a halt not far from the man with the gun.
Immediately the policeman opened his door, stepped onto the sidewalk, and—BANG! BANG! BANG!—the fleeing offender quickly
swung around and fired three times. The policeman had no time to
react. All three bullets connected—one in the stomach and two in
the arm—causing the policeman to drop his weapon. Staggered, he
hobbled to a position behind his vehicle and collapsed onto his back.
Al watched on in shocked horror as the injured officer clutched his
wounds, the gunman looming just paces away.

Al's brief time on the force had not quite prepared him for what
he had just witnessed. And, so, in the silent moments that followed
the sharp crack of the three gunshots, he struggled to overcome his
stunned inertia and take action. He was alone, in a dark and desolate
neighborhood, and standing just twenty feet away was a big man with
a hot pistol who most certainly would not hesitate to use it again.

The moment seemed to freeze in time. *The shooter winded and
heaving. The wounded officer prostrate, speaking in agonizing bursts into
his shoulder radio. Al's eyes as wide as saucers, his heart thumping uncontrollably. The V8 engine of the Olds Aurora rumbling like a distant freight
train.* Then it happened. The mysterious offender took a step toward
the downed officer. Then another step. Then another.

Al gripped the steering wheel with sweaty palms and breathed as if he were preparing to bench press two hundred pounds. He closed his eyes briefly to summon the courage. Then his instinct and training took over. He kicked open his car door and emerged onto the now-empty city street. In one smooth, mechanical motion, as he had practiced one thousand times before, he unholstered his sidearm and pointed it firmly toward the gunman's center of mass.

"Police!" Al shouted. And, although he meant to follow that with "Drop the weapon!" he blurted something along the lines of "What the fuck are you doing?!"

The gunman, his pistol now at his side, stopped progressing toward the downed policeman. He pivoted his eyes, and then his head, toward Al. The man did not appear to be in the midst of a murderous rage, but he most certainly was calculating the risks and rewards of his present scenario.

Al found the words. "Drop the gun!"

But the man did not comply. He simply stood there.

At this point, Al began to have a conversation with himself. *What the hell am I supposed to do here? Do I just shoot this guy? He's not dropping his weapon. But we're only supposed to shoot if there's an imminent threat, right? Is the threat over? I mean, he isn't shooting any more. Is he done shooting? If I just go ahead and blast this guy am I in violation of departmental policy? Is it justified? Will I get in trouble?*

This internal inquisition played out for seconds that seemed like hours while Al kept his Sig Sauer 9mm leveled. Then, without warning, the man twisted his body toward Al and began to raise his shooting arm. The doubts in Al's head silenced immediately. He squeezed the trigger, firing off a well-aimed shot, and then dove for cover behind the Oldsmobile. The gunman returned fire with two blasts of his own.

Al huddled against his car, his frantic breath puffing into the midnight air. It was silent, but he strained to listen, aware that the loud booms of the gunshots had temporarily compromised his hearing. He did not detect the sound of approaching footsteps, and so, after a few moments, he peeked over the hood of the car. Strangely, the gunman had not moved. There he stood, almost larger than life, in a big white T-shirt, stark against the sordid background of the neighborhood. His arms were at his sides, and he was motionless, right where Al had left him.

Al was certain that first shot had found its mark, but the big man looked absolutely unscathed. No blood. No gore. No wretched expression on his round face. Al quickly squatted back into his defensive position and cursed. He readied himself, popped up once more and squeezed off two shots—boom! boom!—before ducking back down. Now, he was almost completely deaf. A few more cold breaths, and then Al peered over the hood once again. *What the hell!?!* The dude was in the same position, broad and imposing and steady, no evidence that any of Al's bullets had done any damage.

Frustrated and increasingly frightened, Al decided to give it one more go. He sprang up, pulled the trigger three more times, and then hid. And again, his ears ringing, the musty odor of gunpowder tickling his nostrils, he waited—for something—a sign. Hoping against hope that this last volley had ended the surreal stand-off, Al raised his head and surveyed the scene once more.

There, like some malicious cyborg, or like an indestructible, expressionless urban zombie, stood the offender.

This sent Al into a panic. *What is going on here? Am I really such a poor shot? Had I missed with all six bullets, or are there more sinister forces at play? Is this guy hopped up on some kind of juice that make him impervious to the pain and destruction of gunshot wounds? Am I hallucinating? Am I dead already, and this is hell, and I'll just have to keep shooting at this freak for the rest of eternity?*

Al blinked and snapped out of it. He decided to phone for back up. He reached into his car and grabbed his cell phone, jamming 9-1-1 into the dial pad as fast as his fingers would allow.

A woman's voice responded.

"9-1-1. What's your emergency?" she intoned dismally.

"This is Al O'Connor. I'm an off-duty police officer and I've been involved in a shooting." He announced urgently. "I need backup."

"Where are you located, sir?"

"59th and Normal Boulevard."

"And someone has been shot?"

"Yes! A cop has been shot and I've shot someone."

"So, do you need two ambulances or just one?"

Al was on the verge of losing it. This conversation had already gone on too long. "Didn't you hear me?! I need backup! Now! Send everyone!"

"Okay, sir. Help is one the way."

Al hung up and was relieved, but only for the briefest of moments. There was what seemed to be an unstoppable force just yards away. Also, Al realized that, during the emergency call, he had lost track of the offender's status. At any moment that nightmarish villain could appear around the side of Al's car and fire a fatal round. Al leaped up for one more quick peek. But now, inexplicably, the gunman was flat on his back in the dirt, unmoving.

Al took a moment to exhale a tremendous sigh. Then he turned his attention to the downed police officer. He strode hurriedly over to where his comrade lay on the ground. As he walked, Al began to hear the distant wail of police sirens. It was music to his half-deaf ears. The cavalry was on the way. He was almost out of the woods. Then he noticed that his gun hand was empty. *Damn.* In the confusion, Al had left his piece on the driver's seat of his car. This was not good. First, he did not know whether the offender had a partner in crime lurking somewhere nearby, waiting to strike at the opportune moment. Second, it was commonly said on the force that "a gun doesn't bounce twice in the hood." As soon as you lose hold of a pistol, somebody else will snatch it up. Al ran back to his car, and the approaching sirens grew louder.

Al's gun was there on the seat cushion, its barrel still warm. He grabbed it, shut the car door and made a few steps back toward the wounded officer. Suddenly he was awash in white light. Several squad cars surrounded him, their spotlights creating a dome of brightness that forced him to squint hard. More than half-a-dozen patrolmen had emerged from the vehicles and were aiming their weapons at Al, shouting madly.

"Stop right there!"

"Do not move!"

Al froze right where he was. Because he was still in plain clothes, these unfamiliar officers could not readily determine whether he was a perpetrator or a good guy. He raised his arms over his head, gun still in hand, slowly and very, very carefully. The policemen eyed him like hawks.

"Whoa, guys!" Al called back. "I'm the police. Please relax. I'm the police."

The officers did not respond. They kept their guns pointed rigidly.

Like a surgeon in the midst of a critical procedure, Al reached with his free hand and pulled the flap of his shirt to the side, revealing the shiny silver of his city badge.

"I'm going to holster this gun now," he announced. Then he lowered his weapon slowly and tucked it into place. At last, the responding officers withdrew theirs as well.

The police began processing the scene like a swarm of industrial ants. The man who took the reins was Joe Keenan, a sergeant from the mobile strike force. Although Al regularly worked in close geographical proximity to Keenan—they both serviced the 7th district—the two had never come in contact. But tonight, Al could sense from the sergeant's demeanor that he was good police; he knew exactly how to handle complicated situations. And this situation—an officer clinging for life, a dead offender in the dirt, mysterious motives and details, no witnesses besides the last man standing—could certainly get complicated. Although his heart continued to race, as Al watched the older man call the shots, he felt more comforted than intimidated.

Keenan barked instructions to his subordinates about where to tape off the scene, how to redirect what little traffic flowed through the area, and how to go about surveying the neighborhood for witnesses and other possible participants in the crime. Then, shortly after getting things under control, he approached Al.

"You must be the shooter," the sergeant huffed, his voice sturdy and reflecting years of experience with these sorts of things.

"Yes, sir," Al rasped nervously. Being referred to as "the shooter" set him on edge.

Keenan peered closely into Al's eyes.

"I can tell. Your pupils are the size of silver dollars."

Al chuckled, for lack of a more appropriate response. The older man put a strong hand on Al's shoulder.

"You did good work here," he said plainly. "They're taking Officer McCormack to a hospital in Oak Lawn. He's responsive."

Keenan was somewhat hard to read. Al assumed that meant that the injured patrolman would live, but he didn't feel in his rights to inquire further.

"Now," the sergeant continued. "Where's the pistol?"

Al's hand went to his waistline. He was relieved to confirm that his gun was holstered properly. Then he realized that the captain was referring to the dead offender's weapon.

Confused, Al stammered, "It . . . it should be next to the body, Sarge."

Without a word, Keenan strode to where the gunman's body still lay inanimately in the dirt. Al followed. This was the first time that he actually took a close look at the person that he had shot. He wasn't quite as big as Al had first perceived—maybe only 5'10"—but he was a good bit overweight. *Why did a guy that fat think he could outrun a police car?* Al wondered. Then he looked at the face. In fact, this was barely a grown man; he was a youngster, maybe twenty years old. Based on the poise the man had demonstrated during the gunfight, Al would have expected someone fifteen or twenty years older.

The dead man wore an oversized white T-shirt, jeans, sneakers— more or less the uniform for gangster types in this part of town. He lay fully extended on his back, arms wide, as if he were sprawled atop a waterbed. His eyes were wide open, staring fixedly into the universe above. The only sign of trauma was a single red blotch on his T-shirt in the center of his chest, about the breadth of a slice of plum tomato.

A few days later, Al learned that all six of the bullets that he had fired had made contact with the gunman. It was the very first one, the one that Al had properly aimed, a chest shot, which proved fatal. The other five ended up in the offender's legs, not surprising since Al had been scared witless while squeezing those off and had hardly aimed as he popped up from behind his car to engage.

So why had the man stood there for so long after Al had shot him through the heart with his first pull of the trigger? The medical examiner suggested that the trauma of the projectile tearing into the man's cardiac muscle must have caused him to go into an intense state of shock. Thrown into autopilot, his body stiffened up where it stood. Then, even the leg shots didn't send him to the ground.

Al had never killed someone before. And, despite his assignment to a very rough inner-city district, he had never even *shot at* someone before. He expected, in this moment, to have some sort of unprecedented emotional response. Perhaps he would get choked up. Perhaps he would get sick to his stomach and have to excuse himself quickly. But that was not the case. Al was glad to be alive—very glad. Beyond that, nothing. What had happened here, the grim display laid out before him, this wretched tableau, was an all too common part of the job for a beat cop on the south side of Chicago.

Al was introduced to this gruesome feature of his vocation very early on. His police academy training included visits to the city morgue to observe and inspect cadavers in varied states of decay. The point of these field trips is to help young officers prepare for the emotional response that they will experience upon witnessing carnage on city streets. Al remembered watching a medical examiner remove a man's cranium in order to conduct a cerebral examination on one of these visits. On another visit, an autopsy was being performed on a child laid upon a frigid slab. That one was almost impossible to bear.

For patrolmen who were assigned to the rough parts of the city, however, these morgue visits were hardly the tip of the iceberg. Al had witnessed depraved violence nearly every day that he worked a beat on the south or west side in his first two years. Especially here in Englewood, there were constant calls about "shots fired." Sometimes these turned out to be nothing more than a couple of kids playing in the alley with firecrackers. But often enough, Al would arrive on the scene to find a man with a bullet in his gut or his chest, or a woman with one in her leg, or a schoolkid who was the collateral damage of the cross fire between rival gangs. And, plenty of times, he would roll up to the scene to find someone sobbing over a dead body on the ground. It doesn't take more than a dozen of these calls to get anesthetized to the carnage. *This must be what it's like for one of those army nurses on the front lines of a war,* Al would think to himself.

Despite all of this, the hardest part about the job for Al was the fact that, regardless of his intentions, the majority of the people he encountered on the streets despised him. He learned this very early on in his career, and for a time he wondered whether he had chosen the wrong path. People of all walks of life, not just the gangbangers in the hood, would see Al in his police uniform and reflexively mutter insults under their breaths, even shout them openly. Civilians generally did not recognize Chicago cops as public servants or keepers of the peace. Most seemed to view Al and his colleagues as a corrupt mafia of sorts, capriciously exercising their power and acting first and foremost out of self-interest.

This cynical perspective may not be without merit. Chicago has a long, infamous history of political graft and official misconduct. A significant stain on the reputation of the police department is the Jon Burge torture scandal. Between 1972 and 1991, Commander Burge and officers under his direction used violence and abuse to coerce confessions—some false—from more than one hundred criminal suspects, almost all black men, on the south side of the city.[10] Burge was investigated and ultimately imprisoned, but that did not put a stop to the seemingly rampant employment of controversial police tactics. Between 2004 and 2016, Chicago dispensed over $600 million on judgments, settlements, and legal fees related to police misconduct.[11] A 2017 US Department of Justice investigation concluded that the Chicago Police Department (CPD) was deeply flawed at all levels, that inadequately trained policemen routinely used excessive force—disproportionately targeting people of color—and that a "code of silence" and toothless disciplinary oversight impelled officers to cover up misconduct with little fear of consequences.[12]

However, Al has always felt that the majority of officers conduct themselves appropriately, and that the overarching reality has been distorted. After all, the most publicized incidents involving police tend to be the most scandalous. It is relatively rare to turn on the evening news and see a headline report about a policeman tending to an ailing homeless man, or helping a frantic mother find her missing child, or mobilizing in a community where there has been a spate of burglaries.

Once, while assigned to the Englewood district, Al and his partner, Officer Cortez, responded to an early-morning domestic violence call. When they arrived at the address, it was just past three in the morning, and the building was dark and foreboding. The sound of angry voices resonated from an apartment on the second floor. The two patrolmen ascended an unlit stairwell and found the residence that appeared to be the source of the disturbance. Al climbed over onto the front balcony to see if he could get a view of whatever might be occurring inside. He observed a paunchy, shirtless man standing over a disheveled, naked woman, who was sprawled on the floor. The woman was screaming at the man to stop his assault and leave her alone. It was clear from the man's state of arousal that he intended on raping the woman. Not more than five feet away, three young, doe-eyed toddlers were seated on a couch, witnesses to the assault.

Al rapped sharply on the balcony window. Seeing him, the seething man nearly jumped out of his sweatpants. The woman shrieked for help as her assaulter fled the room and headed for the back of the apartment. Al and Cortez jumped off of the balcony and sprinted around to the rear of the building, where they witnessed the offender burst out of the back door and bolt for the alley. They tackled him, pinned him to the ground, and began to cuff him.

"Get that molester motherfucker out of here!" The victimized woman was now standing in the doorway to the apartment, still nude, yelling loudly enough to rouse the entire neighborhood.

"What do you think we're doing, lady?" Al shouted back.

"Fuck you, pig!" she replied. "I don't give a fuck what you are doing. I hate you motherfuckers! Get the hell out of my yard and take that fat fuck with you, you ugly pig bastards!"

"This guy was about to rape you!" Cortez snapped at her.

"Go to hell, asshole!" was her response.

The woman refused to sign a criminal complaint against the man, and instead continued her profane tirade while the officers packed her assailant into the rear seat of the patrol car. As they pulled away and drove down the street, she stood in the middle of the street in her lingerie and cursed into the night.

So much for making the world a better place, Al thought. *So much for being a man for others.*

"You were saying?" Sergeant Keenan interrupted Al's train of thought as they stood over the dead offender.

"I was saying?" Al echoed.

"You said that it should be over here somewhere." Keenan was referring to the dead man's pistol.

Al looked around the perimeter of the body. The weapon wasn't in the man's right hand or his left hand, or near his hip, or anywhere within a few feet of the body. Al knew for certain that the guy had possessed and used a gun. He shot an officer for Christ's sake. *Where did it go? Did a local swoop in during the chaos and abscond with the piece? After all, guns don't bounce twice in the hood . . .*

"What the hell?" Al spoke aloud.

"All right folks, we have a missing weapon," Keenan announced. "Stop all nonessential tasks. I want everyone with a free hand looking for it."

In ten seconds a dozen uniforms were combing the area. One got low and tried to peek under the corpse without disturbing it. Others waded through nearby weeds and crabgrass. Others inspected the street gutters.

In a few minutes there came a shout. "I got it right here, Sarge!"

"Everybody freeze!" Keenan bellowed. "Stay right where you are until we secure this evidence!"

Keenan made his way over to the officer who had announced the discovery. That man was on his hands and knees, peering, to Al's surprise, underneath Al's sedan. Al and the sergeant both crouched to take a look. Sure enough, right there, on the pavement below the engine block, a stone's throw from the final resting place of the gunman, lay a 9mm semiautomatic pistol.

Al stood up and looked blankly at Sergeant Keenan.

"Well, how do you explain that one, O'Connor?"

"You got me, Sarge," Al replied.

Later, investigators recovered two bullets embedded in a house across the street. They were traced back to the offender's gun and had surely been intended for Al. Those were the last two bullets in the pistol's cartridge. The investigators concluded that the final, desperate, conscious act of the dying man, his heart shot-through and bleeding out, was to heave his gun in the direction of Al and the black 1997 Oldsmobile Aurora that shielded him.

It was another two hours before Keenan, having been occupied with other investigative matters around the scene, reappeared.

"Come with me, O'Connor," he instructed, and began walking south down the alley off of Normal Boulevard. Al scurried to catch up with the sergeant, who headed for an overgrown lot in the middle of the block. The area was barren and unlit except for what appeared to be a few police personnel swinging flashlights to and fro.

Near the center of the lot, Al and Keenan came upon three patrolmen and two detectives who were bent over, examining something dumped among the weeds. As one passed the beam of his flashlight across the object, Al realized with shock that it was another dead body.

Keenan stared down at it. "This is what was going on before you showed up, O'Connor," he spoke gravely.

Al peered at the corpse. It was a trim, young black man wearing nothing more than a grass-stained pair of white briefs. He was on his back, duct tape covering his mouth and wrapped tightly around his arms, binding them together. And, in the middle of his forehead was a dark bullet hole.

Al was flabbergasted. He looked to the sergeant for an explanation. Keenan pointed to the west. Al squinted to make out something in the distance, perhaps fifty yards from the weedy patch in which they stood.

"See those railroad tracks? That's the Norfolk Southern. The man you saved—McCormack—is a railroad officer, assigned to look after the freight trains that come through here. Sometimes they get jacked when they slow down or stop. When this shit here went down"— Keenan gestured to the violent scene at their feet—"McCormack was sitting over there on Normal Boulevard in his cruiser. He saw this guy fleeing across the street in his underwear followed by your offender, and, as you know, gave chase."

"Jesus," Al muttered in near disbelief. "I can't believe it." He tried to process what must have transpired in the moments before his intervention. He looked down at the cold, stiff man, who had bled profusely among the dandelions and ragweed that shrouded him.

"What the hell happened here?" Al asked Keenan.

The sergeant lifted his cap briefly to scratch his scalp and then shook his head. "We're trying to get to the bottom of it right now, kid."

A week or so earlier, a couple of small-time hustlers from the neighborhood, Terrell Jones and Larry Johnson, conceived of a crude scam. They recruited their friends, eighteen-year-olds Tameka Newson and Martha Jean, to play central roles. One of the girls would call into a local "party line" in order to connect with eager local bachelors. She'd hook a victim, and, after some steamy back-and-forth banter, invite him over for a private, in-person "party." The bait laid and the web spun, the young man would arrive primed and ready for action only to be set upon by Terrell and Larry, who would then rob the victim at gunpoint.

A few hours before Officer O'Connor rolled to a stop at the red light on 59th Street, perilously late for work, "Paradise City" ringing through his factory-installed speakers, Wallace Ross and Darius Williams walked up to the front door on south Normal Boulevard, ready to meet a woman who looked at least half as sexy as she sounded on the phone.

They were not disappointed when Tameka and Martha answered the door. Wallace and Darius followed the alluring woman to an upstairs apartment. The girls cheerfully offered the young men some cold beers, and the party began. Unfortunately, the good times were short-lived. Terrell Jones and big Larry Johnson emerged from the next room with handguns. They forced Wallace and Darius to the floor and instructed them to strip down to their underwear and hand over their valuables. Then Larry and Terrell bound the men and pistol-whipped them.

Tameka and Martha watched on, somewhat surprised by how aggressively their partners in crime were behaving. Larry was incredulous as he examined the piddly handful of cash that the young men had given up—just sixty bucks. He and Terrell discussed the possibility that their captives would go to the police if set free. They decided that the most prudent course of action would be to silence the men for good.

Leaving the girls in the apartment, Larry and Terrell pulled Darius and Wallace to their feet and roughly yanked them down the stairs and out of the apartment building. The idea was to stuff them into the trunk of Larry's car, drive them to a secluded area, and finish them off. But things didn't go according to plan. Upon emerging from the building, Darius made a break for it. Gagged and barefoot, his arms bound, he sprinted into the dark. Terrell and Wallace watched as Larry immediately gave chase. He caught Darius in a nearby empty lot and deposited a bullet in the young man's head, execution style.

Terrell ushered Wallace back up to the apartment, then abandoned him and fled. Upon hearing police vehicles arrive at the scene— the vehicles responding to Officer O'Connor's call—Wallace crept out of the apartment. Some neighbors untied him and provided him shelter until the coast was clear and he could approach the police officers safely.

At around 3:00 a.m. on Easter morning, Sergeant Keenan sent Al to the Area 1 headquarters at 51st Street and Wentworth Avenue for additional processing. By this time, there was no uncertainty as to his role in the incident. Al was not the perpetrator; he was a victim who had defended himself, and he was a hero who had intervened in an attempted homicide of a member of the law enforcement community. The officers at the station treated Al with great deference. When he arrived, one of the on-duty cops asked Al if there was anything that he needed—coffee, a sandwich.

"Where can I go have a smoke?" Al asked, in desperate need of a few nicotine puffs.

"Wherever the fuck you want, my friend," the officer replied. "Smoke right here at my desk. No one will say shit. You've earned it."

As Al continued to answer questions and described the happenings of the previous hours, he burned through half a pack of Marlboros. When other cops in the station walked by, they patted him on the back and offered some congratulatory words. Al felt a bit like John Wayne. For once, some real appreciation for the risks that he took out on the street. For once, some validation of his life's work. Yet, two men paid heavy prices for Al to feel this way. One was in the hospital, and the other one would be pushing daisies. Al wanted to bask in the glory of the moment, but, at the same time, he was in a state of emotional limbo. He didn't quite know how to process the whole ordeal. As he puffed a square nervously, his gut felt like a knotted rope.

The sun had come up when Al walked through the door of his home on Foster Avenue that Easter morning. Sandra was up waiting for him. He had called her from the Area 1 office and offered a very brief overview of the situation. She took Al's jacket and wrapped him up in the biggest hug that her arms could offer. Then she directed him to a seat at the kitchen table, where a large glass of whiskey awaited.

"I figured ye could do wit one of deez, Alfie," she said sweetly, smiling.

"Ye know what?" he replied. "Jameson for breakfast sounds quite good this mornin', darlin'. Quite good."

Ten years and eight months later, on November 24, 2015, Officer Al O'Connor and another dozen-or-so policemen were assembled for a strategy meeting at CPD Headquarters on South Michigan Avenue. It was nearing the end of yet another long shift, and Al, as always, was ready to go home. His wife, Meghan, would probably have dinner waiting for him, as she so often did. She was generous and maternal in her care for Al. Sometimes it was hard for Al not to become irritated when Meghan voiced her concern for his safety. But, at the end of the day, it was simply an expression of her love. And coming home to her each night went a long way toward washing away any anger or cynicism that had accumulated over the course of his shift. Meghan was a youthful ginger, with eager eyes, rosy, freckled cheeks, and a toothy smile that could brighten a room. Al didn't know where or what he would be without her.

Al and Sandra had split seven years earlier. They had never had an especially bitter or caustic relationship. In fact, until the end, they had tended to get along. However, the magic just wasn't there. Al woke up one morning in 2008 and decided to take action before too much of his own life and too much of Sandra's slipped away.

Meghan and Al met in 2013 when the two were invited on a vacation to Cabo San Lucas by some mutual friends. The spark was immediate, and it wasn't just an illusion created by the romantic beaches and ocean breezes. They began dating, and shortly thereafter moved in with each other. In July 2015, they married. Now, some five months later, Al was as happy as a clam. He was thinking about his wife and smiling when Captain Amanda Gunter entered the room and interrupted the meeting.

"Guys, we're gonna have to put this on hold for a few minutes," she announced. Then she instructed one of the officers to turn the television to CNN. Gray-haired and hirsute anchor Wolf Blitzer was in mid-sentence: " . . . we warn our viewers that what you are about to see is a disturbing video of this, uh, this police officer shooting and killing this seventeen-year-old teenager. We'll show you the video right now, but if you don't want to see it, this is a good time to turn your head away."

CNN then cut to a low-quality dash-cam video from a Chicago police vehicle:

> *It's night time, and the flare of halogen streetlamps slightly distorts the picture as we progress through an industrial southwest neighborhood of Chicago. After turning a corner or two, we speed onto Pulaski Road, northbound. In the distance, in the middle of the street, we notice a dark, upright figure. To the left of him is a police SUV and, further on, there appears to be a few more approaching police vehicles with blue roof lights flashing. As we get closer, we can discern that the figure is a trim man in dark clothing, jogging in the middle of the roadway, on the yellow line separating the northbound from the southbound traffic. Another police SUV stops right in front of the man, who slows to a jaunty walk and redirects to avoid it. As we follow, the first SUV swerves around to a new tactical position further*

down the road. The walking man, in a hoodie and jeans, angles away from the SUV, boldly striding, swinging his right arm loosely. Two officers emerge quickly and draw their handguns. They take a few steps from their vehicle toward the subject, aiming firmly in his direction. The hooded man continues walking, perhaps intending to circumvent the officers. When he passes within a car lane's width of the officers, one of the them opens fire. The first few gunshots spin the hooded man around three hundred and sixty degrees clockwise and send him flopping him to the ground, incapacitated. Another dozen or so bullets kicked up puffs of smoke as they pierced the man's body. Seconds later, one of the police officers approaches and kicks something from the man's lifeless hand.

Wolf Blitzer continued his commentary: "There you see the seventeen-year-old Laquan McDonald . . . he is lying there on the street . . ."

Then Captain Gunter snapped off the television. "This," she said loudly, "will present a problem. As you may have heard Cook County State's Attorney Alvarez has, today, charged a Chicago policeman with murder."

Gunter's voice was quickly drowned out by the din of reactions and protests from the seated officers.

"Quiet! I want quiet!" she barked.

The officers quickly clamped their mouths shut. "We are not the judge and the jury here. I know that this news probably upsets you. But what matters is that this video will have an impact on the public perception of this police department. Justified or not, the people of this city do not respond well when they see a video of police putting bullets in a young offender. We're going to have to work together to get through this."

Again, a hubbub erupted from the officers. Many, as before, were protests and curses—officers pissed off at seeing one of their brothers charged with murder for doing his goddamn job. But, mixed in now, there were some conciliatory tones. Some of the cops in the room might have been starting to realize that the situation was a bit more complex.

Departmental policy permits the use of deadly force as a last resort "when necessary to protect against an imminent threat to life or to prevent great bodily harm" to the officer himself or to another person. An erratic dude walking down the middle of the street, ignoring the orders of the police and wielding a knife—maybe the right thing was to put him down. But a civilian, one who is not familiar with those kinds of circumstances, might consider sixteen bullets an excessive response. Maybe, in hindsight, a Taser should have been utilized, or a diplomatic effort to deescalate the situation employed. Unfortunately, police on the street do not benefit from hindsight at the moment of encounter. Al believes that it is very hard to determine the appropriateness of an action unless you are the officer responding to the incident and experiencing the extreme tension and uncertainty of the moment. He learned that the hard way back in 2005.

The captain raised her voice over the discordant murmur. The men and women quieted again. "We don't know what's going to happen tonight, folks. This might turn ugly. This might end up in the streets. We have to be prepared for that, and prepared to act. I know that some of you are at the end of your shifts right now, but nobody can go home. I need you all to make sure that you have your helmets and batons on hand. And for now, just hang tight."

The Captain left the room and a dozen conversations erupted at once. Al was unsure of how to appraise the whole situation. For the past few months there had been rumblings of an ugly situation that was about to be exposed, but he did not know any of the details until five days ago, when the news came that a county judge had ordered the release of the dash-cam video showing the death of Laquan MacDonald. It would become the most publicized and consequential police-involved shooting in the history of Chicago.

Laquan was a disadvantaged inner-city teen who had spent a good part of his life as a ward of the state. His mother—a young teenager when Laquan was born—was early on deemed unfit to serve as caretaker for him and his little sister. There was an incident in which the two toddlers were left home alone and the girl burned herself badly on a radiator. They were taken into state custody for thirteen months before being returned to the care of their mother and her boyfriend. Not long after, the boyfriend beat six-year-old Laquan in full view of daycare workers, and the agency was forced to intervene again. Laquan was moved from foster home to foster home. During one of his placements, he was sexually abused.

The neighborhood where Laquan lived as a teenager—Austin—was a rough one. Shoddy, disregarded, grossly impoverished, it was one of the most murderous square miles in Chicago. His prospects were not bright, but things could have been worse. He was enrolled in a high school for at-risk youths, and was far from failing. Some of the teachers and counselors there thought he was doing all right, liked him, even observed a flicker of potential, a resiliency.

Laquan had a juvenile rap sheet marked with relatively mundane and repetitive stuff: minor drug possession, a violation of probation, truancies, and so on. He was loosely, and perhaps of necessity, affiliated with local gangs known as the New Breeds and the Four Corner Hustlers. He may have slung some dope for them, but did not appear to have been caught up in the violence or turf warfare that had sent so many of his peers to the big house.

He started smoking marijuana when he was only ten or eleven years old. He claimed that it helped him cope with the residual issues of his turbulent childhood. He was placed in a psychiatric hospital three times by the age of thirteen and diagnosed with post-traumatic stress disorder. A post-mortem toxicology report indicated that traces of PCP, a dissociative hallucinogen, were found in his blood and urine.

It has been reported that, prior to his run-in with the police, Laquan had been breaking into vehicles in a trucking yard. Patrolmen first confronted him shortly before 10 p.m. They spotted what turned out to be a three-inch folding knife in the boy's hand and called for a taser. They followed him, and, at some point, cut off his path with their vehicle. He stabbed one of the tires and smashed his blade against the windshield.

Laquan then jogged in the direction of a Burger King. Intercepted by a different police cruiser, he redirected down Pulaski Road, where the dash-cam video picked up the action. The lethal shots were fired by Officer Jason Van Dyke, who would become the first Chicago policeman charged with first-degree murder since 1980. Three additional officers who were present at the scene were later indicted on felony counts of conspiracy, official misconduct, and obstruction of justice.

The CPD and various officials, including Mayor Rahm Emanuel and Cook County State's Attorney Anita Alvarez, were heavily criticized for keeping the incident under wraps for more than a year. During that time, the Chicago City Council approved a $5 million settlement with the family of Laquan McDonald, even though the family had not yet even filed a wrongful death lawsuit. For many in the media, and for many of the citizens of Chicago—especially the disadvantaged black residents—the whole thing stunk to high heaven.

Would there be mass demonstrations? Riots even? Was this going to be Chicago's Rodney King? As Al retrieved his helmet and stick from his locker, he pondered the consequences of the visceral images that had just been broadcast by all of the major American networks and that were now making their way around the world. He was going to have to call Meghan and tell her that he was stuck at headquarters indefinitely tonight. She wouldn't be happy about that. Meghan did not come from an anti-authority background like Sandra, but she was a good deal more disquieted by the dangers that Al had to face on a daily basis. That's the main reason why he had put in for a transfer, which had recently been granted. Just this month he was pulled off the street and made a full-time instructor within the department, teaching "investigatory stops." The curriculum would cover issues like the difference between "reasonable suspicion" and "probable cause," and the criteria that an officer must use when deciding whether to "seize the freedom of movement" of a citizen. Basic stuff, but Al enjoyed discussing the nuances of the law. Moreover, he was happy to put Meghan's mind at ease.

Al headed back to the conference room. Seeing his colleagues geared up, some even with riot shields, he felt unsettled. And he was not the only one on edge. There was a sense among some members of the police force that the Black Lives Matter (BLM) movement was spiraling out of control—as if it were an avalanche, and, at this moment in history, the Chicago police were standing at the foot of the mountain. BLM coalesced in 2013 when a Hispanic man in Sanford, Florida, George Zimmerman, was acquitted of shooting to death an unarmed black teen named Trayvon Martin. Zimmerman claimed self-defense. From there, organizers and protesters began to focus intensely on incidents of police violence and injustice against African Americans, particularly those who, like Trayvon, did not appear to pose a mortal threat.

- In July of 2014, Eric Garner of Staten Island, New York, was placed in a chokehold and forced to the ground by police officers who confronted him for selling "loosies"—individual cigarettes—on the street. Restrained and face down on the sidewalk, Garner reportedly stated "I can't breathe" eleven times. During the episode, Garner had a heart attack and died one hour later.

    The medical examiner determined the death to be the result of "compression of neck (chokehold), compression of chest and prone positioning during physical restraint by police." And, although he cited asthma, heart disease, and obesity as contributing factors in the mortality, he ruled the incident a homicide.

    In July of 2015, the city of New York agreed to pay $5.9 million for damages to the estate of Eric Garner. In December of that year, a state grand jury elected not to indict the officer who had utilized the chokehold—a prohibited tactic—on Garner. BLM protests erupted in New York, San Francisco, Boston, Chicago, and around fifty other urban centers worldwide. The US Department of Justice immediately began its own investigation and, in February of 2016, convened a grand jury to hear evidence.

- On August 9, 2014, eighteen-year-old Michael Brown was shot to death by officer Darren Wilson in Ferguson, Missouri, north of St. Louis. Wilson confronted Brown and his friend Dorian Johnson after the two allegedly stole cigarillos from a nearby convenience store. Although the facts of the case are disputed, both sides agree that Brown and Wilson had a physical altercation through the window of Wilson's police vehicle. At that point, Wilson drew his gun and fired twelve shots at Brown, who was unarmed, killing him.

  Protests broke out almost immediately. For a period of six days, peaceful demonstrations were mixed with civil disorder and looting. Intensifying the outrage was the widespread, though unproven, belief that Michael Brown had his hands up and was surrendering when the fatal bullets hit him.

  Once again, a grand jury was convened to determine whether Officer Darren Wilson should be indicted on a to-be-determined criminal offense. Legal experts, and concerned observers, were critical of the handling of the grand jury process by St. Louis county prosecutor Robert McCulloch whose own father was a police officer who had been killed in the line of duty by a black suspect. On November 24, 2014, McCulloch held a press conference to announce that Officer Wilson would not be indicted. Protests, some violent, took form in St. Louis, Philadelphia, Albuquerque, Los Angeles, and many other cities across the United States.

  In February 2016, after months of negotiations with the US Department of Justice, the Ferguson City Council agreed to a proposed reform of its criminal justice system, which, according to a federal report, had been severely corrupted and biased against people of color.

- Just two days before prosecutor McCulloch's announcement of the findings of the grand jury in Missouri, twelve-year-old Tamir Rice was playing with a toy gun at Cudell Recreation Center, a park in Cleveland, Ohio. A witness called 9-1-1 and informed the dispatcher that the suspect, "probably a juvenile," was pointing a weapon, "probably fake," at people in the park. This qualifying information was not relayed by dispatch to Officers Timothy Loehmann and Frank Garmback, who responded to the call. As they rolled up to the scene, they witnessed Rice reach for the toy—an Airsoft replica—in his waistband. Within seconds of arriving, Loehmann fired twice. One bullet connected with Rice's torso. The boy died the following day.

  A thirteen-month investigation followed. Cuyahoga County Prosecutor Timothy McGinty then moved forward with grand jury proceedings, recommending that the jurors not bring charges against Officer Loehmann. They followed his lead. On December 28, 2015, Loehmann was cleared.

  BLM demonstrations followed in Cleveland and other cities. Local protesters focused their anger at prosecutor McGinty, even marching to his home and demanding his resignation. On March 16, 2016, McGinty lost his reelection campaign. A month later, the City of Cleveland settled a wrongful death claim with the family of Tamir Rice for $6 million.

- Freddie Gray, a twenty-five-year-old black man, was arrested by Baltimore police in April 2015 for allegedly possessing an illegal switchblade. During his transport to central booking in a police van, Gray suffered severe injuries to his spinal cord, including three fractured vertebrae, a spinal severance, and damage to his larynx. Gray went into cardiopulmonary arrest, was resuscitated, but never emerged from a coma. He died one week after his arrest.

Angry protests ensued following the funeral service. The impact was staggering: twenty policemen injured, two hundred and fifty arrests, and up to three hundred and fifty businesses damaged. A state of emergency was declared in the city of Baltimore and thousands of police and national guardsmen were deployed.

On May 1, 2015, Baltimore City State's Attorney, Marilyn Mosby, announced that she would recommend charging each of the six officers involved with multiple felonies, including murder, involuntary manslaughter, reckless endangerment, and assault. She alleged that Gray was improperly arrested for possession of a legal folding knife. Further, she asserted that Gray suffered his grievous injuries because he was shackled but not seat-belted in the back of the police van, and because police took no action as his medical condition visibly deteriorated. Two weeks later, the grand jury affirmed these indictments.

The first three trials resulted in a mistrial, and two acquittals. In July 2016, prosecutor Mosby dropped all charges against the three remaining defendants.

Al O'Connor understood the frustration of the Black Lives Matter folks. The Laquan McDonald shooting was a horrible situation no matter how you looked at it. And it was just one among countless senseless tragedies the black community in Chicago had to process that year. Indeed, legions of young black men were getting gunned down on urban streets across America—mostly by each other, and occasionally by a uniformed policeman. It had gone on like this for decades with little improvement. Al dealt with the shit every other goddamn day. Every time he looked down on a cold corpse sprawled across a sidewalk, part of his soul turned to ash. No doubt about it—something drastic needed to be done. How could you not want the problem fixed?

But Al did not feel that the answer lay in scapegoating and persecuting, legally or publicly, all or even most policemen. He felt that, as much as the BLM movement was about calling attention to the perils, inequities, and violence faced by black Americans, it also stood for demonizing law enforcement in this country. Yes, sometimes cops make mistakes, horrible ones. But a bad apple does not the whole bushel rot. The Black Lives Matter movement, in Al's view, was, in fact, not as black and white as many perceived and portrayed it to be.

"Blue lives matter, too," was the refrain throughout police departments across the United States. The cops that Al knew well just wanted to do their jobs right, make their livings, put food on their families' tables, and get home in one piece at the end of the shift. Al felt that if people could watch a Chicago policeman work the streets around the clock for just one week, they'd have a whole different perspective. If they saw the kind of grit, and perverse monotony, and perpetual risk that it entailed, and if they could understand the kind of extraordinary restraint the officer exercised out there every day, they wouldn't be marching, and rioting, and calling for his head.

Al believed that, if anything, a solution to the problem of violence in impoverished urban neighborhoods would be cultural. Many of these poor kids, for the most part, only learn one path, one way of life: make some money on the corners, and if someone crosses you, put him in the ground. It was a vicious cycle, with generation after generation perpetuating the same dead-end mentality. And the victims of these circumstances were almost entirely black men.

Simply put, the situation had become dire. In fact, more Chicagoans were murdered between 2001 and 2016 than Americans killed in the wars in Iraq and Afghanistan during that same time period—a total of 7,916 in the city. The year 2015 was rough: 468 people were murdered in the city, mostly with guns, and 2,939 people were shot. By comparison, in the same year, New York saw 339 killings and 1,309 shootings, while Los Angeles tallied 280 killings and 1,097 shootings. To make the discrepancy even clearer, 22 percent more people were shot in Chicago in 2015 than in New York and Los Angeles *combined*. In 2016, the Chicago numbers spiked further: 762 murders and 4,331 shooting victims.[13]

There is much debate over the recent surge in gun violence. Some point to the decentralization and spread of gang activity after the demolition of two major public housing projects.[14] Others cite political developments, changes in policing guidelines, or even the weather. Regardless, in Al's opinion, handcuffing the police, so to speak, would in no way help the situation. What we need to do as a society is get into those neighborhoods, disrupt the culture, break it apart from the inside, and show the young people a new path. We need to make them believe that there is another way to get ahead that doesn't involve slinging dope or gangbanging. Al suggests investing in those neighborhoods with a belief that our investment will pay off in the future. Every drug dealer that we take off the streets, every gun that we take out of the game, means fewer dollars the police have to spend in that neighborhood, and fewer lives that have to be placed on the line.

In his thirteen-plus-year career, the only time Al had put bullets in someone, the only time he had even discharged his service weapon in the line of duty, was when he had saved Officer McCormack's life. But, especially during the years Al was assigned to the 7th and 11th districts—the Englewood and Harrison neighborhoods, respectively—he had unholstered his sidearm on a daily basis. There were, it seemed, numerous other times when it may have been justified for Al to fire his weapon with lethal intent, but was able to employ less violent means for resolving the situations. In Al's view, what so few people can truly understand—can barely begin to empathize with—is the fact that, unlike attorneys, or roofers, or real estate agents, or dermatologists, or longshoremen, police officers on the west and south sides of Chicago quite literally encounter "kill-or-be-killed" dilemmas while on the clock. Many times in a career, an officer in the field will have but a fleeting moment, a split second, to assess whether the civilian he has engaged has murderous intent. In that moment, the officer must decide whether the use of lethal force is justified and/or necessary. He must determine whether that time has come in his tour of duty to deprive a civilian of his right to life. And, he must make these choices all the while knowing that his career depends on doing what is right, his legal status depends on making a sound decision, and his family's welfare depends on his snap judgment. God forbid he's overworked, or sick, or out of sorts, or bitter, or simply tired when that moment arrives.

A few years after his fatal run-in with Larry Johnson, Al had another close encounter. It was a dreary, rainy Friday in early autumn, and Al and his partner, Officer Dariush, were at work at the station. Al, in the wake of his heroism, had twice been transferred into more desirable roles within the force. First, they moved him off the beat and into an "incident car." This meant that, rather than rolling through the hood and dealing with every low-level call that came across dispatch, Al and his partner responded only to major incidents: felony assaults, arsons, big drug busts, homicides, and the like. From there he was placed on a tactical team. In that position, he didn't just obey the dictates of dispatch. He had some autonomy over what busts he pursued and how he used his time and energy. He could request and execute search warrants. He could call in other personnel and resources to get the job done.

Al's superior, Sergeant Pagano, entered the room and announced, "We've hit our head-count for the week, fellas. Let's take it easy today unless something worth our attention arises. If not, we'll just go grab a burrito or something."

Not a few hours later, reports of a robbery came over the radio. Pagano decided to call dispatch for the details. The suspect had run together a string of brazen armed robberies on the west side of Chicago during the previous ten days. A black man in his thirties, he typically targeted lower-class Hispanic people who worked on the street, selling fruits and other items from rolling carts—immigrants, often undocumented, who might have had thirty or forty bucks on them, and who would be very unlikely to go to the police due to their alien status. The suspect always worked with a female accomplice. When he jumped out to shove his pistol in some poor sap's face, she would wait in the running car—a black Ford Mustang—and keep watch. Among the police who were tracking the situation, the duo had already become known as "Bonnie and Clyde."

Al, Dariush, their colleague Nowak, and Sergeant Pagano used available details to plot Bonnie and Clyde's scores on a paper map. Sure enough, the crime scenes roughly traced a circle with its center in the 11th district, near Harrison and Pulaski. *Criminals can be so damn stupid*, Al thought.

"There can't be more than three black Ford Mustangs in the whole district. We're going to find them right there," Al suggested confidently. "I goddamn guarantee it."

The four policemen set off in two vehicles—Al, Nowak, and Pagano in an unmarked squad car, and Dariush in a covert minivan. They crisscrossed the checkerboard streets of the 11th district, peering into driveways and parking lots, searching for their target. After a surprisingly brief period of time, Dariush called with some news.

"I have eyes on a black Ford Mustang with very dark tints," he announced excitedly. "Gas station on Cicero and Washington. He's filling his tank."

Al replied into the radio. "What's the plate?"

Pagano referenced his notepad, on which was scribbled partial license plate information that had been collected during a previous encounter with the suspect vehicle. Dariush read off the digits.

"That's Bonnie and Clyde," Pagano confirmed. "No doubt about it. We're three blocks over."

The men knew to be extremely careful. Not only were the two suspects certainly armed, they had already led police on a previous high-speed chase down I-290 after a stick-up in the 15th district. If

Al and his team spooked Clyde, he'd put the pedal to the metal and a dangerous situation would ensue.

After topping off his gas tank, Clyde drove east down Washington Avenue. Dariush followed from a safe distance. Nowak piloted the squad car on a parallel route on Lake Street. When Clyde reached Pulaski Road, he turned right and arrived at a red light at Madison Avenue. Dariush positioned his minivan directly behind.

"It's time to make a move," Pagano announced.

Nowak turned up Pulaski and screeched into position across the path of the Mustang.

"Get out of the car! Get out of the car! Let's go!" Pagano hollered.

Al, Nowak, and Pagano jumped out with their guns drawn. Dariush tried to pin the Mustang into place with his van. But Clyde was quick to act. He threw his car in reverse and rammed the van. He burned rubber, nearly plowing into Nowak as he weaved onto westbound Madison.

"Get back in the car! Get back in the car! Let's go!" Pagano bellowed, an almost comical echo of his previous order.

The two police vehicles gave chase. But Bonnie and Clyde made it only another few blocks. Turning onto Karlov Avenue, Clyde lost control of the vehicle. It fishtailed on the wet pavement and slammed hard into some parked cars. This time, Nowak and Dariush wedged the Mustang tight. There was no place to run.

All four of the officers emerged and approached the vehicle sharply, aiming their weapons at the driver-side window. Nearest to the vehicle, Dariush peered in through the tinted glass before quickly stepping back.

"Gun in hand!" he shouted to the team. "He's got a gun!"

Dariush then hurried around toward the rear of the vehicle for a better tactical position. However, the pavement was slick with fresh rain, and he lost his footing and fell hard onto his back with a loud grunt. At that moment, Al stepped forward aggressively, his finger on the trigger. He grabbed hold of the driver's side door handle and thought, *Here it comes. If this guy is even holding a piece, I am putting him down. There's no ifs, ands, or buts about it.*

The door popped open. But Clyde did not emerge with his gun. Instead, the pistol tumbled out of the vehicle and landed on the pavement with a clank. Al and the other officers held their fire. Then Clyde pushed the door a bit wider, shouted, "Fuck you, cop mother-fuckers!" and threw a large handful of ten- and twenty-dollar bills into the air. The loose cash fluttered like autumn leaves in the windy drizzle and landed quietly on the damp, black pavement.

The night the Laquan McDonald video was released, there were, indeed, demonstrations, and angry people did take to the streets. But there were no riots in Chicago, per se, and the police from Al's unit were not deployed with helmets and batons to quell the unrest. After several more idle hours, they reconvened in the meeting room, where Captain Gunter appeared once more before them.

"It appears that things are not going to get out of hand. And we don't feel like paying you guys any more overtime. So pack up and get out of here."

Al drove home and climbed wearily into bed next to the sweet, warm body of his sleeping wife.

The Monday following Easter Sunday, 2005, the front page of the *Chicago Sun-Times* ran with the following banner headline:

OFF-DUTY COP DROVE BY AT THE RIGHT TIME
Officer credited with killing gunman, saving victim's life

It was tremendous publicity for the CPD, which had continually struggled with perception issues among a cynical populace. The department enthusiastically embraced such a clear-cut case of good guy versus bad guy—one of Chicago's finest doing what he knew he had to do to save a life and keep his city safe. Within the department and beyond, Al was quickly recognized as a hero. However, he had limited opportunity to bask in the glory of his achievement. The initial press that the incident received did not mention him by name. At the time, the police were not sure whether Larry Johnson was affiliated with a gang, and there was concern that Al would become the target of a retaliatory attack. It didn't bother Al, though. Publicity was never his aim. He was proud of himself for doing his duty, acting rightly, and boldly facing the greatest fears he had ever faced. He got plenty of pats on the back from his colleagues and his family; he didn't need to become a household name.

Moreover, immediately after the shooting, Al was placed on a three-day psychological suspension, which was required for any officer who had shot someone in the line of duty. On the third day, he sat down with a department therapist, a well-groomed, middle-aged woman in a pressed pantsuit. She marked a legal pad and stepped through what seemed to be a standard line of questioning with Al, to determine the psychological impact of the incident and to deem whether he was fit to return to action.

Toward the end of their session, the therapist said, "At the end of the day, there is really only one question that matters." She leaned forward to look directly into Al's eyes. "Inside—in your heart—are you okay with what happened?"

She was the first person to ask him this question, and, surprisingly, he hadn't fully considered the emotional consequences of the event prior to that moment. Al thought back on the incident: the instant he recognized that a violent crime was in progress, the moment he stepped out of his vehicle with his gun drawn, the look in the eyes of the offender as he raised his weapon and pointed it toward Al, the sound of Officer McCormack's voice as he pled into his radio, the image of the bloody corpse in the abandoned lot, the pressure of the trigger on Al's finger as he squeezed it.

"I didn't make the decision to kill that man," Al replied. "He made that decision for me."

CHAPTER 5

IN ISOLATION

Brittany Aden

"You are a dirty whore, just like your mother."

The words were as stabbing in Brittany Aden's nightmares as they were when spoken by her father. And, to be sure, they had been recited on numerous occasions. Brittany awoke and sat up in the darkness, a sour taste in the back of her mouth. It was very early, around five, on the morning of November 7, 2000. Normally, she would sleep as late as possible, occasionally missing the school bus. Slumber was her refuge. No one could bother her while unconscious, the ugly world held at bay by her sealed eyelids. But, this morning, her mind was disquieted by painful memories and dire premonitions. She scooted to the edge of her bed, in her small bedroom, in her father's triple-wide mobile home, and wrung her clammy hands.

At age fifteen, Brittany felt that she had suffered as much as she could conceivably handle. Ready or not, today would be the day.

One of us has got to go.

That candid sentiment echoed through the recesses of her consciousness, ricocheting back and forth across her skull, multiplying, crescendoing like the shrill howls of a pack of Tennessee coyotes.

One of us has got to go.

There were no other options, it seemed, no happy endings to this tragic tale. It would not get any better.

One of us has got to go.

One of us has got to go.

One of us has got to go.

Brittany was born in Bartlett, Tennessee, although she remembers little of that town, just glimpses. Her family's house was not far from a corner store. She often scribbled on the front sidewalk with chalk. And, of course, she bore witness to her parents' frequent angry disputes. Her father, Danny Aden, was a firefighter in nearby Memphis, and sported the requisite vocational mustache. By the time Brittany was born, his hair had disappeared and a rotund potbelly had taken shape, but he was tall and always a strong man. He had won both a purple heart and a bronze star for service in the Vietnam War.

Danny was well-liked and respected by his coworkers and neighbors. However, beleaguered by problems with alcohol abuse, and repeatedly the subject of domestic violence allegations, Danny was reportedly pushed into early retirement. He then moved the family about one hundred miles to the northeast, to a town called Westport in rural Carroll County. He had always wanted to do some farming, and had found a suitable piece of a land out there.

One might say the Aden family was unusually assembled. When Brittany was born, her mother, Kellie, was married to a man named Billy Barnes. However, she was sleeping with Danny on the side, and, during that period, became pregnant with Brittany. Convinced that Danny was the father, Kellie left Billy.

When Brittany came into the world, her birth certificate listed the surname Barnes. Her name was legally changed to Aden not long thereafter. There was no paternity test involved in that decision, however, and Brittany would forever wonder whether Danny was, in fact, her biological father. She has always hoped not.

Brittany had five older half-brothers. Two, whom Brittany never met, came from Danny's previous marriage: Jimmy and another whose name Brittany cannot remember. Jimmy committed suicide in his twenties, and the other was run over by a drunk driver when he was little. Chris and Johnny, also sons of Danny, were the products of yet another marriage. Johnny died in a motorcycle wreck in 2008. Chris lives in upstate New York. The fifth half-brother is David, who

Brittany did not connect with until she was sixteen years old. He is Kellie's son from a previous relationship. She lost custody of him when he was a young child, and he was subsequently raised by his paternal grandparents. David lives in Louisiana. Brittany has one full brother, Dallas, who is three years her junior.

Danny, Kellie, Brittany, Dallas, Chris, and Johnny squeezed into the trailer home on the edge of the Carroll County property. They were, to put it mildly, not the paragon of familial contentment. Danny and Kellie fought constantly, their altercations frequently physical. Danny would slap and punch and beat Kellie, sometimes leaving her bruised and bloody. Brittany remembers an incident in which her parents engaged in a horrible fight in the kitchen of their triple-wide mobile home. They began throwing things at each other—coffee mugs, utensils, a cutting board—and Brittany found herself trapped in the corner, too afraid of getting caught in the cross fire to run from the room. Kellie called 9-1-1 so frequently to report the violence that the responding policemen joked about installing a coffee machine on the Aden property for law enforcement use only. However, as Brittany recalls, on only one or two occasions did they actually haul Danny down to the station, and those interventions never resulted in serious criminal charges.

Danny also laid hands on the children. He beat them with just the slightest provocation: disobedience, disruptiveness, impudence. Brittany remembers a time when Danny dragged her into the bathroom, stripped her naked, and whipped her with a belt for about half an hour. She was only six years old at the time. When Kellie returned home to find her daughter in a miserable state, she took photos of the scarlet abrasions and bloody welts and threatened to send Danny to prison. Nothing came of it. Brittany, however, did not incur corporal punishment as frequently, or as severely, as her brothers did. Danny seemed to find reason to whoop one of them nearly every day when they were young. Johnny got the worst of it. One particularly vicious flogging turned most of Johnny's face black and blue. He told everyone at school that he was in a bad dirt bike accident.

Kellie was neither the most attentive nor the most reliable of mothers, but, during Brittany's elementary school years, she was vivacious and loving. She often played the role of savior when Danny was on the warpath looking to mete out punishment. She told Brittany, "No matter how bad you acted out, I could never bring myself to lay a hand on you. I didn't want to add to the suffering that your father created."

As a young woman, Kellie was short and considerably overweight, but, with thick drapes of red hair and a contagious smile, undeniably beautiful and readily pursued by men she encountered in western Tennessee. Besides occasionally filling in behind the bar at a local hole-in-the-wall, she rarely held a job. She was the kind of woman who liked to have men, like Danny, look after her. For most of her life, she did not struggle to find someone to take on that role.

Though geographically isolated from their school friends and neighbors, the Aden kids found myriad ways to entertain themselves and stay out of their father's way. They chased each other through the woods and upon the hills, and swam and fished in Big Sandy River. They zipped around on dirt bikes and old Honda three-wheelers. They even had a horse or two on the property that Danny permitted them to ride so long as the animals were groomed, fed, and tended to. Brittany, like her mother, cherished animals of all sorts. Rarely a week went by when the girl was not trapping a lizard or a field mouse and bringing it back to live in a fish tank in her bedroom. At one time, there were as many as fifteen dogs living out in the yard. Kellie had a tremendous soft spot for cats. There were, indeed, a clowder of them prowling around the property, and mewing for food, and investigating the shadowy nooks of the barn. She and Brittany often picked up strays on the side of the road. When people around the county learned of this habit, they started abandoning their unwanted felines at the very edge of the Aden property.

It is not surprising that Brittany, in these environs, raised by a rugged war veteran and surrounded by a contingent of grubby-faced, scabby-kneed brothers, was a tomboy. She sported a plain-Jane haircut that framed a rosy, chubby face, wore overalls and grubby hand-me-down T-shirts, and rarely hesitated to roughneck with her siblings. "You act like a goddamn boy," her father would snort. "Why don't you clean yourself up and try to be a lady for once?" At a young age, however, Brittany hardly knew what her father meant by that.

Among the Aden kids, scorn and animus were the currencies of the realm. They cursed at each other and engaged in fistfights and tore at each other's hair. The mildest of affronts often resulted in a bout of screaming and slapping. Brittany was not exempt from the attacks by dint of being a girl. The older boys terrorized her, often chasing her, crying, around the property. There were numerous occasions when she ran out to the pickup truck and barricaded herself inside to escape the abuse.

Brittany and her brothers attended the Clarksburg School near Route 22. She wasn't a very good student, but she didn't mind attending class. It was often a welcome escape from the madness of her domestic situation. She even had a few friends that she could talk to and pal around with, although they rarely saw each other outside of school hours. As time went by, Brittany grew out of her tomboy phase and tried to dress more like the girls at school, donning tighter jeans and low-cut tops. She had hoped that her father would be more approving of her new stylings than he was of the old. However, instead, he reminded her that she was too fat to wear clothes like that and that they made her look like a tramp.

Brittany stood up slowly, breathlessly, and tiptoed out of her bedroom. In the living room, she quietly lifted Danny's deer rifle off a wall rack. She had never fired that gun before. Its sturdy, wooden heft surprised her. She pulled the bolt handle back once, loading a cartridge in the rifle's chamber, then snuck toward Danny's bedroom.

Danny was asleep on his side, facing away from the door when she entered. He snored mildly and steadily. Moonlight faintly illuminated the

white sheets that draped his frame. Brittany stepped cautiously around the
bed to get a better vantage. If her father awoke to find her looming there
gripping his rifle, she was likely a goner. The closer she approached, the
more the weapon seemed to weigh her down. For a moment, it felt like a
giant walnut log, and Brittany worried that she would drop it. Shivering,
she raised it, placed her finger on the trigger, and pointed the muzzle
toward her father.

Suddenly, Brittany began hyperventilating. She lowered the rifle and
turned away from the bed, struggling to stifle the sound of her gasps. She
dropped to the floor and sat cross-legged against the wall, the loaded gun
balanced across her thighs. She feared that she would pass out and later
awake to stare down the barrel of the same rifle as Danny aimed it between
her eyes. But, after a few minutes, the panic attack passed. Brittany strug-
gled to her feet, reset the rifle on its rack, and retreated to her bedroom.

Kellie divorced Danny when Brittany was ten years old. The two
had separated numerous times before, and Kellie had repeatedly filed
papers, but, despite the domestic unrest, she never quite had the guts
to follow through. The county clerk finally told her, "If you don't go
through with the divorce proceedings this time, I don't want you to
show up at my desk ever again." Kellie complied. She packed up Dallas
and Brittany and relocated to a shelter for abused women in Trenton,
Tennessee, about an hour from Westport. They were given a private
bedroom, although most of the women slept on thin cots in a large
public area. Dallas and Brittany were the only children in the facility,
making the experience both intimidating and confusing for them.

After a few months, the three moved in with Kellie's friend Dara
and her family, which included Dara's husband and two daughters.
There was not much room to spare, and Dara seemed to resent the
presence of the newcomers. She was bitter and foul-mouthed, and
frequently snapped at Brittany and Dallas.

During this time, Danny maintained visitation rights. At first,
when Danny would show up, Kellie and Dara would have to physically

drag Brittany from her bedroom down to her father's waiting pickup truck. However, post-divorce Danny grew increasingly amiable. He stopped raising his hand to them and spewed insults less frequently. He even bought Dallas and Brittany each their own horse, albeit old nags that had barely enough energy to graze. For Brittany, Danny's demeanor seemed to present a whole new world. *Maybe my daddy is a good person now*, she would hope with crossed fingers.

At the same time, Kellie began drinking heavily and doing a lot of drugs. Her narcotic of choice was Dilaudid, an opioid painkiller, which she would liquefy and inject. She got a part-time job at a nearby saloon, and, for a period of months, was almost never around. The role of tending to the kids fell on Dara, who did not hide her acute frustration with the situation. And so, less than a year after departing Westport, Dallas and Brittany decided to move back in with their father.

It did not take long for Danny to fall back on old ways. He began walloping and tormenting the kids again. Brittany found herself perplexed and on the back foot. Her father had made a notable effort to woo the children back into his life, but, as soon as he got what he wanted, he seemed to resent the circumstances. The situation grew dire. She had nowhere to turn. Here was a father who made her feel like lowly horse shit. There was an invisible mother who was circling the drain of drug addiction.

Brittany began cutting herself. Mostly she made shallow slices in her forearm with a steak knife. For the eleven-year-old, there was something deterministic, even empowering, about self-harm. When slicing herself, *she* had the control—no one else. *She* decided how badly she would injure herself, how heavily the blood would flow. And then, with a satisfaction that she derived from almost nothing else, she could watch as her body healed itself, the wound inevitably fading away. As time went on, Brittany pressed the knife more firmly, making deeper, longer cuts, some on the cusp of nicking an artery. She viewed suicide as a potential solution, but always stopped short of inflicting a mortal wound. *There must be a way out of this*, Brittany would think to herself. *Just be patient, and things will improve.* Only, as time went on, that did not happen.

Brittany did not hide her anguish while at school. Sometimes, in the middle of a lesson, she would bury her head in her arms and sob. The teachers were likely aware of her grief, but it was not until a classmate told a teacher about Brittany's cutting that anyone took action. A counselor pulled her out of class one day. Brittany admitted to injuring herself, and confessed that she had often considered committing suicide.

"In that case, I need to speak to your father," the counselor said.

"Please don't," Brittany begged between convulsive wails. "That will only make the situation worse."

The counselor ignored her protests.

When Brittany returned home that afternoon, Danny was steaming. "How many times do I have to tell you not to bring other people into our business?" he bellowed, shaking her by the shoulders. "Do you know how this makes me look, you little shit?"

Soon a social worker, a pleasant middle-aged woman, began making visits to the Aden house. During these sessions, the kids would sit around the kitchen table and answer the woman's questions about how school was going and what hobbies they enjoyed and whether they were happy. Brittany felt like shrieking about how horrible the situation was, but Danny was always present during the interviews. She knew that if she made so much as a peep, there would be hell to pay later on. The visits, as a result, were a big waste of time.

When Christmas rolled around, the social worker lady showed up with a big bag of gifts for Brittany and her brothers. This set Danny off. "What the hell do you think you're doing, lady?!" he shouted. "Do you think we are a goddamn charity case? Get out of this house and don't ever come back!"

Danny all but chased the poor woman to her car. Brittany expected that to stir up some sort of trouble with the authorities, but, as far as she could tell, there was no backlash. The social worker never returned to their house, and that was the end of that.

This unfortunate status quo persisted. Kellie had visitation rights, but did not make her child support payments regularly. This gave Danny the leverage to limit her time with the kids. Then Kellie remarried to a man named Gene, and, preoccupied with her new life, had minimal engagement with Brittany and Dallas for about two years. Johnny, unable to endure the situation any longer, ran away from home, taking refuge with his maternal grandmother in Mississippi.

The escape inspired Brittany. In 1999, at the age of fourteen, she ran away from Danny for the first time. Kellie, now separated from Gene, was living in a rooming house in the neighborhood of Frayser, on the north side of Memphis. Brittany called her one day and said, "Either you come pick me up, or I am hitchhiking to Memphis." Kellie sent one of her housemates, a lanky eighteen-year-old named Clayton, to retrieve her daughter.

The rooming house did not offer the tidiest or fanciest accommodations, but it was spacious and decently appointed. Brittany had no trouble settling in. She was given a mattress on the floor of the basement playroom. The other rooms were occupied by Clayton's mother Sandra and a woman named Dinky who had an infant daughter.

One afternoon, Clayton showed Brittany a secret hiding space where Kellie kept Dilaudid pills, syringes, and a pipe. Though she had always suspected that her mother was an addict, this was the first time that Brittany encountered direct evidence of the problem. Examining the paraphernalia, she felt rather confounded. In school, the teachers warned of the dangers of narcotics and implored the students to steer clear of drug dealers and abusers. So, did this contraband mean that her mother was a bad person? A criminal? Or were the teachers misleading Brittany all along? At the time, Brittany could not imagine that her mother would engage in something that was as horrible as the authorities led one to believe. Maybe hard drugs were like beer: you're

supposed to stay away from them until a certain age, but almost everyone tries them out at some point.

Not long thereafter, Clayton introduced Brittany to the wonders
of his favorite narcotic, crack cocaine. The two youths started smoking
a few rocks together every day. They also began a casual sexual relationship. Brittany was truant from school during this time, allowing
her plenty of time to mess around and experiment. But, all of this—
the highs, the intimacy with an older boy—was a lot to handle for a
schoolgirl who was too young for a driver's permit. Brittany went with
the flow and did her best to avoid thinking about the consequences.

Danny filed a police report regarding Brittany's disappearance and
truancy. It was clear to Brittany, however, that he was not acting out
of concern for her welfare. He had two motivations, in her view. First,
as legal guardian, Danny wanted to cover his ass; neglecting to report
the disappearance of a minor is not especially prudent. Second, he
exploited his custodianship to torment Kellie. He felt spurned by the
divorce and viewed his authority over the children, his ability to control their whereabouts and their level of interaction with their mother,
as a way to exact revenge on his ex-wife. Danny seemed to relish the
opportunity to disrupt Kellie's relationships with her children.

The police showed up at the rooming house one morning. While
Brittany hid in a bedroom, Kellie claimed that she did not know where
her daughter was. She explained that the girl had run away from an
abusive domestic situation, and implored them to turn their attention
elsewhere. The police left, but made it clear that this would not be
their final visit. Brittany and Kellie decided to go into hiding, relocating to the low-rent Cascade Motel not far away. Brittany felt that they
should have fled the state, headed to Mississippi maybe, but Kellie was
insistent that this plan made the most sense. Either way, their whereabouts were not a well-kept secret. The following night, while Kellie
was out somewhere, two cops came banging on the door of the motel
room. Brittany tried to hide and stay quiet, but the hotel manager
unlocked the door. She ran to the bathroom and attempted to squeeze

out of the window. One of the policemen grabbed her, dragged her back into the bedroom, and handcuffed her. The officers then searched the room, uncovering a bundle of crack pipes and hypodermic needles. They stuffed Brittany into a squad car and transported her to the juvenile detention center in Memphis.

Danny showed up the following morning. Brittany protested, but was ultimately compelled to get into his pickup truck. They drove back toward Carroll County. At each red light, she contemplated jumping out of the vehicle and sprinting off into the night, but decided against it because Danny was spry for his age and would likely have chased her down. As an alternative, she began demanding that they stop at a gas station so that she could relieve herself. Sensing a ploy, Danny firmly objected until Brittany screamed, "If you don't stop, I'll piss right here in the seat!"

They pulled into a truck stop along I-40. Brittany's plan was to climb out of the bathroom window to make her escape. She noticed a squad car parked out front—not ideal; Danny would surely involve the cops the moment he noticed something amiss. The concern was irrelevant, however, because, upon entering the bathroom, Brittany discovered that there was no window to escape by. Stifled, she finished her business and reemerged. Danny grabbed her by the collar and escorted her back to the truck.

The next day, Brittany appeared before Judge Logan at the Carroll County courthouse. He was well acquainted with the Aden family, having presided over Danny and Kellie's divorce proceedings. He gave the troubled girl a choice: either participate in a punitive juvenile boot camp or enter an addiction treatment program. Brittany opted for the latter, figuring that some downtime in a therapeutic environment would be better than months of push-ups and sit-ups and standing at attention.

The rehab facility was called Sunflower Landing and was located near Dublin, Mississippi. It comprised a lush rural campus buffered by plowed farmland, but was just a stone's throw down the road from the maximum-security Tallahatchie County Correctional Facility. Signs on the shoulder warned drivers not to pick up hitchhikers under any circumstances.

A counselor informed Brittany that her residency would last twelve to eighteen months, depending on her levels of commitment and progress. Expecting to do just a fraction of that time, Brittany began to experience some buyer's remorse about the choice she had made in court. On the other hand, she was taken with the beauty of the surroundings and relieved to be a three-hour drive away from Carroll County.

Life at Sunflower turned out to be fairly rehabilitative. Brittany shared a room with a friendly girl named Mallory, and the two quickly developed a bond. Days consisted of breakfast and mild exercise in the mornings, followed by classroom instruction and group therapy in the afternoon. There were all sorts of animals on the grounds: cats, dogs, livestock. During their free time, the residents were permitted to ride horses, a perk that Brittany and Mallory indulged in as frequently as possible.

However, the honeymoon period did not last very long. Brittany experienced intensifying friction with a girl named Summer who seemed to be envious of Brittany's friendship with Mallory. This quickly escalated into a major problem. Brittany was and has always been acutely defensive of, almost obsessive about, her personal rela-tionships. In the rare event that she finds someone that she connects with emotionally, she tends to become inextricably attached. This was the situation with Mallory, and now Summer was interfering. What the irritating girl may not have realized, however, is that anyone who dared attempt to drive a wedge into one of these relationships was playing with fire. And in the Aden household, physical violence was always the first recourse against a personal affront. Summer talked shit about Brittany to anyone who would listen and complained to super-visors about Brittany's flirtatious behavior toward some of the male residents. Brittany decided to retaliate by punching Summer in the nose a few times. The administration responded by limiting Brittany's recreational time and stripping her of her horse-riding privilege. Brittany stopped participating in class, refused to cooperate with the therapists, and told everyone to fuck off. She was subsequently expelled from the program.

In her bedroom, again, Brittany was overwhelmed. She lay on her bed and sobbed into her pillow, enduring alternating waves of horror about the violent act she felt compelled to perpetrate and of panic that her window of opportunity was closing, perhaps never to be reopened. Outside, a pale lemon blanket sheathed the eastern sky. Seconds passed, then minutes. Soon, Danny would open his eyes and all would be lost. Brittany was paralyzed by the bitter amalgam of emotion that enveloped her heart. But the voice in her head was undeterred: one of us has got to go.

Brittany thought about where she might be in a week, a month, a year, if she were not able to follow through with this morning's plan. I will be dead. I will kill myself, and soon. I will cut myself deeper than I ever have before. I will drown myself in the river. I will throw myself into traffic. *There was no doubt in her mind about this inevitability. This moment called for action. Brittany realized that, if she could not summon the spirit to answer that call, then, perhaps, she did not deserve to live. Perhaps none of this suffering was worth experiencing.*

In time, the stream of tears ran dry. She stopped shuddering and sat up. Like a whisper, a house cat tiptoed to the threshold of the bedroom door and poked its head inside. It peered up at Brittany, a silent inquisition. She returned its gaze for a moment, inhaled deeply, and clenched her fists.

After the expulsion, Brittany returned to her father's custody in Carroll County. He was none too pleased with the circumstances, and, per usual, vented his boiling anger with regularity. Brittany was helpless. When she wasn't crying, she forced herself to sleep, sometimes guzzling Nyquil until her head became foggy. She stayed in bed for days at a time, only emerging to use the toilet. One night while cutting herself, she decided to swallow a whole bottle of sleeping pills. As she grew groggy and weak, and as her vision grew blurry and dim, she was certain she had seen the last of this world. Sixteen hours later she woke up with a pulsing headache and churning stomach. Her sliced arms had leaked crimson all over her sheets. But, alas, Brittany had not passed in her sleep.

While visiting her maternal grandmother in Memphis for Christmas, Brittany decided to run off again. She had begun dating a local boy named Myron, who agreed to steal her away in the middle of the night. They absconded to his mother's place in Orange Mound, on the east side of the city. Yet, this, too, was a very temporary refuge. Myron quickly tired of the relationship. Three days later, he took Brittany to the Oak Court shopping mall and, when her back was turned, ditched her. Devastated, Brittany called her mother.

Kellie and her husband Gene had reconciled. They picked Brittany up and brought her back to Gene's place, a charming country house in Michie, Tennessee. Gene was a mechanic and a part-time driver for the local school district. There was a barn full of old disassembled cars, and a big yellow school bus parked out front. Brittany actually loved staying there. However, Danny soon filed another police report. Within a few days, the cops came looking for Brittany. She was elsewhere, but they arrested Kellie for custodial interference. When Brittany returned the following day, Gene drove her over to the police station. The police agreed to release Kellie upon her daughter's surrender.

When Danny arrived, Brittany had an unfettered meltdown. She screamed and thrashed and cried, collapsed to the floor, and threatened to kill herself if she were forced to return with her father. The police, unsettled by her behavior, felt that they could not in good conscience, nor without exposing themselves to certain liabilities, release Brittany into her father's custody. They opted to transport her to Lakeside, a mental health center on the east side of the city. Brittany knew the facility well; her brothers Chris and Johnny had already spent time there for behavioral issues.

A psychiatrist there diagnosed Brittany with major depression and bipolar disorder, and prescribed her two medications. Brittany liked Lakeside—a bright, verdant campus centered around a small private lake—and faced with miserable alternatives, hoped to stay for a long time. But, because Brittany's health insurance did not provide sufficient benefits, the facility turned her out after only two weeks.

It was back to the Aden farm. Shortly thereafter, an incident occurred in which Danny, enraged, hurled some cooking pans at Brittany. She called the police and then locked herself in her bedroom. A pair of patrolmen arrived and addressed the situation with her father. Convinced that it was yet another run-of-the-mill disturbance, they soon returned to their vehicle and drove off down the road.

Brittany called her mother and began crying and pleading for help. Suddenly the line went dead. Danny appeared in the doorway. He had ripped the phone cord out of the jack.

"You think I'm playing around, girl?" he rasped.

Brittany ran out of the room, chased by her father. She sprinted from the house and into the adjacent woods. Tears streaming down her cheeks, she could just make out the departing squad car through the trees. It was rolling down a gravel road, away from the Aden property. Brittany screamed for the policemen as she scrambled over brush and through dense stands of oaks and poplars, but the vehicle was out of earshot. In a moment, it disappeared around the bend. Brittany waded deep into the trees, found a hiding spot, and cried until late in the night. This, of course, was not the first time that she took refuge in the wilderness.

Around the same time, Chris and Danny had a major altercation. Brittany does not remember the origin of the dispute, but it involved Danny smacking her seventeen-year-old brother repeatedly. Chris retaliated by spraying hairspray into his father's face. Danny fought back furiously. Chris then tackled Danny at the knees, driving him into a chest of drawers. Danny howled.

"You broke my leg, you motherfucker! You broke my goddamn leg."

Chris scrambled to his feet and ran out of the house. A few weeks later he called Brittany to tell her that he had joined Johnny at their grandmother's place in Mississippi. Neither boy ever returned to the farm.

And so, by late 2000, the Aden clan had been halved. In Carroll County, it was down to three: Danny, Brittany, and Dallas. Escape seemed all but impossible. Running away had failed twice, and there was no hope of transferring into Kellie's custody; her addiction was spiraling out of control. Opioids, crack, meth—if it gave the woman a buzz, she would smoke it or shoot it without a second thought. Moreover, Kellie was broke and, at times, homeless. No judge in his right mind would have deemed her an appropriate guardian.

The school year began again. Brittany, zombie-like, shuffled from day to day. In her heart, all hope was lost. There had been fleeting moments of optimism. The year prior, Danny had suffered a heart attack. That could have been a natural resolution to the situation. However, Chris drove him to the emergency room, and the doctors were able to perform an emergency angioplasty.

Brittany was livid with her brother because, when the chest pain began, Danny was vehemently opposed to seeking medical treatment. He had wanted to sleep it off. "You're an idiot," she told Chris. "Why didn't you just leave him in bed? He'd probably be in hell by now!"

There seemed to be no way out. Brittany felt as if she were being held captive in a torture dungeon, occasionally on the verge of escaping, but inevitably foiled by her tormentor.

Those days, Danny was on medications for all sorts of maladies: arthritis, depression, heart disease. However, he never slowed down, and worked the land most days until dusk. Occasionally, he forgot to take his anti-inflammatories and would return home at the end of the day suffering from severe joint pain. Because he was always ready and willing to punish the children for his suffering, Brittany took it upon herself to bring him his pills each day when she returned home from school. She'd hop on a dirt bike and track the old man down in the fields. She did not like the idea of providing him relief of any sort, but it was better than the alternative.

One day, Chris told Brittany that he found out that too much nitroglycerin could make a person's heart explode. This was one of their father's medications. Brittany, intrigued, devised a nefarious plot. Each evening Danny prepared a big thermos of iced tea, which he would drink while out in the field the following day. One night while he slept, she crushed up a half-dozen nitroglycerin pills and mixed them into the tea. In the morning, she headed off to school with her fingers crossed and her heart racing.

That afternoon, Brittany returned home expecting her father to be on his back on the kitchen floor, bloated and blue-faced, his heart having ruptured violently. But, no. He was on the tractor as usual, chugging across the field, a cigarette dangling from his lips, fit as a fucking fiddle.

Brittany snatched the rifle from its rack once more. She stiffened her lip and marched boldly through the trailer home to her father's bedroom. She hoped that, by approaching with a more determined demeanor, she would generate enough momentum to follow through with the dismal task that lay before her. Relatedly, a few days earlier, she had declared to two of her classmates that she was going to kill her father. She knew it was a risky thing to broadcast, but felt that expressing her vision openly would perhaps hasten the event.

Brittany crept into Danny's bedroom. It was nearly six, and dawn's first sunrays were trickling in through the dusty curtains. Her father was still asleep, in the same inert position as before. Brittany stepped around and determinedly raised the rifle. Again, she began shaking, nearly seizing. Tears welled up and burned her eyelids. Her breath grew shallow. She placed her index finger on the trigger, and it felt like an icy fang. Struggling to aim, she stepped forward and pointed the rifle in her father's direction. She closed her eyes firmly, her mind racing wildly, then reopened them.

A pause.

An inhale.

A heartbeat.

Brittany pulled the trigger.

The moment was surreal. She did not hear the discharge, nor feel the kick of the powerful rifle against her shoulder. Her surroundings seemed to have frozen in time and gone mute. It was as if the bedroom were a vacuum, and all indications of life had been sucked into the ether. Danny had not moved from his position, had not even spasmed. But, Brittany knew that she had fired the gun because she saw a fiery flash emerge from the muzzle.

In a daze, she began to wonder whether she was imagining all of this. She felt weak in her knees. Perhaps she had momentarily blacked out and done nothing. Was this all a dream? A lucid nightmare? She began to retreat from the room, carefully stepping backward around the bed. Danny appeared to be resting peacefully still. Brittany flipped the light switch. Her eyes adjusted and the room came into sharp focus. Her breath caught in her throat. The pillow next to her father's head was splattered with blood and bone and pink chunks of flesh.

Brittany exited Danny's bedroom, her body numb and unfamiliar, as if the squeezing of the trigger had detached her from her earthly senses. She felt partially incapacitated, not by fear, but by the confounding rush of emotions that now swamped her head. Her eyes dropped to the rifle gripped tightly in her hands. An acrid waft of spent gunpowder filled her nose. In a moment, she recovered from her paralysis and hurried outside.

Brittany was not preoccupied with the criminal consequences of her violent act, nor had she duly contemplated them prior to this morning. At heart, she did not view the killing of her abusive father as an illegitimate act. *It just makes sense,* she had thought to herself. *What else am I supposed to do? People will understand.* However, Brittany had watched plenty of police shows on TV over the years, from which she learned that a killer has to cover her tracks. She dropped the gun into the bed of her father's F150 and pulled a canvas tarp on top of it.

Brittany returned to the house and checked on her brother Dallas. Despite the blast of the rifle, he was still asleep. Brittany roused him and urged him to dress quickly.

"We have to go to school early today," she announced.

The eleven-year-old, barely awake, rubbed his eyes and followed her instructions.

Brittany drove the truck to her friend Jerry's house across town. Her brother rode along in silence, fully unaware of the morning's violent event. Brittany decided not to inform him. She figured that involving Dallas would only make things more complicated. The kid had enough trouble as it was. Arriving, she made sure he boarded the school bus, then knocked on Jerry's door.

Jerry, though seventeen, was in the same ninth-grade class as Brittany. He was surprised to find her standing on his stoop that morning.

"What are you doing here?" he asked.

"Just get in the truck," Brittany replied.

As they pulled away, Brittany came clean. "I just killed my dad."

Jerry's reaction was to laugh. Clearly, Brittany was making an absurd joke.

"I'm not fucking kidding," she continued. "I just shot him where he slept."

Jerry's grin disappeared. "That's not funny. That's not something to goof about."

"I'm not goofing, Jerry. He's laid out in his bed. He's dead."

Jerry's eyes widened as he internalized the news. They bumped along in silence for a minute, before Brittany spoke up again.

"I have to get rid of the gun."

"What gun?"

"My dad's deer rifle. It's in the back. I think I'm going to throw it off the bridge."

"This is fucked up, Brittany!"

"I know. I know it is, but I had to do it."

Jerry nodded solemnly. He was well aware of the situation in the
Aden household. All of Brittany's friends were. "Well," he sighed,
"that's a good gun. There's no reason to throw it into the river. I'll
take it."

"It's all yours," Brittany replied.

They met up with a classmate named Brandy, who agreed to ditch
school and drive the group up to Memphis. Jerry and Brittany opted
to keep their friend in the dark regarding the shooting.

During the ride up the interstate, a police car tailed them and
turned on its emergency lights. Brandy pulled over. Jerry and Brittany
shared a nervous glance as the highway patrolmen approached the
driver's window. However, he did not inquire about a homicide in
Carroll County. He informed Brandy that he pulled her over for failure to wear a seat belt. And, when he discovered that the three kids
were underage, asked why they were not in school.

"We're taking my friend to the doctor," Brandy replied, gesturing
to Brittany in the back seat. Brittany offered a weak smile. It was a
half-baked excuse, but the cop bought it. He wrote Brandy a ticket
and sent them on their way.

In Memphis, Brandy and Jerry left Brittany at a house owned by
a drug dealer. His name was CJ, and Brittany had been buying crack
from him for the better part of a year. Brittany rapped on the door,
and he appeared, a brown beer belly protruding from the bottom of
his wrinkled T-shirt. He looked the girl up and down.

"It's a school day, isn't it?"

"I have a problem. Can I come in?"

"Mi casa es su casa."

Brittany described the morning's happenings to CJ: the anguish,
the fear, the adrenaline, and, ultimately, the relief. He listened closely,
withholding comment.

"If you don't want to be involved," she said, "I'll leave right now."

He narrowed his eyes and leaned back. Despite the transactional
nature of the relationship, Brittany felt an intimate affinity with CJ.

Ironically, although he supplied dangerous narcotics, he had always shown more concern for her welfare than just about anyone else. The two were introduced by Clayton. At first CJ was reluctant to sell her dope. She was a naïve, underaged cracker from the sticks. It just wasn't business that he wanted. But, at the same time, CJ knew Clayton all too well. If he didn't serve Brittany, and keep an eye out for her at the same time, that dumb wannabe hustler would take the poor girl somewhere far worse. CJ figured that the next time he encountered this chubby little white girl she would be turning tricks on Crump Boulevard.

And so here they were. And now she was a murderer.

After a long moment, CJ exhaled. "You're my girl, Brit. You know I would never turn you out."

Brittany handed two hundred dollars to CJ, bills she had grabbed from her dad's stash before leaving. "Give me as much as you can."

She spent the entire morning and afternoon in CJ's kitchen, burning crack rocks until she was so intoxicated that she began vomiting. She took a long, hot shower, and then another one a few hours later. Even so, the stench of the gunpowder seemed to linger in her pores.

Early the following morning, the police came for Brittany. She did not resist. They cuffed her and directed her to one of the patrol cars. It was rainy and dark. As they drove to the station, Brittany gazed out at the ashen clouds and the soggy streets and wondered whether she should feel something more than she did.

Dallas had discovered his father's body after returning home from school on the day of the shooting. Danny's girlfriend called looking for Danny around that time. Dallas answered and told her that daddy was dead. Then he went and watched cartoons on television until the police arrived.

Dallas pointed the investigators to Jerry. When they tracked down the teen, he spilled his guts. He handed over the murder weapon and told them where they could find Brittany.

Brittany refused to speak to the Carroll County detectives assigned to her case. They held her in a juvenile detention center for a night,

under suicide watch, and then transferred her to the Timber Springs
Adolescent Center for a mental health evaluation. She was detained
there for thirty days. Public defender Billy Rowe was assigned to
Brittany's case. There was a preliminary hearing, during which Kellie
tearily testified on her daughter's behalf, narrating incidents of abuse
that the children suffered at the hands of their father. A few Carroll
County policeman testified as well, recounting the many times they
responded to domestic disturbances, and painting a picture of an unstable and chaotic household. These testimonies were helpful, Brittany
thought. Yet none of the adults seemed particularly optimistic.

One of the policeman bumped into Brittany in the courthouse and
put a hand on her shoulder. "If your father had been awake, Brittany,
this might be a whole different ballgame. If only he was awake."

Rowe entered into negotiations with the prosecution, and, five
months later presented a plea deal to Brittany. She would be given sixteen years, less about two years of good time, if she pled guilty to second-degree murder. Otherwise, the prosecution would move forward
with knives out. They would seek a first-degree murder conviction,
which could carry a life sentence. Brittany, however, was not ready to
accept. She put faith in very few people at this juncture, and absolutely
did not trust men in particular. She questioned how much Rowe cared
about her fate and felt that he hadn't done enough to procure the
best possible option. He was clearly swamped with other cases, as are
most public defenders. In fact, she had interacted with him only two
or three times prior to the presentation of the deal. He brought her a
coke and a candy bar on each occasion. The interactions were generally
terse and unproductive, though. Embittered and defensive, Brittany
was very hesitant to cooperate.

Brittany recalls Rowe explaining that, if she did not sign the plea
deal, she would likely be tried as an adult and face life in prison. She
wanted to talk it over with her mother, but Rowe felt that there was not
enough time to track down Kellie and that the woman's input would
not change the grim predicament. Also, he pointed out that Danny's

girlfriend seemed ready to implicate young Dallas as an accessory in the crime. Rowe was concerned that, if they did not come to an agreement with the state immediately, a whole new can of worms might open up.

Brittany stared angrily at Rowe. Was he trying to manipulate her into doing something stupid because he was too busy or lazy to make a real effort? After all, what, exactly, was his stake in this whole process? Whether she lived or died, he would probably carry on just fine. He'd go home and have a steak dinner with his wife and then hit the golf course on the weekend.

But, regardless of her hesitations, Rowe had planted a seed. Brittany could not help but fret about her younger brother. Dallas was an innocent little rug rat. The idea that these proceedings would somehow ensnare him, that she could possibly drag the poor kid down with her, made her sick to her stomach.

It was a confounding predicament. Brittany accepted responsibility for the act and knew that she would have to bear the full burden of it. Yet, she longed for a way out, and racked her brain for a better alternative. Unfortunately, she knew nothing about the law that would be helpful in making an informed decision. She couldn't hire a new attorney. She couldn't act as her own attorney in court. She could produce no star witnesses who would somehow exonerate her. She was up shit's creek without a paddle.

Rowe held out the plea documentation and a pen. Brittany sighed. There seemed to be little point in holding out. She snatched the pen and scribbled her signature.

The judge approved the plea and sentencing. Fifteen-year-old Brittany was remanded to the Carroll County Jail. A minor, she had to be separated from the general population, and was isolated in a single room for virtually the entire eight months of her stay there. The accommodations were painfully austere. There was no television, no radio, no commissary, no recreation yard. Brittany was allowed to retain very few personal items, not even photos. Aside from tasteless meals, the department provided her with two sheets of paper, two envelopes, and two stamps each week, and little more. Her mother came to visit a few times. However, the two interacted from opposite sides of a reinforced glass barrier, and the communications were limited to thirty minutes per visit.

Unexpectedly, a local elderly couple came to visit Brittany at the jail. Billy and Marth Gooch lived not too far down the road from the Aden house. One of their grandchildren was Brittany's high school classmate. Mr. Gooch explained, "We know that you don't have much support. We want to be here for you. So you let us know whatever you need, and we'll do our best to provide it. Money, toiletries, reading material—whatever, honey." Sweet Mrs. Gooch smiled pleasantly and offered additional words of consolation and encouragement.

At first Brittany could not understand why these strangers were offering to help her. They, as far as she knew, were barely acquainted with her parents, if at all. In fact, Brittany had never heard of them before their appearance at Carroll County Jail. Now, here they were offering all kinds of generosities. Brittany instinctively suspected that the old-timers had an agenda. This sort of unadulterated altruism was virtually unthinkable in her world. Yet, she could not imagine what sinister considerations would have motivated Mr. and Mrs. Gooch. She accepted their offer of help and gradually developed a trusting relationship with them. With time, Brittany arrived at the conclusion that they must have been aware of her travails with her father, and of the delinquencies of her mother, and decided that the Christian thing to do was to fill in as caretakers. They were remarkably giving, and continued to provide support for Brittany throughout the years. Later, when her fellow inmates inquired, Brittany referred to the Gooches as her "grandparents."

In late summer of 2001, Brittany turned sixteen and was transferred to the Tennessee Prison for Women in Nashville, the primary penal institution for female offenders in the state. Still underage, she was again segregated, assigned to a room in B Pod of Unit 3, which was where all special-case inmates were housed. In that same sector were women who were so unruly that they had to be quarantined from the general population, others who required protective custody for one reason or another, and even a death-row inmate. Any time Brittany left her cell—to see a doctor, for example, or to get some fresh air out in the prison dog run—the entire cellblock had to be locked down. Needless to say, field trips were rare. For the two years that Brittany was confined there, she had no face-to-face interaction with any other prisoner. Occasionally, an inmate would yell to her from a cell down the hall. At first, Brittany would respond. But the inquiries were typically inane or harassing and that quickly got old. After a few weeks, she ceased participating in these hollered conversations.

Here, Brittany was provided with quite a few recreational items: a television, a radio, books, arts and crafts. She completed more paint-by-number paintings than she could count. But, in the end, it was not enough to keep her occupied, and not nearly enough to stave off depression. The isolation drove her mad. Her preferred method of escape—as was the case prior to her imprisonment—was to sleep excessively. She stayed in bed most days until four in the afternoon, woke up for a bite to eat and a little television, then nodded off again around ten or eleven at night. It was interminable and mind-numbing, yet, in some ways, Brittany was more content than she had been on the outside. In here, she did not have to fear her father's abuse. Furthermore, there was no longer any day-to-day uncertainty. The routine was the same, sun up and sun down. The minutes and hours melded with each other. The days and weeks floated by without care or concern. There were no decisions to be made, no challenges to face, no dreams to be quashed.

Nonetheless, Brittany's past haunted her. She experienced post-traumatic stress that manifested in various ways. In particular, Brittany once had a vivid nightmare in which her father came to see her in prison. As she walked to the visiting room to meet him, she began to panic. She had not seen or heard from him since the shooting. Was he here to bring her back to the farm? Was he here to kill her? She sat down at a steel table. Danny entered and took a seat on the opposite side. He smiled, but Brittany could not determine what the expression indicated.

"Where have you been?" she asked.

Danny's smile was replaced by a dark, smoldering countenance. He leaned forward on his elbows. "I've been dead, Brittany. You killed me."

Brittany thought back to the moment of the shooting. Although she had glimpsed the gory aftermath, she had never actually confirmed her father's fate with her own eyes. She did not witness his final interment. Until this moment, some part of her had remained unconvinced of his death.

"What . . . what are you doing here?" she stammered.

"You know why I am here."

Brittany's heart raced. Fear and confusion overwhelmed her. She would have called out for help, but the words caught in her throat. Even death, it seemed, could not stop her father from tormenting her.

She managed a whisper. "But . . . but . . . how is this possible? Who let you in?"

"I let myself in. Nobody knows I'm here." The grin returned to Danny's face, this time malicious.

The dream abruptly ended. In the morning, Brittany placed a tearful call to her mother. Kellie confirmed that Danny was, in fact, deceased and not coming back.

On Brittany's eighteenth birthday, the unit manager, an affable but by-the-book officer named Deborah Johnson, gifted Brittany a new set of prison blues and escorted her to Unit 2, the general population sector. The juvenile had become an adult, at last, and from that day forward she would share facilities and resources with the big girls. This was a bumpy transition for Brittany, who had spent nearly the last three years by herself. She had grown used to having her own space, not having to consider the wants or needs or idiosyncrasies of another human being. Additionally, she had never in her life been a fan of crowds, which gave her anxiety, and found it burdensome to have to manage multiple relationships at once. Moreover, the prison drama irritated her to no end. There was constant bickering, and backstabbing, and emotional squabbles. Within a week or two, Brittany was requesting to be returned to the segregated unit. Those appeals fell on deaf ears.

Nonetheless, Brittany made a few friends: a spunky lesbian tomboy named Champagne, who had a smile on her face no matter what the situation; a skinny, pigeon-toed city girl named Mozella, who, at age fifteen, was incarcerated for carjacking, kidnapping, and assault; and a sweetheart hair stylist named Nikki, who always sang while she braided Brittany's hair. Nikki had a daughter on the outside, but was doing life for the stabbing murder of an ex-girlfriend. Deborah also introduced Brittany to an older couple, Cassandra and Pookie, who agreed to look after the girl as she acclimated to the new environs. As it turned out, these two women functioned as excellent surrogate guardians for Brittany. They not only protected her from some of the cellblock riff-raff, they made sure that she was healthy and well-fed and got what she needed from the commissary even when she didn't have the money. The three of them evolved into a tightly knit family unit, a phenomenon that was quite common within the prison. Cassandra and Pookie referred to themselves as Brittany's prison "parents." Brittany was their "daughter." All sorts of familial and interpersonal roles were mimicked and recreated there behind the walls: sisters, aunts, grandparents, even wives and ex-wives. Brittany attributed the web of relationships to the tendency for women to form emotional bonds no matter their whereabouts or circumstances.

Most of the ladies in the facility were in active lesbian relationships, or were open to them. The inmates referred to it as being "gay for the stay." Relatively few of the them had participated in same-sex relationships or homosexual activities prior to incarceration, and few participated in them after release. However, within the facility, it was quite normal. Although sexual activity was prohibited in the public spaces, women had clandestine rendezvous in their cells, in the laundry room, in a closet, in the bathroom, or in the chapel—wherever the opportunity presented. Brittany linked up with her first girlfriend,

Lolita, within a year of moving into Unit 2. During her sentence, she had numerous other jailhouse romances.

On the outside, things were not proceeding well for Brittany's brother or mother. Kellie's drug use was still out of control. She was unable to provide for Dallas, and, for a time, the two of them were living out of a car. At some point during high school, Dallas abandoned Kellie and moved in with his girlfriend's family. Brittany spoke to him on the phone from time to time, but he never visited her in state prison. Kellie came to Nashville only once, in 2010, a decade after her daughter was locked up.

Prison was not quite so volatile as life on the outside, but Brittany did have some extreme ups and downs. A rough stretch began when she required gall bladder surgery about two years into her sentence. After the operation, a surgeon prescribed Lortab for the pain. Then, five days after the surgery, she was given a random urine test. Unsurprisingly, she popped for an opioid, which is the class of drug that includes hydrocodone, an ingredient in Lortab. Brittany explained the situation, but was nevertheless written up by the supervising correctional officer, a man named Colby. He claimed that there was no record of her surgery, and informed her that she would be consequently charged for a narcotics violation.

Brittany responded by lifting her shirt to expose her still-healing wound. "Do you think I cut my fucking gut open and stitched it back together all by myself?" she barked.

Colby obdurately refused to dismiss the violation unless she cooperated by leading him to hidden drug stashes within the complex. Brittany dug in her heels.

"I don't know nothing about any drugs, Colby. You might as well line me up in front of the D-board because I don't know shit, and I'm not gonna know shit tomorrow or in the future."

Colby took Brittany up on her offer. She was hauled before the correctional disciplinary board. She pled innocent, insisting that the opioid dose would be in her medical record, but was found guilty of a class A narcotics violation all the same. This verdict came with five days of segregated confinement and a revocation of earned good time credit, effectively extending Brittany's sentence by two months. Furthermore, Brittany was ordered to relocate to the Mark Luttrell Correction Center in Memphis.

Although all aspects of the punishment were unwelcome, the transfer was especially distressful. Luttrell, also a women-only prison, had a notorious reputation as a black hole within the state system, a wretched dungeon where hopes went to die. In Brittany's view, it looked and operated like a third-world ghetto. The facilities were rusty, moldy, and crumbling. The showers were filthy, crowded concrete boxes where women were compelled to jostle for a spot underneath the shower heads. The air conditioning did not function. Brittany arrived in the middle of summer and spent weeks just sweating through her prison clothes.

Furthermore, the correctional officers and staff demonstrated less concern for the prisoners in this facility. Women got sick more often here than in Nashville, but had to wait longer for inferior medical treatment. It seemed that the directive of the COs was to provide as little care as possible, and, if possible, take no action. Some women with serious conditions, such as cancer, received only mediocre treatment and died quickly. Brittany remembers an incident in which a mentally ill young woman warned the staff not to segregate her without observation as she believed she might hurt herself. They disregarded her warnings and she promptly committed suicide.

The overall level of self-respect and fraternity among the inmates at Luttrell was far below that at the Nashville prison as far as Brittany was concerned. There was considerably more drug use, violence, and general depravity. Whereas she witnessed only a single brawl during her decade at the Nashville prison, at least a dozen broke out during her first summer at Luttrell. Several of the inmates were pregnant, having been knocked up by imprudent correctional officers. The women

there were more predatory. Brittany felt that she had to comport herself like a vile bitch just to keep her antagonists at bay.

Two months after the transfer, Brittany was sent back to the
Nashville prison to have her wisdom teeth extracted. She pleaded with
Deborah Johnson and the mental health personnel to allow her to stay
there, warning that, if she were forced to do her time in Memphis,
she would be dead before the year was out. They refused to accom-
modate her. And so, on the night before her scheduled transport back
to Luttrell, Brittany attempted suicide. She swallowed a bottle of
Tylenol and a handful of antidepressants and, using a leg razor from
the commissary, slit her wrists and inner elbows in at least a dozen
places. The COs found her semi-conscious and covered in blood. She
was admitted to the hospital for two days of treatment and observation, then placed on suicide watch for a week. Ultimately, the prison
administration relented, agreeing to house Brittany in Nashville on an
ongoing basis.

Brittany lived in prison as if she were never to be released. She
did not worry about what was going on outside of the walls, or about
what she may have been missing. Most of the time she kept to herself,
read books, and watched TV. She rarely instigated problems with other
inmates, but, if someone dared step to her, she slashed back without
a second thought. She participated in some of the developmental and
vocational programs the institution offered: completed her GED,
worked toward a certificate in cosmetology, spent a year working on a
crew that repainted the interior of the prison. However, these efforts
were more to keep busy than to prepare herself for reentry.

Indeed, for most of her sentence, Brittany's universe ended at the
prison walls. That's how she wanted it. In her mind, it was simpler to
exist this way than to attempt to stay attached to people and things in
the free world. She felt bad for incarcerated women who had children
on the outside, women who were compelled to live a dual life. There
was enough bad shit to deal with on the inside. These poor women
were importing additional stress and drama.

Roughly a decade into her sentence, Brittany was relocated to Memphis once again. This time, calmer and more mature, she did not object to the decision. She both deserved the punishment and may well have done something horrible had she remained in Nashville any longer. The circumstances that led to her transfer had to do with a love triangle. Brittany had been romantically involved with a woman nicknamed Bay-Bay, who was working a life sentence for a triple-murder. However, the two began fighting often, and, at one point, Bay-Bay (who happened to be six feet tall and over three hundred pounds) was written up for assaulting Brittany. Then, on the sly, Bay-Bay became romantically involved with another gal from the cellblock named January. Brittany grew suspicious and confronted January one day as they hung out near their cells.

"I'm going to ask you right now: are you two sleeping together?"

January refused to reply, and instead laughed heartily in Brittany's face.

That was all the answer that Brittany needed. She leaned in and growled, "You listen here, bitch. I'm going to cut you. I promise you that."

Brittany went back to her cell to retrieve a razor while January retreated into Bay-Bay's room. Brittany returned and attempted to kick the door in. At 5'4" and 180 pounds, she was compact and powerful, and the boot of her foot against the door resounded throughout the cellblock. A big officer named Sergeant Henry responded to the incident. He yanked Brittany away from the door, disarmed her, and marched her out of the unit.

Brittany informed Henry that he'd have to lock her up in segregation forever, because as soon as she got out she was going to kill both Bay-Bay and January. He listened and expressed sympathy for the emotional young woman, but was compelled to make a report to the disciplinary board.

Brittany could easily have faced an assault charge that would have tacked years onto her existing sentence. However, the board found her guilty of lesser administrative charges, which resulted in ten days of punitive segregation and an increased security rating.

Afterward, Deborah Johnson offered Brittany two choices. "I either keep you in segregated, round-the-clock lockdown for a year, or you head back to Memphis."

Brittany, defeated and ashamed, opted for the latter. "I think it's in everyone's best interest that I get out of here."

In the summer of 2014, twenty-nine-year-old Brittany was released from prison. She left with an envelope full of photographs and letters—the entirety of her worldly possessions. A man named Herbert drove up from Virginia to retrieve her. He and Brittany had been pen pals for the final few months of her sentence. He offered her a place to stay, and, facing a dearth of options, she readily accepted. There had been another pen pal fellow in London who had hoped to import Brittany to the UK, but he bailed upon learning that English immigration was not keen on felons.

Things with Herbert unraveled quickly. He was married and, though officially separated, spent lots of time with his wife. Despite the generosity he demonstrated toward Brittany, he was jealous and controlling. If, during a trip to the store, for example, she chuckled at something the cashier had to say, Herbert would spend the rest of the day chastising her for it. He seemed to view Brittany as a clandestine concubine of sorts, and ultimately objected to her ever leaving the house.

Brittany soon found the situation intolerable and decided to crash with her mother for a time. Kellie was occupying a space in a dilapidated rooming house in Memphis, still an addict, still strung out all hours of the day. She was suffering from various severe health conditions, including heart failure. The situation was dismal. Brittany avoided taking up crack use again, but worried that it was only a matter of time before she got sucked back into that vortex. Fortunately, she was introduced to a friend of a friend, a brooding but ruggedly handsome young man named Chris. They linked up and she moved into his place in Frayser.

Not long thereafter, the couple was evicted for nonpayment of rent. Chris was a freelance laborer, and, when jobs were scarce, struggled to make ends meet. They relocated to a small, more affordable residence in sparsely populated Red Banks, Mississippi.

In March of 2015, Kellie passed away. No one in the family knew of the passing for two weeks. The woman who was with Kellie at the time did not take it upon herself to notify loved ones. Police ultimately reached Dallas, who went to the morgue and claimed the body. He arranged a memorial service the following week, but neglected to invite Brittany.

A month or two later, Brittany had a psychiatric crisis. One morning she woke up feeling acutely paranoid and persecuted. The sensation snowballed. She started to believe that someone was planning to kill her. Then she became convinced that she would be framed for a murder charge. Her neuroses spiraled out of control. She began swallowing sleeping pills by the fistful. Ultimately, she called the police and begged them to protect her from her pursuers. Officers arrived and took her to the mental hospital. She was prescribed a few medications and discharged a week later.

An unskilled felon with debilitating psychological issues, Brittany does not harbor much optimism these days. She felt a flutter of hope upon her release from prison, but that sensation quickly drifted away. Her incarceration, in retrospect, had been a bittersweet experience. Of course, no one in her right mind would volunteer to be stuck in a cage for fourteen years. But at the same time, Brittany was on the path to nowhere prior to her incarceration. Had she stayed on the outside, she most assuredly would have killed herself, or would have suffered the same inglorious demise as her mother. She worries, still, that her fate may unfold along these lines.

Brittany does not feel remorse about murdering her father. She does wish that her fifteen-year-old self could have conceived of an alternative, nonviolent resolution to the situation, but she does not beat herself up for it. She knows that, ultimately, she will have to answer to God. However, she finds it hard to believe that He will judge her harshly. After all, He is the one who allows defenseless children to be abused in the first place.

Today, Chris is Brittany's only safety net, and an insecure one at that. She almost never communicates with family members or acquaintances from the past. She has no income or savings. For a time, she received food stamps, but continued benefits required participation in a work program. Brittany does not feel emotionally well enough to regularly interact with others, much less hold down a job. She has filed for disability benefits, but has not been approved. Her psychiatric prescriptions have long since lapsed, and neither she nor Chris have the wherewithal to procure the necessary mental health treatment or medication.

As the world turns, Brittany Aden remains locked inside a small frame house, in an unincorporated rural community, isolated from it all. Depression and fear and anxiety encroach from all sides, assailing her during her conscious hours, paralyzing her. To escape, she sleeps— sometimes for days on end. She closes her eyes. The world disappears to black.

And she sleeps.

And she sleeps.

CHAPTER 6

AN ALL-AMERICAN BOY

Brandon Clancy

The bedside clock beamed 6:50 a.m. in bold, digital red. Brandon Clancy stared at it, hoping that, by some act of providence or trick of physics, the digits would begin ticking backward. And then, if only, they would continue to regress for a half hour, an hour, a day and a half at least, to a time before what happened on Saturday night happened. *Jesus*, Brandon prayed, *let me go back in time, just this once. Let me undo it.* The clock shifted to 6:51 a.m. There would be no such luck. The moment of truth was nigh.

Brandon cautiously stepped out the front door of his apartment building. It was still chilly, uncharacteristically so for San Bernardino, California in the summer, even at dawn. He wore the same clothes he had donned the previous night—expensive jeans, a nice polo shirt—going-out clothes. They smelled faintly of cocktails and cigarette smoke. Did he detect a hint of something else? Something pungent, sulfuric? He slept in those clothes—well, to be true, he didn't *sleep*; he lay on his back all night, stared at the ceiling of his bedroom, and fought back panic attacks and an acute nausea. To say, at this early hour, that the past twenty-nine hours had been the worst span of time in his life would be a gross, laughable understatement.

The nearest newspaper vending machine, Brandon recollected, was outside the 7-Eleven, two blocks down. He trudged, numb, light-headed, beside himself. *How did it happen? How?! Brandon Clancy doesn't screw up like this. That wasn't me! It wasn't me!* He alternated between violently berating himself, literally punching himself in the chest, and praying solemnly, exhaling supplications between his teeth.

Brandon arrived at the newspaper machine and eyed it with utter dread. He clutched two quarters in a sweaty palm, unable to extend his arm and deposit them, as if the machine might suddenly morph into a carnivorous robot and viciously gnaw his hand off. He took the deepest of breaths, uttered one more benediction, then slipped the quarters into the slot. They clunked into the belly of the machine with an echo that resonated through the whole of the Inland Empire. He reached in and quickly ripped out a copy of the *San Bernardino County Sun*, then hurried around the side of the building.

With convulsing hands, Brandon flipped through the sheets, one by one, until he arrived at B2, the "Crime Watch" section. He closed his eyes for a long moment, then began reading.

Brandon's childhood was set in southwest Washington state, in areas along the Columbia River, which turns north between Vancouver and Portland, and then arcs westward, past Eagle Cliff, Cathlamet, and Skamokawa on its journey to the Pacific Ocean. He was born in Longview, nearly fifty miles up I-5 from Portland, and lived there until the age of five, when he and his mother Marie moved in with her parents. His grandfather, a retired logger and millworker, and grandmother, a homemaker, owned a modest farm on the rural outskirts of Vancouver, Washington. There was plenty of room in the house for their beloved daughter and grandson.

Brandon's parents had split when he was only three years old. His father Max—a Santa Barbara native known to many as Buddy—relocated to the High Desert of California, and bounced between towns such as Lancaster, Palmdale, and Victorville, on the north side of the San Gabriel Mountains, which form the northern border of Los Angeles County. Marie and Max were very much in love when they married and bore Brandon, their only child, in 1974.

The two linked up after Max returned from Vietnam. He did a tour and a half there, about twenty months, but was shipped back to the United States when news came that his parents were both nearly killed in a car crash. The war left its mark on Max. For a time, upon returning, he was a lost soul—confused, self-destructive, drifting. He drank heavily and smoked a lot of grass, self-medicating to fog over shrill memories of the jungle and to drown out the voices of the many who jeered at returning soldiers. He was unable to hold down a job, unable to find traction in life in general. Ultimately, the marriage could not endure the instability.

For a time, Brandon had limited relations with Max. And being the kid whose father was out of the picture weighed on him, gave him a chip on his shoulder. However, Marie doted on the boy enough to compensate for the paternal absence. Throughout Brandon's childhood, the two partook in regular one-on-one outings—to the river for some fishing, to the ice cream shop, into the city to explore museums. Marie was a constant presence at his many—and there were *very many*—athletic events.

Brandon was a wound-up ball of kinetic enthusiasm who needed constant outlets for his energy, in his most natural state when active and outdoors. There were endless games of football, soccer, baseball, dirt bike riding, and roughhousing with his buddies. Brandon occasionally engaged in minor mischief, or had run-ins with local bullies, but for the most part, he was through and through a good, all-American kid.

Marie was a free spirit, some would say a hippie. She was intensely caring and worldly, and well-liked by most everyone she came across. She had a gift for homemaking, and was always involved in some sort of do-it-yourself project. She often crafted her own clothes. Although she was typically a calm, kindhearted presence, there was an element of mama grizzly in her disposition. If someone challenged her, or pushed her too far, or, God forbid, imperiled her son, she was inclined to explode.

Brandon, in turn, loved his mother deeply. She was his world. He often fretted about her well-being, an unusual preoccupation for a schoolboy, and would find himself on the verge of a panic attack if she returned home from work more than twenty minutes later than usual. He could not imagine a life without her.

Marie worked tirelessly as an administrative assistant in the hopes of providing their small family with an incrementally improving quality of life. They often moved in pursuit of that goal. Brandon, in fact, attended seven different elementary schools, transferring regularly until Marie linked up with her second husband, Rich. They married when Brandon was ten years old, and, that same year, Marie gave birth to a boy named Micky. Not long thereafter, the foursome moved into a comfortable home in La Center, a distant northern suburb of Vancouver, also situated near I-5.

By this time, the early 1980s, Max had finally pulled himself together. He stopped drinking and trained to become a carpenter, ultimately advancing into positions as a general contractor and construction superintendent. When Brandon was in fourth grade, the two began connecting on a regular basis and, from that point on, Max, despite the geographical distance, was a regular fixture in his boy's life. Throughout Brandon's teenage years, his father was exceptionally supportive and encouraging, especially when it came to athletics. Max, too, married again—three more times to be accurate—and had a child with each of those wives.

Brandon was a natural sportsman, of medium build, but bearing distinctive athletic prowess. Not only did he excel in whichever sport he chose, he embodied an awe-inspiring work ethic that distinguished him from his peers. He attended La Center High School, a small institution that served only three hundred students. There, he became supremely focused on athletics: wrestling, baseball, basketball, but, more than anything, football. That was the sport his father and his father's father had devoted themselves to as young men. When he wasn't on the field or the court, he was a regular fixture in the weight room. The effort paid off. Freshman Brandon was five foot eight and 130 pounds. Senior Brandon was five foot eleven, 180 pounds, and all muscle. As an upperclassman, he earned all-conference and all-league honors in three sports.

Brandon, an affable and open-minded young man, was broadly popular at school. He was friendly with nearly his entire class, and ran with diverse social circles. He wasn't a bully, did not have problems with drugs or alcohol, and typically stayed far away from trouble. He was on the honor roll all four years and was elected the junior class president. And the girls were not blind to Brandon's distinctive attributes. Surely, his athleticism was appealing, but so too were his subtle charm, his abundant sense of humor, and his disarming smile, which he flashed both warmly and self-confidently. Brandon's glory days were *actual* glory days—the sort of robust, invigorating, youthful experience that most of us would cling to given a do-over in life.

Brandon developed an interest in firearms and hunting at a young age. At nine years old, he and his buddies would don padded layers of clothing and protective goggles and have running BB-gun battles in the woods. That was only a fleeting fancy, however, because a boy somewhere else in town took a pellet to the eye and lost his sight. All of the men in Brandon's life were enthusiastic participants in American gun culture, which was pervasive and heartily embraced in this part of the country. Max and Grandpa Don were Marine Corps veterans and avid hunters. They often took Brandon on excursions in pursuit of pheasants and duck, sometimes deer. They taught the boy to have a healthy respect for weapons and, at many an opportunity, preached and reiterated gun safety. All of the family guns were locked up when not in use. Brandon had to ask permission if he wanted to take one out.

When Brandon turned fifteen, his stepfather presented him with his first real gun: a basic .22-caliber rifle. Even though the boy had often handled firearms, it was a big moment. The rifle was a coming-of-age gift, a hand-me-down from a patriarch, a symbol of manhood. He cherished the gun, kept it cleaned and oiled, handled it as if it were the most valuable of relics. It should be noted that many other local boys had bigger, more powerful weapons: larger caliber hunting rifles, heavy pistols and revolvers, even AK-47s. Some of the boys showed up to school with shotguns on the racks of their pickup trucks.

As Brandon remembers it, that was simply the way of things. Guns were part and parcel with the culture in his corner of America.

Despite his successes at La Center High, Brandon opted to relocate to the High Desert and reside with his father in Yermo, California for his senior year. At the time, Max was engaged in contracting work for the nearby Fort Irwin Army Base. He wanted to witness his son's senior year of football, and he felt that Silver Valley High—a larger school in a stronger conference—would provide the boy with a better platform as the collegiate athletic recruiting season approached.

As might be expected, there was a feeling-out period at the new school. Brandon arrived not knowing anyone, and it took some time after the start of the year for him to establish new friendships. His athletic prowess was not immediately recognized either. He earned a starting position on the football team, at slotback, but the coaches seemed relatively unimpressed by his hard work and efforts on the practice field. Brandon recognized that he would have to take his game to another level if he really wanted to stand out at Silver Valley.

The first match-up of the season, in September, was against local rival Yermo High School. As he and his teammates emerged from the locker room and took the field, Brandon felt a massive surge of adrenaline. His father and grandfather, seated near the team's bench, proudly shouted encouragement to their boy. The crowd was three times the size of what he was used to back in La Center, the enthusiasm of the spectators equally magnified. Waves of buzzing energy rippled through Brandon's body.

On the third play of the game, the quarterback flipped the ball to Brandon. He turned upfield, shimmied, sidestepped a few defenders, and then bolted twenty-eight yards for a touchdown. The stadium, filled to capacity with two or three thousand eager fans, went bananas. Brandon's heart felt like it was going to pound through his uniform as his teammates slapped him on the back and smacked his helmet exuberantly. Two possessions later, the Silver Valley coach called for the same play. Again, the quarterback fed the ball to Brandon. This time he plowed through the defense, stiff-armed a cornerback, and rambled sixty yards to the end zone. The celebration, on and off the field, was riotous.

A star was born. The following morning, Brandon went out for breakfast with the family. Max purchased a newspaper on the way into the restaurant and excitedly flipped to the sports section. Filling a quarter of the page was a large photo of Brandon streaking down the field. Underneath, the Silver Valley head coach was quoted as saying that Brandon would be touching the ball much more frequently in the future. The whole family was over the moon. Max rushed back outside and purchased every paper in the machine.

Overnight, Brandon became a household name in Yermo. Kids he had never seen before were high-fiving him as he navigated the hallways. And that was just the beginning. Brandon went on to string together an epic season of football, game after game of highlights and heroics. He led the team to an appearance in the conference playoffs, and, when all was said and done, had established the single-season rushing record at Silver Valley High School: over 1,100 yards in twelve games. Everything he had worked for over the years—all of the extra hours in the gym and miles on the running track—had come to fruition.

Various collegiate football programs took notice, although the interest was more limited than Brandon had hoped. Few Division I schools actively recruited him. The most prominent schools that offered scholarships were California Lutheran University and University of Laverne, local Southern California schools that were not known for their athletic programs. Brandon was, however, fervently courted by San Bernardino Valley College (SBVC), eighty miles south of Yermo, an hour east of downtown Los Angeles. Initially, he would not have considered a community college. However, he learned that SBVC had an esteemed football program, and that many of its players left after a year or two to join top-tier NCAA teams. The coaches at SBVC told Brandon that he was a prime candidate for the same sort of trajectory. Brandon enrolled.

Adjusting to life in San Bernardino was somewhat difficult for Brandon. He did not like being so far away from his mother, and he and his father had barely spoken since he turned down the Cal Lutheran scholarship. Max was royally pissed at what he believed was a harebrained, shortsighted decision. For a time, he would not even answer the phone when his son called. Brandon, meanwhile, was competing in both football and track, and, at the same time, hitting the books hard. He rarely had a moment to himself or more than a few dollars in his pocket. Marie sent a little bit of money from time to time, but he typically had to scrimp and scrape just to buy a bag of groceries once a week.

The move to San Bernardino also came with a fair degree of culture shock. Brandon had been raised in an almost entirely white, middle-class area of Washington, and had advanced with the same classmates from middle school through his junior year of high school. Silver Valley was more diverse, servicing a sizable population of Hispanic students in addition to whites. But it was not until Brandon arrived in San Bernardino that he got a taste of gritty urban society. In the early 1990s, violent crime and gang activity in the county were rampant and spiking further. The Crips and Bloods, two powerful regional gangs, worked the streets, peddled drugs and guns, and battled for turf. Some of the local motorcycle gangs also entered the fray, violently confronting crews who were coming in from Los Angeles and Las Vegas. The *San Bernardino County Sun* commonly featured reports of drive-by shootings and articles about the detrimental and far-reaching impacts of the gang phenomenon. A 1994 front-page headline declared "Teen Boys: A Generation Lost," and cited significant increases in vandalism, car theft, assault with a deadly weapon, and battery of a police officer over the preceding decade. Unemployment exceeded 12 percent around that time, the lack of legitimate economic opportunity driving many young men into illicit pursuits.

When Brandon first arrived in San Bernardino, he moved into an apartment complex that housed about a dozen of his teammates.

Five of them shared his flat, including a couple of very large Samoan and Hawaiian linemen. He knew that he had backup if he ever ran into trouble around town. However, muscle can't stop a bullet. The prevalence of weapons among young people made Brandon wary. There were more than a few times when, during a night out with the boys, a confrontation between late-night revelers featured the threat of gun violence. Sometimes, when the mad-dogging and chest bumping got too heated, one of the parties would walk to his car and retrieve a piece from the trunk. Brandon and other witnesses would head for the hills. There was also the time that one of his teammates produced a handgun after a shouting match in the locker room. Guys were diving for cover and sprinting out of the locker room half-naked. The incidents made Brandon paranoid. He sometimes found himself neurotically wondering whether the guy sitting at the bar, or the dude next to him pumping gas, or the teens buying a six-pack at the convenience store were packing heat, and whether they might consider the look on his face or the tilt of his ball cap an inexcusable affront.

Fortunately, Brandon made it through his freshman year without too much trouble and performed well in his classes. Yet, as much as he would have liked to play in the NFL after earning his bachelor's degree, he recognized that the odds were slim. So he enrolled in a few courses related to aviation. Sports aside, he aspired to become a commercial pilot. He put a lot of thought into joining the Marines after graduating, and working his way through flight school to earn his stripes.

Football went well, too. Balancing a full course load with daily athletic commitments—team practice, weight lifting, strategy meetings— was not easy, but Brandon continued to develop his strength and athletic abilities. He forced himself to work harder than anyone else on the team. No one at SBVC considered him a standout superstar the day he walked in the door. Success, once again, would come only through tireless effort and ceaseless self-motivation.

Although he played only special teams and saw limited field time during the season, Brandon impressed the coaches in time. The offensive coordinator became particularly encouraging. He approached Brandon after practice one day late in the season.

"You're fast enough and strong enough to play Division I, Clancy," he announced. "The Hurricanes are harassing me for new talent."

Brandon's heart skipped a beat. He knew that this coach had a special relationship with the football staff at the University of Miami. There were a couple of guys that he was pushing pretty hard in that direction, but they were having trouble with their grades. Brandon was more than fine in the academic department.

"Tell me what I need to do, Coach," Brandon replied, "and I'll do it."

"I know you will. The first thing we need to do is get you off of special teams and onto the offensive roster. Put up some numbers in the fall and you'll be partying in South Beach come spring."

This was music to Brandon's ears. He had tremendous confidence in his own abilities and dedication, but it was the first time that one of the SBVC coaches had offered such an ambitious appraisal. When the spring practice season rolled around, the head coach reassigned him to the offensive squad and began grooming him to play slotback. Brandon put all of his heart and soul into training his body and mastering his role. Greatness was within reach.

At the end of the spring semester, Brandon moved into a new place. He had enjoyed plenty of good times with his roommates from the old team apartment—wild parties, clubbing, late night visits from local co-eds. However, he did not feel comfortable living in that part of San Bernardino. It was grimy and unattractive, and there were lots of shady characters on the streets in the immediate vicinity. Come summer, Brandon decided to link up with a few guys and rent a smaller place near California State University, in a leafier part of town. He had known one of the roommates, Melvin, since his childhood in Vancouver. The other, Nick, was a few years older, and had grown up in the San Bernardino area.

The football program went on hiatus in May, as conference regulations prohibited formal practices until late July. Around the same time,

Brandon worked things out with his father. They were communicating regularly again. He, in fact, was going to fill in as a laborer for Max's construction company during June and July. Brandon enjoyed getting his hands dirty, plus the work would provide him with savings that would last through the following semester.

In early summer of 1993, Brandon and his new roommates decided that it was time to let loose. It was a Saturday, and they had recently finished all of their final exams, closing out the academic year. San Bernardino was unseasonably cool for early summer, in the fifties, with spots of fog and occasional sprinkles throughout the day. However, nothing was going to deter the boys from cracking open some beers and firing up the barbecue. Some football friends and girls came by for burgers and brats, and by the time the sun set, Brandon and Nick were sporting healthy buzzes. Melvin, for his part, did not drink, having volunteered to function as the designated driver when they went out to the clubs later that night.

Around nine, Brandon, Nick, and Melvin decided to head over to one of their favorite clubs in nearby Redlands. They cleaned up, changed into presentable garb, and then gathered in the dining room for one more communal swig of Jim Beam.

"I'm bringing the shotty," Brandon announced.

"What for, dude?" replied Melvin.

"In case someone wants to fuck with us!"

Brandon walked over to the closet and retrieved a sawed-off shotgun. He had picked up the weapon during his return to La Center for the Christmas holiday. It was a vintage piece, maybe thirty years old, that his grandfather had acquired at one of the regional gun shows. The seller had originally purchased it from a Montgomery Ward's catalog, then modified it by removing the forward half of the barrel.

Brandon's grandfather was surprised at first when Brandon asked if he could take the gun back to San Bernardino. However, the young man went on to describe some of the run-ins he had experienced during the year, and explained that he wanted to be able to brandish an intimidating weapon if it came down to it.

"If you feel that exposed," his grandfather said, "go ahead and take it." He handed the boy a box of home-defense shells. "I trust you. Just be careful."

Brandon proudly held the gun aloft for his roommates to behold. "If someone steps to us tonight, I'm whipping this bad boy out," he declared grinning. Then he snapped open the break-action and loaded a cartridge into each of the chambers.

At the club, Nick and Brandon downed a few more beers and a couple of strong shots. Uninhibited, they hit the dance floor, approaching the cutest of the girls with their smoothest of moves. The repeated romantic forays didn't exactly pay off. Around midnight, the boys departed as empty-handed as they had arrived. They piled into the cab of Nick's Toyota pickup truck—Melvin driving, Brandon squished in the middle, and Nick on the passenger side. Their barrel chests and broad shoulders made the arrangement plenty snug. The shotgun, loaded, lay on the floor below their feet.

They cruised around aimlessly for a while before deciding to swing by the University of Redlands to see if there was a fraternity party they could crash. Discovering no opportunities in that part of town, they then rolled past the Cal State campus hoping to find even a modest soirée lingering late into the night. Again, their efforts produced no results. Around two in the morning, tired and ready to sleep off the booze, Nick insisted that they call it quits.

Melvin began navigating back to their apartment. At a stoplight, the group pulled up next to a small Honda sedan driven by a long-haired white kid about their age. There were attractive, college-aged girls in the passenger and rear seats. Nick rolled down his window, got the girls' attention, and made a nasty gesture, sticking his tongue between his index and middle fingers.

"Fuck you, dude!" the driver snapped in retaliation, flipping Nick the bird. He then stomped on the accelerator and sped off down the deserted street.

Nick, brought back to life by the interaction, shouted at Melvin. "Hit the gas, man! Let's go after them!"

"Nah, man."

"C'mon, man! Just fucking do it!"

"Yeah!" chimed in drunk Brandon. "Let's get those punks!"

Melvin, the most even-keeled of the three, rolled his eyes. Then, relenting, he hit the gas. The boys pursued the Honda through north San Bernardino, making a few turns, before tracking it into a dark residential area. It finally pulled into the driveway of a small, frame house. Melvin brought the pickup to a stop on the street nearby. The girls jumped out of their car and, shrieking, scampered into the house.

The driver emerged into the driveway and began shouting and cussing at the pickup truck. "Get the fuck outta here, assholes! You pieces of shit!"

Brandon reached down and grabbed the shotgun. He shoved it toward Nick. "Show him the shotty, Nick! See how tough he is then!"

Nick paid no attention to Brandon. He was too busy screaming obscenities.

Brandon reached across Nick and stuck the weapon out of the window. "What now, motherfucker?!" he shouted.

At the same time, Nick shouldered open the passenger door. He wanted to jump out and get in the dude's face. Brandon, his arm still hanging out the window, the shotgun dangling, pulled back. The door slammed shut, and –

BOOM!

There was an utterly deafening explosion as the shotgun discharged. It was as if someone had placed a metal bucket over Brandon's head and smashed it with a softball bat. A cloud of gun smoke filled the cabin with a bitter stench. Melvin immediately popped the clutch and peeled out. The boys, in shock, half-deaf, and shouting wildly, sped away from the scene.

For Brandon, the sixty seconds after the gun went off were a complete blur. There was screaming and mindless panic, in slow motion, hazy, like a grainy war film. For a time, all he could hear was a sharp

ringing, like a tornado siren, piercing his eardrums. He could see that
Melvin and Nick were moving their lips, hysterically trying to communicate, but could make no sense of it. The boys were tossed left and
right as Melvin screeched around corners and buried the accelerator.
Finally, he whirled onto a main thoroughfare and slowed to the speed
limit. Brandon's hearing started to recover.

"Holy fuck, dude!" Nick yelled at Brandon. "What the fuck did
you do?!"

"I didn't do shit, man! The door slammed and that's all I know! I
didn't pull the trigger!"

For a long moment, Melvin was silent, a look of horror on his face,
as Brandon and Nick freaked out at each other. Finally, he interjected.
"Calm down, guys. Just calm the fuck down." He turned the pickup
south, away from the area of the incident. "Did anyone see where the
shot went?"

This question amplified Brandon's panic. He worried that he was
about to wet himself. "What do you mean where the shot went? I have
no fucking idea! I thought the safety was on!"

Nick squeezed his head with his palms, in a state of disbelief. "We
might have hit him, guys. We might have shot the fucking guy!"

"Did you see him get hit?" Melvin asked.

"I . . . I don't know what I saw, man."

"There's no way we shot that dude!" Brandon cried, more of plea
than a statement of fact. "There's no way! I wasn't even aiming at him!"

The boys drove around San Bernardino in a gradually diminishing
state of hysteria until the eastern sky began to offer hints of sunrise.
They returned to the apartment. Nick double-locked the door and
they all took a position around the dining table.

Brandon was still beside himself, pacing and ripping at his hair.
"Jesus, Jesus, Jesus! What the hell just happened?! I'm in a fucking
nightmare!"

"We don't know what happened, brother," Melvin offered. "There's
no point in having a meltdown right now. We just don't know."

"We might have shot him, though," Nick interjected. He had lowered his voice to a near whisper, his face pale as a sheet.

"It's been three hours and the cops haven't shown up at our door," Melvin said. "I'm going to bed."

"Me, too, I guess," Nick conceded.

The two retreated to their bedrooms, leaving Brandon alone in the kitchen. The refrigerator buzzed steadily. Outside the window, a northern mockingbird sang, oblivious to all. Brandon's head throbbed with each pulse of his heart.

Standing around the side of the 7-Eleven, shivering, the fresh Monday-morning copy of the *San Bernardino County Sun* fluttering in his hands, Brandon read through the items listed in the "Crime Watch" section. His heart nearly stopped when his eyes reached the second bullet point:

MAN KILLED IN SAN BERNARDINO
Steven Henderson, 23, was followed by suspects in a mini-truck as he drove home early Sunday morning. A shot from the truck struck him before entering his residence in north San Bernardino. Officers did not provide a description of the assailants or their vehicle.

Brandon felt the lifeblood drain from his face. He staggered and put a hand against the wall to steady himself. It was as if his greatest horror had been scripted into real life. He smacked himself in the face a few times, hoping to wake himself from the nightmare.

He returned to the apartment, and immediately locked himself in the bathroom. He vomited repeatedly, over and over until there was nothing but bile left in his system. Then he vomited bile. Melvin awoke to the commotion, and took a position outside of the bathroom. He could hear Brandon sobbing, heaving, wailing.

"Brandon, what happened, man? Talk to me. What's going on?"

Brandon could barely form words. "The . . . the . . . paper. On . . . on the . . . the table."

Melvin found the newspaper open to the Crime Watch section. He read the headline and nearly fainted himself.

The boys spent the morning somberly evaluating what their options now were. More than a day had passed since the incident, and, although they continued to stress and fret—especially Brandon, who had not eaten or slept a wink—the more time went by, the more it seemed as if the shotgun blast may have been much ado about nothing. Now that their gravest fears had been confirmed, however, the boys were as hysterical as they had been in the moments after the gun blast. They discussed turning themselves in, but, rather quickly, decided against that option. Brandon would face murder charges if caught; perhaps all of them would. California had the death penalty, they knew.

"My life is over," Brandon lamented, just ten days shy of his nineteenth birthday. "My fucking life is over."

Brandon decided he had to skip town and head back to Washington. He had an uncle up there who was a criminal attorney. He'd take refuge at his mom's place and buy some time until he could piece together the best course of action. Melvin—his family also in Vancouver—agreed to accompany Brandon. Nick would stay in San Bernardino. He would ditch his truck and hole up at his mother's house, not far away. All three were in survival mode. No official plan was settled upon, but they knew that remaining at the apartment made them sitting ducks. Before departing, they agreed to stay closely in touch over the coming days, and to decide on a final strategy together.

Brandon and Melvin drove into a remote area of the High Desert. They stuffed the gun into a trash bag and buried it under some rocks off the side of Barstow Freeway. They then drove straight through, over one thousand miles, to La Center.

They stopped at Brandon's mother's place of work, an office of the public utilities district. She was shocked but over the moon to see her dear son.

"What are you doing here, Brandon?!" she exclaimed, embracing him tightly.

"I wanted to come see you, Mom," he replied wanly. "I'm kind of sick of San Bernardino. It can be a shitty place. I think I might talk to the coach at Portland State and see about transferring."

Marie tilted her head and gave Brandon an inquisitive look. He had just spoken to her about how well things were progressing at SBVC, and about how the coaches were giving him a boost. However, she opted not to address those concerns. It may not have been the right time for that.

"I'm so glad to have you here," she exhaled, offering Melvin a warm hug as well.

Brandon settled into his mother's house and waited for the moment of reckoning. Marie and his stepfather Rich suspected something was amiss. They repeatedly inquired about why Brandon was so on edge. His reply was that he was simply upset about how things had turned out at SBVC and that he was at a challenging turning point in his life. Even Brandon's half-brother Micky—only nine years old at the time—seemed to sense a disturbance in the force. None of them, however, interrogated Brandon extensively. Marie had recently been diagnosed with thyroid cancer and was scheduled to have surgery. Everyone else was preoccupied with work and school and life. Perhaps, had the saga extended for weeks more, they would have been able to extract the truth from Brandon. That did not happen.

Brandon felt as if he were continuing to operate in a dream state. He simply could not come to terms with the fact that he had committed such a depraved atrocity. A momentary indiscretion had ended an innocent life and certainly destroyed his own. As the days passed he was shocked that his chickens had not yet come home to roost. One day, Melvin called.

"Yo, man, your birthday's tomorrow," he announced with some enthusiasm.

Brandon had forgotten. He had not put a moment's thought into the occasion. There was no point in celebrating. That's the last thing that he felt he deserved.

Melvin continued. "We should catch up with some of the boys in Vancouver . . . blow off some steam."

"There's no way I can do that," Brandon replied. "I can't go out in public. I would be miserable. I have to figure this whole thing out. I have to figure my life out. How do I carry on? Is my life even worth living?"

"What are you going to do then?"

"I have to figure out how to approach my uncle about this. He's my only hope. Otherwise, I might have to head to Canada."

"Canada, dude? That's not going to solve the problem."

"That's the thing," Brandon replied ruefully. "There is no solving this problem."

Melvin offered some sympathetic words, but they had no impact. Brandon knew, in his heart, that life would never be the same. Everything that he had worked for, and pushed for, and aspired to, had vanished like butterflies in a tornado.

Marie made a special dinner for Brandon's birthday, along with a big chocolate cake topped with nineteen candles. She and Rich and Micky sang "Happy Birthday" heartily. Brandon forced a few smiles and feigned a modicum of delight. However, the festivities deepened his despair. That people were celebrating him, Brandon knew, was a vast insult to the memory of the man he had carelessly slaughtered some ten days earlier. Each bite of cake tasted like a forkful of bitter ash.

Two days later, Nick rang. It was the first time Brandon had heard from him since fleeing San Bernardino. There was not a hint of levity in Nick's voice. He got straight to the point.

"Brandon, we need to turn ourselves in."

"Nick, I . . . I just don't know if I can do that right now. I don't know if I'm capable of that."

"I've been talking to my pastor, man. The guy we killed did not deserve what he got. He did nothing wrong. Absolutely nothing wrong."

Brandon's stomach sank. Nick was speaking the truth. And, even though it was a truth that Brandon had danced around from the outset, it was pure anguish to hear the sentiment put into words.

"Let me talk to my uncle," Brandon pleaded. "He has to help me figure this out. I don't even know how to turn myself in—the right way to go about that."

"I hear you. I hear you. We just . . . we have an obligation to do the right thing. That's what my pastor says. We have to do right by God."

They boys agreed to revisit the issue the next day.

Nick's invocation of the almighty stung sharply. Brandon did not resent him for it, but incorporating faith into the situation added another layer to the already complex hash of legality, morality, self-preservation, and fear. Brandon had been reared as a Southern Baptist, but had all but abandoned the religion by high school. Over the last five years, although he maintained a steadfast faith in God, he had rarely prayed or considered religious mores. As busy and driven as he was, taking time to properly observe an evangelical doctrine seemed more effort than he could afford.

Since the shooting, however, Brandon had frequently spoken to his Savior, had even begged Him to resolve the crisis. Yet, those supplications were more reactionary, self-serving, and desperate than pious in nature. Nick's reference to God was different. It brought to light the metaphysical, the spiritual implications of what had transpired. How Brandon proceeded, perhaps, was not just about taking steps that society might consider ethical or prudent; his actions, at this juncture, could resonate for eternity. Already ravaged by his conscience, Brandon barely slept that night.

The next evening, a Friday, the phone rang again. Brandon knew that Nick would be expecting a decision, but he was still not ready to commit to any particular course of action. He felt paralyzed, immobilized by the great weight of the circumstance. Guilt ate at him like an insatiable carnivorous beast, but the thought of stepping out of his mother's home, making a decisive move in one direction or the other, filled him with the most horrible, crippling dread. Nick, he knew, was losing patience, and could possibly give up the game soon. Brandon steeled himself before picking up the phone and holding it to his ear.

"Hello," he spoke quietly.

"Hello, may I speak with Brandon Clancy?"

A shrill alarm went off in Brandon's mind. The voice was neither Nick's nor Melvin's. It was an older man. The hair on his arms stood on end. "This . . . this is Brandon," he stuttered.

There was a moment of quiet, then, "Brandon, this is Sergeant Porter of the Clark County Sheriff's Department. My associates and I are outside of your mother's house. I think you know what this is about."

Brandon's blood ran cold. His mind went into overdrive. Should he run out the back door? Should he barricade himself in a bedroom? His poor mom was in the next room. Good God! How would she react? This would destroy her.

The sergeant interrupted Brandon's thought process. "Brandon, we'd like you to come outside and speak with us."

Brandon swallowed hard and closed his eyes. There was no way out. The moment of truth had arrived like a long-awaited train, except instead of climbing aboard, he was about to be run over.

"Yes, sir," he whispered. "I'll be right out."

"That's good to hear."

Brandon hung up the phone gently, as if it were an unstable stick of dynamite that could blow the whole house to kingdom come. He stepped carefully into the dining room, where his mother sat flipping through a magazine. She looked up at him, and realized immediately that something was very wrong.

"Brandon? What is it?"

Brandon began to cry. "Mom, I . . . I did something horrible."

"Horrible? What are you talking about?" She stood up, alarmed, and took a position in front of him. "Tell me what it is, Brandon."

There was no time to waffle. Brandon decided to give it to her straight, like a sledgehammer to an anvil. "Two weeks ago . . . in San Bernardino . . . I . . . I accidentally shot someone."

"What? What are you saying, Brandon?"

"Mom, I shot a man to death," he declared weakly between sobs. "That was the Clark County Sheriff. On the phone. They're outside. They're here to arrest me."

Marie went pale. There was a pregnant moment as the gravity of her son's words became evident. Then she collapsed to her knees and began screaming and sobbing. "No! No! Brandon! Oh my God! Brandon!" She had a complete, unrestrained meltdown.

Brandon dropped to the floor as well and held his mother as tightly as he could. They sobbed deeply, together, with loud wails. She shrieked "No, Brandon! No!" over and over again. Brandon felt as if he were going to die, right there, on the dining room hardwood. They held each other for a matter of minutes before Brandon realized that police might become suspicious. He stood up. His mother clung to his legs. Brandon pried himself away and then stepped to the front door. Only days ago, the world was his oyster. In this moment, though, a cornered fugitive, a man condemned, he slowly turned the knob and pulled the door open.

There were four squad cars in a line on the street. Eight policemen had emerged and taken tactical positions on the far sides of the vehicles. They had guns drawn and trained on the house.

"Show us your hands, Brandon!" one of them shouted.

Brandon, in the doorway still, raised his arms over his head.

"Now walk toward me! Slowly!"

Brandon identified the source of the voice. It was a tall man with salt-and-pepper hair. He beckoned to Brandon. This must have been Sergeant Porter. Brandon took three or four uncertain steps forward.

"Stop right there, Brandon!" Porter bellowed.

Two of the officers approached Brandon. Cautiously, they turned him around, pinned his arms behind his back and snapped on a pair of handcuffs. As they walked him over to one of the squad cars, young Micky pedaled up to the scene on his BMX bicycle. Another officer prevented the boy from getting any closer. Seeing his innocent little half-brother, Brandon began to weep heavily again. He wanted to say something, to explain the frightening situation to Micky, but the words stuck in his throat. Porter read Brandon his Miranda rights, and then tucked him into the rear seat of the squad car.

As the squad car pulled away from his home, Brandon, unexpectedly, felt a mild wave of relief. The uncertainty of the past ten days had been absolutely agonizing. At least now, the wait was over. Part of him did not care what came next. On the other hand, no longer consumed with anxiety and fear, Brandon found himself overcome with grief and shame. He was absolutely convinced that life as he had always known it had ceased to exist the moment the shotgun went off. As he rode through the old neighborhood on his way to the police station, he realized that he would likely never see those houses again, or those broadleaf trees, or those children playing in the park. He'd never smell the warm river breeze, or eat an ice cream cone from the drug store. And he'd probably never hug Micky again, or see a smile on his mother's face. Brandon was gone. He was gone, gone, gone.

"Man, what happened?" The voice of the police officer in the driver's seat extracted Brandon from his melancholy reverie.

Brandon could barely find the breath to respond. "It was a mistake," he intoned. "It wasn't supposed to happen. I didn't mean for this to happen."

The officer glanced in the rearview mirror. His eyes seemed to express concern, maybe an ounce of empathy. "Well, what happened, then? Get it off your chest."

"I accidentally shot someone," Brandon confessed. His eyes burned with tears. His stomach churned.

"Accidents happen, man," the officer replied comfortingly. "One minute everything's cool. The next, your world is upside down." He eyed Brandon in the mirror again. "How'd it go down?"

"What?"

"The shooting. How'd you end up accidentally shooting someone?"

Though woozy and distracted, Brandon began to sense that the officer's inquiries were not as innocuous as they had seemed at first. Maybe he had an agenda. Maybe the officer was trying to get Brandon to say something damning while his guard was down.

"What does it matter?" Brandon grumbled. "I'm dead."

"What do you mean you're dead?"

"I'm fucking already dead," Brandon repeated.

"Do you think that you want to hurt yourself?"

Brandon was done with this conversation. He clammed up for the remainder of the ride.

At Clark County Jail, Brandon was placed under suicide watch. He was stripped of all of his clothes, made to wear a paper jumpsuit, then locked in a padded cell. He had never experienced emotions anything like what he was experiencing now. He was beyond regretful, beyond inconsolable. Crushed. Absolutely destroyed. Brandon ruminated incessantly about how many lives he had destroyed in a single careless moment—with a flick of the wrist. He remained in a fetal position in the corner of the cell for two or three days, sobbing endlessly. A policeman pushed food through a small hole in the door a few times per day, but Brandon could not stomach even the thought of eating.

He was then moved to an observation cell, which he shared with a scrawny young man in his early twenties. Uncle Scott finally paid a visit. Although he now ran a private litigation practice, Scott had begun his career as a criminal attorney, and was well-versed in the law pertaining to this situation. He read Brandon the riot act about keeping his mouth shut.

"Don't speak about the incident to anyone other than me, Brandon. Not a soul. Not your mother, not the man who brings you food, not your cellmate—especially not your cellmate."

"I won't," Brandon affirmed.

"Okay. But, I'm going to say it again, because it is very, very important: do not discuss your case with anyone but me until we get a proper criminal attorney assigned to your case."

Brandon nodded solemnly.

The next day, Brandon was directed to an interrogation room, where he was introduced to Detectives Cole and Loukas who had come up from San Bernardino. Judging by their imposing statures, along with their steady, piercing glares, Brandon inferred that the two men had more than enough experience dealing with lowlife perps. Cole was a bear of a man, graying with a heavy mustache. Loukas was muscular and swarthy. This, Brandon figured, was sure to be an uncomfortable experience.

On the contrary, the two men were convivial and relatable. Before getting into the details of the case, they spent some time bantering about Brandon's football background and how the two detectives were long past their high school glory days, but still played in exhibition games on the local law enforcement team. Brandon knew that he had the right to remain silent, but these men were disarming, and it felt as if the best move would be to stay on their good side.

"We know you are a good kid," stated Cole while scanning Brandon's file. "You've never been in trouble—not even a speeding ticket. This just doesn't add up. Tell us what went wrong."

With that, Brandon was ready to sing. In hindsight, he realized how calculated and crafty these two detectives were. To properly fill that position—to be able to interrogate effectively, to extract sensitive information, to induce confessions—a person has to be intelligent, acutely insightful, and, to some degree, sociopathic. Every case, every suspect requires a different approach. Detectives must be able to adopt motley, incongruous personas during an interview, often switching back and forth between them at the drop of a hat. The good ones, like Cole and Loukas, can be abrasive and frightening when the situation calls for it. Or they can play the suspect's best friend, his prime hope for salvation. They can be his counselor when he needs advice, his priest when he needs to confess, his father when he needs protective love. And, in this case, Cole and Loukas knew exactly how to manipulate Brandon: they would play the roles of his trusted coaches. They knew that a jock like the one that sat cuffed before them must have spent a lifetime placing faith in coaches, older men who possessed the experience, the know-how, and the fortitude to guide him through life's mine fields.

"Talk to us," Loukas said to Brandon, "and we'll help you figure this thing out. We are the only two people who can come to your aid right now. You are in an ugly spot, and if you make the wrong move, it's only going to get worse. There is no moving forward, no containing this situation, until the truth comes out. Help us help you."

Uncle Scott's exhortations echoed in Brandon's head. Divulging anything to these men would create a legal hornet's nest. However, he was desperate, disoriented, weakened by three days without food, with minimal sleep. Cole and Loukas were presenting the lifeline that he had been waiting for. *Maybe they* can *make this better*, Brandon prayed. Then he described what happened on the night of the shooting.

The following day Brandon was shackled and transported to the courthouse for his extradition hearing. As he took his position opposite the bench, he saw that his mother and grandfather were in attendance to observe the proceedings. Marie appeared wan and deflated, as if she had shed ten pounds in the past couple of days. Brandon felt a warm knot congeal in his throat. When the judge inquired, he, as Uncle Scott had advised, waived his right to challenge the extradition. He was then escorted from the courtroom. During the walk he made direct eye contact with his grandfather, who carefully mouthed the words "I love you." That was the last time Brandon ever saw the man.

Brandon flew with Cole and Loukas, sandwiched between them on a commercial flight, from Portland, Oregon, to Ontario Airport in California. They transferred him into the custody of another police officer, who would transport Brandon back to San Bernardino. This man showed Brandon none of the courtesies that had been offered by the detectives.

"You fuck around and I'm going to blow your head off. That's the deal. Sit in the back and shut the fuck up."

Brandon did exactly as he was told. Upon arrival, he was booked and fingerprinted at West Valley Detention Center, a large county jail. He was placed in a concrete cell with a few dozen other inmates who, like Brandon, were in pretrial limbo. The room was equipped with a few benches, a steel sink, and a toilet (into which a haggard young man was vomiting). As Brandon settled in, he warily eyed packs of rough dudes who congregated in different areas of the cell. Brandon was a strong guy, and could hold his own in a fight if he needed to, but his baby face and fish-out-of-water disposition made him stand out in exactly the wrong way. Several guys stared him down or cursed him out if he looked in their direction. When lunch was served, a vicious-looking man snatched Brandon's milk carton off of his tray, flashing an evil eye that suggested a willingness to take a man's life over a trifle.

The next morning, after another sleepless night, Brandon was bussed over to the old courthouse in downtown San Bernardino. He was shoved into a medieval-looking holding cell with at least fifty other irritable inmates awaiting arraignment. There was no lighting in the cell, except for some ambient fluorescent flickers that filtered in from the next room. It was stuffy, oppressively hot, and stunk of body odor. The men were packed in like sardines and practically had to elbow for breathing room. It was a menagerie of unseemly characters. There were black and Latino gangbangers, and skinheads, and junkies, and other unstable-looking dudes who surely should have been committed to a mental health facility. Heavily tattooed roughnecks kept approaching Brandon to size him up and interrogate him.

"Where are you from? Who do you know?" they would ask.

"I don't know anyone," he would reply.

"What are you doing in here?"

"I killed somebody."

"Who? A woman? A child?"

"No. Not a woman or child. Why don't you mind your own business?"

"Or what, motherfucker? What you gonna do? I'll mind whatever business I want to mind, bitch."

It went on like that for hours. Brandon had no clue how to placate these thugs or how to stay out of their way. He felt like a baby wildebeest who had been separated from the pack, and now the hyenas had him surrounded and were nipping at his flanks. The hours ticked by.

Finally, after what seemed like an eternity, Brandon was extracted from the cell and taken to a room to meet with his attorney, a public defender. Her name was Sandra Mukai, and she was a very petite Japanese woman. Brandon had been expecting, indeed hoping for, a slick, broad-shouldered man in a power suit, the kind of imposing litigator who could throw his weight around in the court room, even shout down the opposing counsel if it came to it. He wondered whether this prim and proper lady could summon the fortitude that the case most certainly called for.

Brandon was dropped into a seat across from Sandra and handcuffed to the table. The correctional officer stepped out and, before Sandra could even introduce herself, Brandon succumbed to an emotional meltdown. He put his head in his hands and began sobbing.

"I never meant for this to happen," he wailed. "I can't believe this is real. Is this it? Am I going to jail for the rest of my life? Will I get the death penalty? Am I done for?"

Brandon was nearly hyperventilating. Sandra cleared her throat, then spoke evenly and reassuringly, as far as that was possible. "It's too early to assess those things, Brandon. This is not the kind of case that typically results in a death penalty, but we have a long way to go. There are many facts that we need to analyze, many angles to consider. What I can tell you is that none of this fits. Clearly, you are not a hardened criminal, and you do not match the profile for this sort of charge. I think it is safe to assume that you are not a bad person at heart. That will work in your favor."

Sandra may not have been the archetypal defense attorney Brandon had imagined, but, by the end of their conversation, she had talked Brandon down from his emotional ledge. She was undoubtedly professional and experienced. Her demeanor offered a glimmer of hope.

They walked over to the courtroom and stood before the bench. The judge flatly informed Brandon that he was charged with murder in the first degree.

"How do you plead?"

Brandon, his knees wobbling, his head swimming, replied, "Not guilty, your honor."

Brandon was transferred to Glen Helen Rehabilitation Center, another county jail facility, where he was to remain until trial. The situation here seemed even more chaotic and precarious than what he had already experienced. He was assigned to a bunk in a gymnasium-like dorm room, which he shared with about sixty other inmates. The men were allowed to mingle, and move about throughout the room. Brandon would have much preferred the confines of a private cell. Here, he wouldn't be able to track all of the potential threats. Soon after his arrival, a couple of older white guys approached Brandon and offered to show him the ropes.

A gray-haired man with a ponytail, appropriately nicknamed Silver, summed up the situation. "Here in Glen Helen, you stick to your race. There's no ifs, and, or buts about it. You're going to ride in the white car with us. There is no comingling between the whites and the blacks, period. The Latinos are hit-or-miss. Most of 'em are affiliated with *La Eme*, which can be a problem. On the other hand, we've been getting along with most of the southside *vatos*, but that's all about to change. Some people are not happy with their taxation policies."

Brandon was already lost. "Slow down, please. Who are *La Eme* and the *vatos?*"

"I'm talking about the Mexicans," Silver explained. "*La Eme* translates to 'The M' and it refers to the Mexican Mafia. They run most of the jails and prisons in Southern California, and you generally want to stay out of their way. It's made up mostly of Southsiders, or *Sureños*, who are gang members from SoCal. Then there's their archrivals: the Northsiders, or *Norteños*, from Northern California. You won't see any of them down here, though, because if the two sides aren't segregated it would be a fucking bloodbath. There are hardcore killers on both teams. Just keep that in mind."

Brandon scanned the room and made a quick appraisal of some of the nearby inmates. Many of them looked like feral animals to his eye.

Silver continued. "But the Mexicans aren't the only ones you have to worry about. There's also Crips and Bloods here, and Black Guerillas, and Aryans and Nazi Lowriders. Pretty much all the crews are represented. The only way you can protect yourself is to stick with us peckerwoods and learn as much as you can as fast as you can."

"What about the taxes you mentioned?"

"The Southsiders have been helping themselves to portions of our food and personal items lately. That's called 'taxation.' It's not unusual, but some hardcore skinheads moved in recently and war is brewing."

Brandon needed no further convincing. He followed the guidelines, rarely if ever straying from the vicinity of the other white guys in his crew. They ate together, played cards together, worked out together. The prime understanding was that, whenever the shit hit the fan, they'd have each other's backs.

Brandon learned from Silver that county jails tend to be considerably more dangerous than state prisons. In state prisons, there are deeply established customs or "programs" cultivated by the inmates. These programs, involving regimented activities and habitual

behavior, serve to reduce the chaos and to make a seemingly interminable incarceration tolerable. Most guys in state joints want to do
their time and stay out of trouble long enough to see parole. Also, in
those institutions, there is a respected hierarchy among the prisoners.
Certain long-term inmates, the "shot callers," have a lot of power. They
make the decisions for their respective crews, and they negotiate with
each other about economic and security issues. In state joints, the shot
callers preserve the peace whenever possible and tend to snuff out disputes quickly because a small pissing contest over drugs or gambling
debts could soon engulf the whole prison block.

Things were different in county jail. Here, all sorts of riff-raff
were stuffed under one roof without a clear command structure. You
had murderers mixed with petty thieves mixed with DUI offenders,
child support violators, meth dealers, and so on. New guys didn't
know the rules. Inmates who were prone to causing problems or
carrying out acts of violence had less incentive to toe the line. They
knew that, whatever happened, they would soon be transferred to a
state or federal institution, and would not have to deal with the long-
term fallout.

There were a number of unsettling incidents during the months
that Brandon stayed at Glen Helen. Beatings and stabbings were not
uncommon. Most days there were fights, some of which transformed
into large-scale brawls. The correctional officers used tear gas and
concussion grenades to break up a melee once. This sort of violent
disorder did not bode well for guys who were looking to prove their
innocence or negotiate a lenient plea deal. There was a very fine line
between self-defense and criminal violence in the midst of a riot. If
you weren't careful, you could end up catching a charge that was worse
than the one that put you behind bars in the first place. A few inmates
in Brandon's dorm were charged with attempted murder for their
actions while incarcerated.

Every once in a while, someone would encourage Brandon to seek
revenge on another inmate.

"That motherfucker just disrespected you, man! Why don't you just go stab him in the neck? You're facing a murder beef anyway. What do you have to lose?"

Brandon was willing to do what he had to do to stay alive, but he worked hard to keep his nose clean. He also had a few older guys, like Silver, looking out for him. When they could, they kept him on the sidelines during times of war. But, in a few cases, it was all hands on deck, and Brandon would find himself in the middle of a scrum throwing punches.

The constant threat of violence took its toll. Emotionally unmoored and completely out of his element, Brandon found himself in a chronic state of traumatic paranoia. He was forever looking over his shoulder, darkly envisioning the moment that one of these vile characters would walk up and drive a shank into his heart. But, in a perverse way, he hoped for it. The finality would be nice. In those early months of incarceration, Brandon hated himself and wanted to die. Often, before falling asleep at night, he prayed that he would never wake up again, that his heart would just cease pumping in the middle of the night.

Brandon passed the time by focusing intensely on his legal defense, speaking with Sandra frequently about pretrial procedures and her progress in establishing his defense. She seemed to be doing a thorough job, but Brandon's family wanted him to hire a private criminal defense attorney instead. They were operating on the common perception that public defenders lack the skill and commitment of private litigators. Public defenders are relatively low-paid and quite often litigate on behalf of the dregs of society. Because their workloads are unmanageable and financial payoffs modest, they are often perceived to lack a significant emotional or material stake in the welfare of their clients. Yet, Sandra was demonstrably passionate about Brandon's case from the get-go. She clearly cared about what happened to him, and seemed to be driven to succeed. Perhaps that was her nature. Or perhaps winning a case like this would provide a boost for her career. Ultimately, Brandon did not care what the motivation was. He was convinced that she would fight for him, and do what was necessary to save his skin. He refused to replace her.

He also recommitted to his Christian faith. He studied the bible every day as if it were an academic text, clinging to its teachings about faith and forgiveness. It provided him with not only a wholesome distraction, but also a glimmer of hope. For, despite his legal preparations, he felt deep down that trust in a higher power was his only path to salvation. *If anything goes right for me*, he thought, *it will be by the grace of God.*

Brandon's first-degree murder charge implied a deliberate, premeditated, and malicious action. That is, the prosecution intended to show that Brandon carefully selected his target and thoughtfully planned the murderous act. This sort of allegation is generally the most serious form of homicide in American law. Below it is second-degree murder, which eliminates the deliberate and premeditated aspects of the crime. Under this lesser charge, a homicide might result from the act of wantonly shooting into a crowd or of breaking a bottle over someone's head during a bar fight.

There are also different degrees of manslaughter charges, which are less onerous and punitive than murder. Voluntary manslaughter is commonly thought of as a crime of passion. It is often applied when the circumstances surrounding the homicide caused the offender to become emotionally or mentally disturbed. For example, a man comes home to find his wife in bed with the neighbor, then kills them both.

The least severe homicide charge is involuntary manslaughter. This is warranted when the perpetrator commits a potentially deadly act—be it intentional or negligent—that did not have, as its goal, the death of another person. A woman participates in an illegal drag race and veers off the street into a bystander. A reckless doctor injects a patient with a dose of medicine that is not within safety guidelines.

Sandra believed that, considering Brandon's demonstrable quality of character and lack of criminal record, a plea deal was highly probable. In a perfect world, they would be able to negotiate a suspended sentence for involuntary manslaughter. However, she warned, this was a long shot.

"I'm going to do everything that I can for you, Brandon," Sandra affirmed. "But I am not going to make any guarantees. If the best we can do is a second-degree murder charge, you will spend fifteen years to life in prison."

To make matters worse, Brandon was facing a sentencing enhancement for the use of a gun during a crime. This would potentially add an additional ten years to whatever sentence he received for the homicide. Brandon's emotional state allowed for little optimism. He trusted Sandra, and believed in her abilities, but, at the same time, he was all but fully convinced that he would face the worst possible outcome. He spent much of his time actively imagining a life behind bars. It was an uncontrollable ideation, but, in some ways, emotionally constructive. He wanted to come to terms with the notion of an extended incarceration before it became a reality. *If you do twenty years, you'll be released when you're thirty-nine*, he told himself. *You can still have a life after that.*

Sandra informed Brandon that both Nick and Melvin had turned themselves in and had agreed to cooperate with the prosecution in exchange for immunity. Brandon did not resent them for this. His friends likely would face their own murder or accessory charges if they refused to play ball. The good news was that their stories corroborated Brandon's claims. It was a drunken accident. Brandon was not intentionally aiming at the victim. He didn't mean to pull the trigger. The bad news was that all of their testimonies confirmed that one man, and one man only, was responsible for the death of Steven Henderson. Brandon had acquired the gun. He was the one who insisted that they bring it along for the evening. He was the one who brandished it during the late-night confrontation. In the end, Nick and Melvin told the truth, and rightfully so, but Brandon was still up shit's creek.

He was confined to Glen Helen for a full eight months while a plea deal was hashed out. During that time, there were extensive negotiations between Sandra and the prosecutor, a high-profile litigator named Dave Whitney. Both sides expended significant time and effort on gathering facts and examining the circumstances. For Brandon, the pretrial legal process was agonizingly slow. This, Sandra assured him, was all part of the strategy. The passage of time helped their case. The story would fade from the headlines, and the prosecution would become encumbered with other cases and unrelated political concerns. The longer they postponed things, the better. Sandra wanted the sting of the wound to dissipate some before they ripped off the bandage.

Sandra hired a private investigator to reenact the event and to investigate potential witnesses. She questioned Detectives Loukas and Cole at length. She explored the possibility that the shotgun went off even though the gun safety was engaged. Although the drunken haze of the evening prevented Brandon from positively recalling most details, he was quite sure that the safety was in the "on" position. This would suggest that Brandon had taken some precautions, that the aging gun malfunctioned, and that his claim to an involuntary manslaughter scenario may hold water. Detective Loukas met Sandra at a gun range to test the weapon. He repeatedly attempted to fire the gun while the safety was engaged. Apparently, at least once, he was able to make that happen.

Dave Whitney's pretrial discovery involved, among other things, recreating the shooting. Whitney wanted to observe precisely, physically, how the incident occurred. He decided to use an elevator car as a simulation for the pickup truck cab. He strapped Brandon into a chair, gave him the reassembled shotgun, and made him go through the exact steps that he remembered taking that fateful evening.

At long last, the state presented their offer to Sandra, who relayed it to Brandon. "They've agreed to voluntary manslaughter with a gun enhancement. If the judge approves, you'll be given a total of nine years: six years for the homicide plus three for the gun allegation.

You may be able to shave a few years off of that term if you participate in a work program in prison and, of course, if you stay out of trouble."

The words "nine years" were a punch to the gut. Brandon had attempted to prepare himself for the worst-case scenario, and this was far from it, but the seriousness of Sandra's demeanor and the finality of the offer gave the punishment far greater weight.

"What about trial?" he asked. "At this point, what are my chances of getting off if we put up a strong defense?"

Sandra pursed her lips and leaned forward. "I'll go to trial for you. However, it is not my recommendation. The case is not cut-and-dry. A jury might view it in a variety of different ways."

"So I'd be playing poker with my life."

"That's one way to put it. What the state has offered is the best that you are going to get, and my recommendation is that you take it now. If you turn this deal down, it will never come back."

Brandon took the deal.

Prior to sentencing, a probation officer was tasked with writing an assessment of the crime and of Brandon as a potential threat to society. The analysis was scathing. It concluded that, regardless of Brandon's character and lack of a previous criminal record, his judgment was egregious and he caused irreparable harm to many lives. He recommended the strongest possible sentence and discouraged the judge from offering a parole option. In response, Sandra hired a third-party investigatory firm to conduct a similar analysis. Their assessment was that Brandon was a good kid in a bad situation. They concluded that, given his background and support system, the likelihood that he would reoffend was minimal—less than a 2 percent chance. They described him as a prime candidate for lenient sentencing.

In the end, the judge accepted the plea deal as Sandra had presented it, and sentenced Brandon to nine years, less time served, in state prison.

There was a period of three days before Brandon was to be transferred to state prison. As the inmates say, he was "waiting to catch the chain." Word got around that he was on his way out, and, on his last day at Glen Helen, a mean, musclebound *Sureño* named Jesse approached Brandon in the yard.

"I'll take your shoes, homes," he announced. It was common for departing inmates to leave some of their personal possessions behind when transferred. Brandon had a relatively clean pair of Nike basketball shoes.

"Sorry, man," Brandon replied. "I promised them to Silver."

"I don't care who you promised them to. They're mine now." Jesse stepped forward with his chest out. He looked ready to rip Brandon's throat out. But, by now, Brandon had learned the game. The most ruthless dudes in jail were diabolical sociopaths. They were always testing boundaries, feinting, parrying, looking for weaknesses to exploit. Although Brandon had lost about twenty pounds since his incarceration, he still worked out a few hours a day, so he was well muscled, spry, and able to handle himself. However, if he demonstrated even the slightest vulnerability—fear, uncertainty, a lack of self-confidence— Jesse would find a way to get to him. Maybe he would sneak up and shank Brandon with a sharpened toothbrush. Perhaps he would recruit a couple more *vatos* and deliver a crippling beat down.

Unblinking, Brandon looked into Jesse's eyes and spat on the ground. "If you want these shoes, you'll have to yank them off my feet."

"Are your shoes worth your life?" Jesse growled.

"I don't know," Brandon replied evenly, "are my shoes worth *your* life?"

Jesse scowled and walked off. However, that, by no means, was the end of the situation. Jesse would surely regroup and look for any opportunity to make Brandon pay.

Silver had witnessed the exchange. "Fuck that motherfucker," he proclaimed. "I got your back. You say the word and I'll stab him in the fucking neck."

"It's all good," Brandon answered, hoping to sound more at ease than he felt. "I just have to survive one more night."

Jesse spent the rest of the day glaring at Brandon, mad-dogging him and shouting obscenities across the yard. Brandon tried to play a game of basketball, but struggled to maintain focus. It was as though the two were playing a demented game of psychological chess. It was hard to tell whose turn it was, and there was the risk that even the slightest wrong move could end in checkmate. Brandon considered staring Jesse down, or taking Silver up on his offer. He thought about stomping across the yard and cold-cocking the ugly prick in the face. He considered putting the ball back in Jesse's court by approaching and taunting him. "So do you want my shoes or not?" he could ask.

At the end of the day, the inmates were directed to line up to return back to their dorm rooms. Jesse was assigned to a different wing of the prison than Brandon was. The two made eye contact as they marched slowly back inside. Then they split off in opposite directions. Brandon had survived to see another day, whether he liked it or not.

Brandon was remanded to the central facility of the California Institute for Men—commonly known as "Chino"—a notoriously violent state prison complex. Every hardcore gang one could think of was represented there. Although Brandon had had lengthy conversations with other inmates who knew all about life in a state institution, he felt extremely apprehensive during the bus ride north. It was hard enough to withstand nine months in county jail. Now he had to find a way to persist, and to survive, for up to nine years.

Chino was a high-security institution with prisoners locked up in individual cells. The place was dilapidated. Many of the windows had been busted out, so birds were constantly fluttering in and out of the complex and shitting all over the place. Some guys tried to make pets of the birds by feeding them crumbs and crackers. There was incessant commotion in the corridors—dudes arguing, or freaking out about one thing or another. Inmates were constantly calling out to each other to bum cigarettes, a highly valued commodity there. Some guys made wicks out of toilet paper, which they would then use to light the cigarettes. The prison constantly smelled of a combination of burning paper, bodily fluids, bird droppings, and manure from nearby cow pastures.

Despite his increasing bulk, Brandon continued to stick out like a sore thumb. There were simply few clean-cut, young white boys in the system. For the first few weeks, numerous other inmates tried to intimidate and take advantage of him. Even the correctional officers were relatively sadistic.

"Do you know how to fight?" one had asked Brandon on his first day at the facility.

"Why do you ask?" Brandon replied.

"Because you're going to have to fight for your life in this place, boy."

And so, Brandon continued to persist in a state of hyper-vigilant anxiety, wary of predators around every corner.

The Chino prisoners were given optional recreation time in the yard some days, a refreshing change of environment from the oppressively tight confines of the cells. The older guys in the white crew insisted that all the peckerwoods go outside for each recreation period. It was a safety precaution as they were far outnumbered by the Latino and black crews. There were two gun towers overlooking the yard, on each of which was nailed a sign reading "NO WARNING SHOTS." If violence erupted, the COs were within their rights to begin firing their weapons immediately.

During Brandon's second day in the institution, there was a stabbing in the yard. Brandon did not witness the incident, but he was not far away, lifting weights as usual. A commotion erupted, and prisoners began shouting and jostling. Then came the sharp crack of gunshots. Everyone scattered. A voice boomed over the loud speaker instructing the prisoners to immediately lie down on the ground. Within two or three minutes the incident was under control. All of the inmates were on their bellies. The COs had not fired actual bullets, but rather bean bag rounds, which hurt like hell and, though non-lethal, quickly subdued their targets. The incident involved two rival gang members. The attacker had stabbed his victim roughly thirty times. The victim—as often was the case—survived.

Officers poured into the yard with shotguns. The prisoners were ordered to remove their shirts or strip their jumpsuits completely. They were forced to stay still while the officers investigated the situation and interviewed every single prisoner who was within eyeshot during the attack. The process took an agonizingly long time. The men, many of them now donning only boxers, remained prostrate in the dirt for about eight hours. It was early March and far too chilly to be half-naked. Brandon was nearly hypothermic when the prisoners were finally returned to their cells around eight o'clock that night.

A month later, Brandon was transferred to Chino West, a lower-security facility in which the men were housed in large bunkrooms similar to those back in Glen Helen. The atmosphere was more relaxed, but the leaders of the white crew were still vigilant. One explained the deal in simple terms, "If you man up, we have your back. If you show cowardice, you're on your own." Brandon took that to heart.

In this facility, the men entertained themselves with a weekly event that they called "Friday Night Fights." Every Friday after dinner, a large group would gather in the restroom to watch ragtag boxing matches between various prisoners. Brandon was surprised to learn that the fights were good-natured, competitive affairs, rather than belligerent manifestations of bad blood between rival factions. Whoever volunteered was given the opportunity to engage. Sometimes the fights were between members of the same race, other times mixed. Many of the men who attended gambled on the outcomes. Some even tried to fix the bouts.

The participants abided by what they called "gentlemen's rules": no biting, eye gouging, or head-butting. A technical knockout would be declared if a man was sufficiently battered and struggling to defend himself. Each fighter wrapped his hands in socks so as to avoid leaving lasting marks on his opponent's face. The correctional officers had a don't ask, don't tell policy regarding the Friday Night Fights. They warned that, if it got out of hand, or if guys started walking around with black eyes and torn lips, they would come down hard on the people involved.

An older Mexican guy named Turtle attempted to discourage Brandon from participating. "You're not in here forever, boy," he said. "This is not how you do time. A lot can go wrong in these fights. You bust someone up too much and you can catch a charge. You get hurt bad and you might become a target. If I was you, I would steer clear of this bullshit."

Yet Brandon felt that building some credibility and demonstrating that he had a fairly sturdy pair of balls was the more important concern at this time. He was tired of being challenged by jailhouse predators. It was time to show that he could hold his own, that he wasn't a pussy.

Brandon engaged in seven bouts. They were ugly, unrefined scraps, each man winging wild haymakers until he ran out of gas. Brandon received his fair share of hard licks, but also delivered some punishment. His record during his time at Chino West was 5-2, a respectable run that generated some hard-fought respect. Soon enough guys were patting him on the back rather than fucking with him.

As time went by, Brandon settled into a consistent, almost mechanical routine. He ate during mealtime, lifted weights during yard time, and read and studied when confined to his cell. The weight pile—a rudimentary cluster of rusty fitness equipment—was his sanctuary. He spent time each day, sometimes up to six hours, pumping iron and exercising in the yard. A few years into his sentence Brandon was built like a monster, his physique shredded and bulging with muscles everywhere. He had put on thirty more pounds of muscle. He could easy bench press over 400 pounds and was able to squat press nearly 600. He was a far cry from the baby-faced kid who had been easy pickings for the hyenas back in county jail.

Though Brandon seriously doubted that he would ever see the day that he was released from prison, he did take measures to develop himself while behind bars. He enrolled in some correspondence courses through the University of Ohio: calculus, statistics, business management, and so on. Later in his sentence, when he was trans- ferred to Donovan Correctional Facility in San Diego County, he participated in a vocational welding program. The training was quite extensive—six hours per day, four days per week. Later still, at low- security Avenal State Prison in central California, Brandon took on a job as a day laborer maintaining and repairing facilities. He enjoyed the constructive exertion and, as a plus, figured that the skills he built through these various endeavors might have some value on the out- side, if he ever had the opportunity to breathe fresh air again.

Consistency was the key to survival for Brandon. He, like many of the inmates, religiously adhered to his own personal program. He abhorred changes that altered his day-to-day activities. He spurned distractions that drew focus away from his work and caused him to step back and contemplate the direness of his predicament. His fam- ily members occasionally visited, but, for this reason, Brandon did not fully enjoy the occasions. When they were around, he was forced to think about all the good stuff that was going on outside of the prison—all of the experiences and happy times that he was missing out on. He found himself mourning the carefree, ambitious person he had once been and would never be again.

His mother and Micky came for an overnight visit once. Brandon was permitted to spend the night with them in a sparsely appointed trailer home on the prison grounds. His mother was allowed to bring in a home-cooked feast. It was the first time Brandon had eaten his fill or slept in a proper bed in over three years. But, in the end, the visit was more painful than productive. His concerned mother pried into how Brandon was coping from day to day. The questions dragged up dark emotions and created tension. Brandon responded with half- truths and directed the conversation to other topics.

The experience knocked him out of his zone of stability. He found himself crying at night and struggling to summon the emotional resilience that he needed so badly. It took him weeks to get back into the swing of things.

Eventually, Brandon learned that his avoidance of trouble would pay dividends. Thanks to the "good time" sentence-reduction system in California, he would be serving far less than the nine years he was levied. He would likely be paroled after just four years and eight months in the California state prison system (in addition to the eight months he had spent in county jail prior to his conviction). In 1998, Brandon was transferred to a level-one facility near Tehachapi. Although there were gun towers looming overhead, he enjoyed freedom of movement throughout the grounds. And, suddenly, the prospect of becoming a free man again became palpable. However, as Brandon's day of reckoning approached, his anxiety ballooned. He grew acutely paranoid and hypochondriacal. He was convinced that he would succumb to a rare prison infection or have his throat slit by a psychotic inmate.

Brandon's sense of self-loathing, too, amplified. He hadn't had a single remorse-free day since the shooting, but now, more than ever, the guilt staged a full-frontal assault on his spirit. *I can never, will never feel good about myself again*, he would think. *I am a worthless fuck-up who took an innocent life and destroyed families. I don't deserve to get out of here. God won't let it happen. I don't deserve anything good.*

Brandon's lack of faith in the penal system further fueled his pessimism. There was always the chance that his sentence would get extended. The COs had a disconcerting degree of control over when he would be released. At their discretion, a prisoner could lose some of his good time credit for any of a myriad of infractions. Get into a shoving match with another prisoner? How about another week behind bars? Get caught with contraband? That might cost you a month. Some of the officers developed god complexes, enthralled by their ability to toy with the fate of an inmate. Once, at Avenal prison, a CO repeatedly dared Brandon to throw a punch at him. Brandon politely refused, but the officer grew insistent, taunting and cursing.

"Suck my dick," Brandon finally suggested.

The CO shoved Brandon to the ground and began grinding his face into the filthy concrete. As strong as a grizzly bear, Brandon could have fought back and snapped the officer's arm. However, he refused to resist. It surely would have cost him time, and could have culminated in a felony charge. The officer knelt on Brandon's back and pressed on the back of his head.

"Admit you're a pussy, Clancy!" he demanded. "Say, 'I'm a pussy!'"

Brandon laughed at the man and spit some blood to the side. "You got me, asshole. I'm a pussy."

The incident was reviewed by prison officials. Brandon was stripped of fourteen days of good time credit for "verbal disrespect."

Brandon also fretted about the issue of recidivism. In his time behind bars he had witnessed numerous prisoners walk free, only to return months later for a different infraction.

"What the hell are you doing here?" Brandon asked one of these return customers. "Why wouldn't you do everything in your power to stay out of this place?"

"What do you want me to say?" the man sighed. "I fucked up. It's harder than you think. You'll find that out for yourself someday."

And so it seemed like the whole system was set up for prisoners to fail. Reentry to civilian life is a bitch, the older guys told him. If the parole officer doesn't like you, you're coming back. If the victim's family is angry and vigilant, you don't stand much of a chance. Furthermore, many penal institutions were operated by for-profit corporations. These outfits really have no incentive to help you succeed and stay out of prison, Brandon conjectured. The more bunks they fill, the juicier their bottom line.

But, with just weeks to go before his scheduled parole date, Brandon had to accept that he, now twenty-four years old, now a grown man, would soon be stepping out into the free world. Until this point, the prospect had seemed utterly unfathomable. He began to focus on drafting achievable, concrete plans for the future. To begin, he would work for his father's contracting business. Then he would

apply to San Diego State as a business major, maybe even walk on to
the football team while he progressed toward a bachelor's degree.

There were, however, plenty of naysayers in the big house. "Son,
you'll be lucky to get a minimum-wage job, much less go to college
or play sports," they admonished. Nonetheless, a sprout of enthusiasm
began to push its way up from the depth of Brandon's spirit. He had
always been someone willing to fight tooth and nail for his dreams.
Five years of incarceration had not fully extinguished that gritty deter-
minism. And so, every once in a while, Brandon would lay awake at
night, while the rest of the prison slumbered, and allow himself to
dream big.

The final day of Brandon's sentence, in the spring of 1999, sprang
up like a startled deer. There was a brief pre-parole counseling session
the day prior, but it was laughably perfunctory. The counselor asked
Brandon whether he had a ride home from prison. Brandon responded
in the affirmative. The counselor sent him on his way.

Some of Brandon's friends had sent him clothes in anticipation of
parole. When the time came, Brandon donned an oversized sweatshirt,
running shoes, and a pair of shorts—his first time in non-institutional
clothing in a half-decade. A correctional officer led him down an
unfamiliar hallway, through a set of reinforced doors, and into a lobby
area that Brandon had never seen before. His father, stepmother, and
half-brother Will were there waiting for him. Brandon hugged them
deeply and wept with joy.

"Let's get out of here before they change their minds," his dad
quipped.

Reentry, as advised, was a bitch. Brandon felt as if he were a toddler
learning how to walk again. He had no clothes, no job, few friends,
and just a few hundred bucks to his name. His mom came down from
Washington for his release and spent a week helping him reacclimatize.
He moved into an extra bedroom in his father's home near Barstow,
but it was understood that the family would be willing to put him up

and support him for only so long. To pitch in, he spent several weeks helping his dad improve the property and clear some land. A letter arrived from San Diego State University informing Brandon that his application had been denied. It was not a surprising outcome, but it hurt, and it was the first clear evidence that the cards were stacked against him. Brandon soon decided that the best move would be to find his own place in San Diego, where job opportunities were more abundant.

Although Brandon's father was not a particularly high-profile member of society, he was well-liked in and around San Diego by the many businessmen he had serviced and contractors he had worked with. One of his associates owned a modest apartment building in Pacific Beach and agreed to rent a bachelor unit to Brandon for $345 per month. Brandon called an old girlfriend named Molly that he knew from high school. She came down and helped him settle in. They purchased an air mattress, a small TV, and some blankets. After arranging his possessions, they had sex, Brandon's first round of intercourse in half a decade. And, quite truly, the act was a consummation—a consummation of his freedom. Brandon had arrived at the conclusion that a man is not truly free unless he can go out into the world and make love.

As they lay there on the air mattress, holding each other, Holly said, "I'm going to help you find more furniture. We need to turn this little place into a proper home. This is no way to live."

"Are you kidding?" Brandon scoffed playfully. "I'm in heaven right now. I can stretch out and look out the door if I want, and breathe in the ocean breeze. I can walk down the street and have a taco whenever I want it. I can sleep with you! Compared to prison, this is the lap of luxury."

Brandon began hunting for work immediately after settling in. He had no time to waste. Each day, he awoke before sunrise and began the arduous process of rebuilding his life. There was a Gold's Gym down the street that agreed to exchange a fitness membership for help with unloading some boxes. Brandon continued to exercise and lift weights a few hours each day. It was about the only thing that was still familiar to him. Often, he passed by a large construction site that was on the same street as his apartment. The crew had gutted a cluster of homes and was busy clearing debris. Brandon hoped that they might consider hiring him in some capacity. Of course, he had welding skills and plenty of carpentry experience, but, if they had even a janitorial position, he would have jumped on it. Yet, he was nervous about approaching the workers. He did not quite know how to introduce himself and feared the possibility that they would reject him outright because of his criminal record. He bought a few Gatorades, then steeled himself and approached. A laborer directed him to the foreman, who happened to be about as much of a muscle-bound gym rat as Brandon himself. Contrary to expectations, the foreman greeted him warmly. His name was Kent, and he ran the project for a construction company called Hutchins.

"I've got some experience, and I'm really hoping that there might be an opening in your crew here," Brandon said, half stammering.

"I'll tell you what," Kent replied. "Show up at our office in Claremont Mesa tomorrow at five and I'll introduce you to Spike. He runs the show. We'll see what happens.

Brandon made sure he was there by four in the morning. Spike was waiting for him. As luck would have it, he knew and respected Max Clancy. They had worked together on several jobs.

"I'll give you a shot, kid. The shift starts at this time every morning. Think you can hack it?"

"I know I can," Brandon replied heartily.

And with that, things began looking up. Hutchins did demolition and hazardous material abatement. Many of the projects were big-money deals, and it showed in Brandon's paycheck. He earned a whopping $26 per hour to start, double or triple what he had originally hoped for. He worked his ass off, fifty hours a week in the hot sun, tearing off roof tiles, sledgehammering concrete, filling pickup trucks with rubble. He made sure that he worked twice as hard as anyone else on the crew. His goal was to be an unstoppable labor machine, so productive that the bosses couldn't help but give him more responsibility and higher-paying gigs. Brandon took the bus home every night covered in muck and sweat, then walked over to Gold's for a vigorous workout. He was a man on a mission.

Brandon's maniacal self-drive paid off. He got plenty of work and was the go-to guy for a foreman named Chuck, who immediately recognized potential in the respectful, young workhorse. However, not long after Brandon got into a groove, he found himself struggling with acute anxiety and depression issues. He had almost no friends, and, aside from Holly, who was rarely around, no women to spend time with. When he wasn't at work or the gym he had not the least idea of what to do with himself. Brandon was still plagued by paranoia and catastrophic thinking. He was convinced that something horrible would go down at any moment—an earthquake, a fire, another accidental tragedy—and all of the hope he had for the future would be summarily and rightfully extinguished. For the good part of a year after his parole he suffered from recurring panic attacks. He struggled to look beyond the legacy of the crime that he had committed, and to cope with the traumatic fallout of five years in a cage. Indeed, Brandon never quite fully recovered from his prison experience.

To cope with his troubling emotions, Brandon began writing down goals and spent lots of time visualizing them. First, he wanted to become a construction foreman within six months. Then, he wanted to purchase a house within two years. He wanted to find a good woman, marry her, and become a devoted father. He knew that he would never achieve most of the ambitions he had set his sights on as a teen, but he believed that he could do something else just as important: have a family and do right by them.

Despite Brandon's frequent bouts of doom and gloom, almost all of these goals came true. His work situation could not have been more rewarding. He became very close with both Kent and Chuck, and was, indeed, quickly promoted to foreman. For a brief time he moonlighted as a bouncer at a local bar, a gig that Chuck had lined up. One night, while Brandon was on duty, a spirited young woman grabbed his hand and asked him to dance. Her name was Lana. Her eyes were electric and she had a smile that made shivers run up Brandon's spine. He, regrettably, had to turn her down because he was supposed to mind the door. But, at the end of the night, she sidled up and gave him her phone number.

Brandon called her shortly after she left the bar and left a message. "Hey, Lana, this is Brandon from the bar. Maybe you remember me. I mean, you probably do because you gave me your number. I was the bouncer. Uh . . . anyway, I just wanted to make sure that you got home okay. Just, uh, call me if you need anything."

Brandon's awkward yet chivalrous gesture won Lana over. They began dating, exclusively and rather intensely. Brandon's heart, which had been so damaged and neglected, began to fill again with a warming lifeblood. However, he knew that, soon, he would have to reveal his past. He would have to expose himself as a criminal, a felon, a killer. The anticipation of that impending conversation caused him tremendous angst, but, several weeks in, he summoned the courage to broach the topic. Lana, her brow furrowed, the corners of her mouth downturned with seriousness, stared intently into Brandon's eyes as he recounted the ordeal of the last six years of his life. When he finished, she embraced him deeply.

"I sensed that you had been through something intense, something life-changing. I do not think that you intended to murder someone. I just know that you are not capable of something so monstrous. It was a horrible tragedy, both for the victim, and for you. This does not change how I feel about you at all."

A year later, Brandon and Lana married.

To be clear, Brandon's story deviates far from the standard for a felon convicted of a homicide. He actually went on to live what many might consider a version of the American dream. Within a year of the wedding, Lana and Brandon purchased the home that he had envisioned. Shortly thereafter, they welcomed a baby girl into the world and named her Joanna. They worked hard to build wealth, advance in life, and cultivate a comfortable lifestyle. And, for a time, that's exactly what happened.

However, a few years in, the marriage hit some turbulence. Lana and Brandon often found themselves at war over various stressors and concerns. The situation became toxic and irredeemable despite extensive efforts to preserve the union. Lana filed for a divorce, which was finalized in 2004.

Despite this personal misfortune, Brandon continued to have notable success in his business life. He earned an associate's degree in construction management, as well as a contractor's license and real estate sales license, neither of which is easy to obtain for an ex-con. In the early 2000s he even dabbled in real estate development, but took some big hits during the Great Recession and subsequently opted to steer clear of that line of work. He also started a general contracting business about five years after his release, an enterprise which he runs to this day. The company provides demolition and lead and asbestos abatement services primarily for institutional and military clients. In 2016, revenue exceeded $5 million.

Brandon remarried in 2007, to Anita, a loving mother of two young daughters. In 2010, their son Roger was born. Today, the family lives happily in a comfortable community not far from San Diego. The girls are in high school, performing exceedingly well in academics, sports, and the arts. Roger is a smiley and energetic little wild-child, just the way his old man was. They all have a great relationship with Lana and Joanna, who live just a few blocks away with Lana's husband. Brandon strives to embrace every moment, and to provide a stable and nourishing environment for his loved ones.

Not a day goes by that Brandon does not ruminate, if briefly, on the monumental mistake he made. He still suffers from some degree of PTSD related to the incident and his years of incarceration.

He endures occasional bouts of anxiety and depression, and struggles to hold back the tears when he recounts that fateful night of nearly a quarter-century ago. However, Brandon made a decision some years back to not allow his past to hold him back. He believes that in life you must choose to move on completely, and forsake the skeletons of history; attempting to proceed with one foot mired in the past is to invite failure and misery.

None of the children know about the homicide. Heretofore, Brandon felt that they might be just too young to process that hard truth or to fully benefit from the lessons it beholds. However, the girls especially are getting to an age in which it is essential to understand that grown-up choices have grown-up consequences. And, at some point, the line between parental discretion and prevarication becomes blurry. Perhaps, with the release of this book, he will finally share his story with them.

Brandon Clancy killed an innocent man. He made a horribly misguided series of decisions that culminated in a grave, perhaps unforgivable mistake. With a careless squeeze of the trigger, he terminated all of the hopes and dreams that his victim held so dearly, all of the joy and love and passion that this young man possessed, and the happy, fulfilling future he must have envisioned.

Shortly after being paroled, Brandon composed a heartfelt letter to the family of the victim. He talked at length about what he had gone through and what he had come to understand as a consequence of the tragedy. Tears pouring onto the paper, he wrote, "I wish I could bring your son back. If I could trade places with him, I would." Brandon believed, deep in his heart, that he meant those words as fully and sincerely as one can. He felt compelled to express his thoughts, even though he was unsure of the impact they might have, and even though he did not, deep down, feel that he deserved the opportunity to do so.

He never received a reply.

EPILOGUE

I was lying in bed on the night of October 1, 2017. It was around 10:30 p.m. and, although I was tired, I knew that sleep would not come for another few hours. I had been suffering from insomnia in recent weeks. I'm not sure what the cause was. Probably too much caffeine. Maybe too much work. I was coming up on the deadline for the first draft of the manuscript for this book, and, on top of that, working about fifty hours a week as a teacher and consultant. I wanted to dig into a good novel, but my brain felt too fried to focus. I grabbed my phone and pulled up Twitter. There were reports of an active shooter at a country music festival in Las Vegas.

The situation was unclear at first. Most news outlets were reporting that there were heavy casualties near the Mandalay Bay hotel and that the situation was developing. Some were relaying rumors of multiple shooters at multiple locations. I decided to search for an online police scanner to see what I could learn for myself. I found one and was immediately horrified by the radio chatter among law enforcement personnel. One officer announced that he was transporting six critically injured people to the hospital. Another reported that he was heading to the New York, New York hotel, where an active shooter had been spotted. A female dispatcher relayed information regarding an active shooter at the Tropicana and a possible car bomb at the Luxor. Later, I heard a SWAT officer whispering urgently into his radio about the progress his team was making within the Mandalay Bay. They were advancing down a hallway toward the suspected position of one of the shooters. Shortly thereafter the scanner went offline, likely disconnected because it was revealing sensitive information about police tactics and movements.

Needless to say, I was very concerned. I presumed, as I am sure many did, that this was a coordinated terrorist action, likely perpetrated by ISIS-backed operatives. After all, as far as I knew, there were few other notable terror organizations who had the motive or wherewithal to carry out what was proving to be a mass casualty event in a major American city. Although ISIS had staged numerous attacks in places such as Istanbul, Brussels, Baghdad, and Paris, the United States, to this point, had remained relatively unscathed. *They have finally gotten to us*, I remember thinking. *It was just a matter of time.*

But, I was wrong.

The perpetrator was not a foreign Islamic militant, but rather an Iowa-born Nevada resident named Stephen Paddock. Although there have been reports that he had recently lost a significant sum of money, Paddock was a multimillionaire real estate investor and heavy gambler. Before that he worked as a mail carrier and an IRS agent. Aside from a traffic violation or two, he had virtually no previous run-ins with law enforcement.

Yet, in less than ten minutes of shooting, Paddock exacted a terrible toll, one that was historic in magnitude: fifty-eight dead and 546 injured. The carnage was and is almost incomprehensible. It was a seemingly unforeseeable act perpetrated by a lone, white, American man. And, to this day, nobody seems to know for certain why he did it.

This lack of explanation has led to rampant speculation and debate about why Paddock transported twenty-three firearms up to his thirty-second-floor suite in the Mandalay Bay and began raining bullets on the crowd of roughly 22,000 concertgoers who had assembled for the Route 91 Harvest music festival. Like me, many observers immediately hypothesized a political or ideological basis for Paddock's actions. Indeed, ISIS asserted that they had radicalized Paddock and orchestrated the attack—an assertion that, at this point, has been dismissed by most experts. Some conspiracy theorists have alleged that, because he was shooting into a mostly white, presumably Christian crowd, Paddock must have been affiliated with an extreme leftist group, such as Antifa.[15] However, officials have pointed out that Paddock was not known to express strong political views other than that he "was happy with Trump because the stock market was doing well."[16]

Alternatively, there has been extensive inquiry into Paddock's mental health, with some pundits reducing the tragedy to the apparent fact that Paddock was insane. "He was a demented, sick individual," President Trump declared in the days after the tragedy. Paddock had been prescribed diazepam, an anti-anxiety drug whose "common" side effects may include panic, delirium, instability, rage, and psychosis.[17] Some suggest that he may have demonstrated a degree of cognitive instability in the years prior to the shooting. There was an incident in 2012 when Paddock filed a $100,000 lawsuit against the Cosmopolitan Hotel, claiming pain and suffering related to a slip and fall on the premises. Paddock may have faked the fall, and, indeed, the lawsuit was thrown out by the court. The attorney defending the hotel described Paddock as "slovenly," "careless," and "bizarre." Yet, aside from this, there have been few reports of erratic or antisocial behavior on the part of Paddock.

Perhaps we can attribute Paddock's behavior to his upbringing or genetics. His father was a notorious armed bank robber who had been on the FBI's ten-most-wanted list. Law enforcement viewed the man as a dangerous psychopath. He was sent away to prison when Stephen was just seven years old. Then he escaped and set up an illegitimate bingo parlor in Oregon. He was apprehended again, paroled, and then arrested once more for racketeering. He lived out his life in Texas before passing in 1998. The elder Paddock's rogue disposition may have been a dark harbinger of the crime against humanity his son would commit decades later.[18]

Or maybe the culprit, in this case, is American gun culture. The United States is home to roughly half of the civilian-owned firearms in the world. That comes to slightly more than one gun per person—the highest rate of gun ownership in the world.[19] Gun laws here, in general, are relatively limited. There is only a short list of federal criteria that would prohibit an American from owning a gun—among them a felony conviction, a dishonorable discharge from the military, or a restraining order. The federal government requires background checks for the purchase of a weapon only when the seller is a licensed firearm dealer. It is estimated that 40 percent of gun sales are outside of the scope of this regulation. There is currently no national law mandating a waiting period for the purchase of a gun. The Center for Disease Control and Prevention is effectively prohibited by law from studying the causes of gun violence. Although fully automatic weapons were banned by the Firearm Owners' Protection Act of 1986, semiautomatic rifles are legal in many states. Stephen Paddock owned over forty guns, some of which had been modified to mimic automatic assault rifles. It has been reported that most, if not all, of Paddock's gun purchases and modifications were legal. It seems fair to say that, in a country where there are so many weapons floating around and so few obstacles to acquiring them, a tragedy of this magnitude was an inevitability.

Indoctrination, mental illness, family history, culture—the Stephen Paddock case demonstrates how complex motivations for and causes of gun violence can be. The six narratives you have read about in this book explore additional underlying issues, including domestic abuse, drug trafficking, alcohol consumption, law enforcement methods, and poverty. If only we could distill the situation down to a single, fundamental factor and then focus energy and resources in that direction. Some want a nationwide ban on certain weapon types: assault rifles at minimum. Others, conversely, believe the key is to reduce gun control regulations. We could improve mental health screening for gun purchasers or invest in blighted urban communities. Perhaps restricting violent video games and movies will do the trick. Then again, maybe we should enhance policing capabilities and criminal penalties.

But, of course, the scourge of gun violence in this country cannot be so reduced. It is a manifestation of pervasive and multifaceted societal ills. A meaningful amelioration of the problem will likely require coordinated action on many fronts, over many years or decades. And I suspect that policy and governmental intervention will not be enough. In my estimation, such efforts must be accompanied by, if not preceded by, a sweeping change in worldview among the citizenry: an empathetic reevaluation of the underlying conditions that breed gun violence and of the at-risk populations who are inclined to resolve their issues with firearms, along with an enduring commitment to consider diverse and innovative remedies, even if it means sacrificing certain long-held principles. I have been challenged, during this project, to allow for such pliancy in my own perspective. I understand that asking the same of tens of millions of others is no small request.

Alas, although the bodies continue to pile up, and although we, as a nation, have born witness to a succession of unspeakable massacres over the past two decades, there appears to be ever greater partisan entrenchment and less willingness to embrace alternative viewpoints and solutions. Consequently, the question, in my mind, is not, What, in particular, should be done? It is, Are we, as a nation, ultimately capable of doing enough? If the answer is yes, then I hope that this book will contribute to a loosening of the ideological deadlock and an opening of hearts and minds.

During the process of writing this book I felt a resonant urge to make generalized judgments about the individuals I chose to feature. Not just to assess the merit of their actions, especially as related to gun violence, but to place the aggregate of what I gleaned of each individual onto the scale and make an overarching moral judgment: Is this a good person or a bad person? Many of my associates expressed a similar inclination, often framing it, however, with a different vocabulary. Usually, the question was: Are all of the people in the book criminals? (The word "criminal" seems to be commonly employed as a synonym for "bad person," at least in this country, especially among those who have never been incarcerated.) Furthermore, I believe that the shooters featured in this book may have felt a related need to make a simplifying assessment, but, instead, directed the analysis inward. Perhaps this is the fundamental reason why they each chose to participate. The act of recounting one's life narrative—reviewing and revealing the whole picture, in detail and with candor—allows one to better appraise the moral worth of that life.

If by "criminal" we mean someone who has been convicted of a crime, then five of the six individuals featured in this book are criminals. Except for Officer Al O'Connor, who used his gun to save another officer's life, all were deemed guilty of illegally shooting another human being. Although some would consider that judgment a transcendental moral stain of which the perpetrator can never be rid, a more even-handed analysis reveals the waters to be far muddier. People make mistakes. Others commit offenses that run contrary to their otherwise admirable values and characteristics. Moreover, human attributes are often temporary in nature; although one may behave in generally unscrupulous or reckless or destructive ways for a period of time, there are likely few individuals who do so for their entire lives, or even their entire adult lives. Even Stephen Paddock seemed to straddle this blurred line. In the aftermath of the tragedy, his brother Eric talked about how Stephen supported their mother and gave her a comfortable retirement. "Steve took care of the people he loved. He helped make me and my family wealthy. He's the reason I was able to retire . . . This is the Steve we know, we knew."

Especially in the wake of this project, it seems to me that to endeavor to judge an individual as "a good person" or "a bad person" is a fool's errand. Although I did not have a premeditated message that I wanted to push across in this book, this theme emerged of its own accord, loudly and clearly.

Think of Marvin Gomez. He had never committed a crime prior to the shooting, nor has he committed one since. His account of the incident seems plausible despite the outcome of his trial. Where, exactly, do we draw the line between self-defense and illegitimate aggression?

Think of Brittany Aden, who suffered sustained physical and emotional abuse, whose mother was a drug addict, who experienced acute psychological problems. Did she deserve to be imprisoned for thirteen years?

Think of Brandon Clancy. Cherished by his friends and family, driven to succeed in the world via strength of spirit, he made a dreadful mistake and served time for it. Should he forever be condemned for killing another man?

Think of John Frizzle. What is worse than shooting your own mother? one might wonder. Yet, one could also reasonably conclude that he committed the crime in the midst of a psychotic episode. Is John fully accountable for his crime? Does that moment of madness supersede everything he has done since then?

Think of Lester Young Jr., who murdered an innocent man over a handful of crack cocaine—a wanton, depraved act of violence. After nearly a quarter century in prison, he is committed to being a constructive member of society. Which man do we judge: the reckless teenaged drug dealer or the reformed ex-con? Prior to our interactions, a part of me expected to dismiss Lester as a corrupted soul, a menace to society, a monster. He is most certainly none of those things—at least, not anymore. None of these people are.

And what if we take this analysis to the extreme? How should we view those, like Stephen Paddock, who have committed the most atrocious and depraved crimes against humanity? How should their life narratives inform the actions we take and the choices we make as individuals and as a society?

I am not answering those questions; I am asking them.

I discussed this project with many friends, family members, and acquaintances during the roughly twenty months that I spent working on it. Almost everyone expressed a variation on the same sentiment: this topic is very relevant *right now* because of the recent mass shooting that just occurred. My response, after dozens of these conversations, has become rote. The issue of gun violence is not relevant only right now. It has been relevant continuously for decades and, barring a cultural and political upheaval, will be relevant for the foreseeable future. This is the state of affairs in America, my homeland. In America, we shoot each other.

ACKNOWLEDGMENTS

Endless thanks to my family, friends, and supporters, especially Erin Patinkin, Molly Each, Lady Luna, Maxim Brown, and my parents.

NOTES

1 Peter Nickeas and Megan Crepeau, "Family Business Turned Crime Scene," Chicago Tribune, July 2, 2016, http://www.chicagotribune.com/news/local/breaking/ct-west-side-homicide-scene-20160702-story.html.

2 "Data USA: Riverside, IL," Data USA, datausa.io/profile/geo/riverside-il/#demographics.

3 "Past Summary Ledgers," Gun Violence Archive, http://www.gunviolencearchive.org/past-tolls.

4 Chelsea Bailey, "More Americans Killed by Guns Since 1968 Than in All U.S. Wars—Combined," NBC News, October 4, 2017, https://www.nbcnews.com/storyline/las-vegas-shooting/more-americans-killed-guns-1968-all-u-s-wars-combined-n807156.

5 Roland G. Fryer Jr., Paul S. Heaton, Steven D. Levitt, and Kevin M. Murphy, "Measuring Crack Cocaine and Its Impact," Harvard University Society of Fellows 3, 66 (2006).

6 "2011 New Mexico Statutes Chapter 30," Justia: US Law, law.justia.com/codes/new-mexico/2011/chapter30/article2/section30-2-7/.

7 Bureau of Justic Statistics, www.bjs.gov.

8 Jed S. Rakoff, "Why Innocent People Plead Guilty." New York Review of Books, November 20, 2014, www.nybooks.com/articles/2014/11/20/why-innocent-people-plead-guilty/.

9 "Trends in US Corrections," The Sentencing Project, June 26, 2017, www
.sentencingproject.org/publications/trends-in-u-s-corrections/.

10 Noah Berlatsky, "When Chicago Tortured," The Atlantic. December 17, 2014,
www.theatlantic.com/national/archive/2014/12/chicago-police-torture-jon-
burge/383839/.

11 "How Chicago Racked Up a $662 Million Police Misconduct Bill," Crain's
Chicago Business, March 20, 2016, www.chicagobusiness.com/arti-
cle/20160320/NEWS07/160319758/how-chicago-racked-up-a-662-million-
police-misconduct-bill.

12 Jason Meisner, Annie Sweeney, Dan Hinkel, and Jeremy Gorner, "Justice
Report Rips Chicago Police for Excessive Force, Lax Discipline, Bad Training,"
Chicago Tribune, January 13, 2017, www.chicagotribune.com/news/local/breaking/
ct-chicago-police-justice-department-report-20170113-story.html.

13 Azadeh Ansari, "Chicago's 762 Homicides in 2016 Is Highest in 19 Years," CNN,
January 2, 2017, www.cnn.com/2017/01/01/us/chicago-murders-2016/index
.html.

14 David Heinzmann, "Leaderless Chicago Street Gangs Vex Police Efforts to Quell
Violence," Chicago Tribune, July 29, 2016, www.chicagotribune.com/news/
local/breaking/ct-chicago-violence-gangs-20160728-story.html.

15 Michael Edison Hayden, "Las Vegas Shooter Stephen Paddock was 'Antifa,'"
Newsweek, October 3, 2017, www.newsweek.com/alt-right-conspiracy-theo-
ries-blame-antifa-mass-shooting-las-vegas-677075.

16 Christal Hayes, "Las Vegas Gunman Was a Trump Supporter, Happy with
President Because Stock Market Was Doing Well," Newsweek, November 3, 2017,
www.newsweek.com/las-vegas-gunman-was-trump-supporter-happy-stock-
market-701597.

17 "Diazepam Side Effects," Drugs.com, https://www.drugs.com/sfx/diazepam-
side-effects.html.

18 Don Bishoff, "Bingo Bruce a Pro at Cons," Eugene Register-Guard, Section D,
February 9, 1998, news.google.com/newspapers?nid=1310&dat=19980209&id
=a1VWAAAAIBAJ&sjid=gusDAAAAIBAJ&pg=6214,2238858&hl=en.

19 Christopher Ingraham, "There Are Now More Guns than People in the United
States," Washington Post, October 5, 2015, www.washingtonpost.com/news/
wonk/wp/2015/10/05/guns-in-the-united-states-one-for-every-man-woman-
and-child-and-then-some/?utm_term=.bf213d2bf7cf.